D1154471

*Tragedy*
*and the Paradox of the Fortunate Fall*

HERBERT WEISINGER

# *Tragedy and the Paradox of the Fortunate Fall*

MICHIGAN STATE COLLEGE PRESS

5-6-92

*First published in 1953*
*Printed in Great Britain*

# Contents

# *Acknowledgements*

I SHOULD like to thank the administrations of Michigan State College, The Institute for Advanced Study, and The Warburg Institute of the University of London for their generous assistance in making this work possible by grants of leave and by fellowships. My thanks are also due to the staffs of the Library of Princeton University, the Princeton Theological Library, and the Library of The Warburg Institute for their courteous help.

The manuscript was read by my friends and colleagues, Professors Lawrence Babb, V. E. Leichty, and Arthur J. M. Smith. It was given an especially close scrutiny by Mr. Stanley Edgar Hyman and by my wife; I regret now that I did not always take advantage of their sharp eyes and sharper tongues.

I owe to Professor Arthur O. Lovejoy of The Johns Hopkins University the discovery of the paradox of the fortunate fall; he is of course not responsible for what I did with it.

My sense of obligation to Professor Erwin Panofsky of The Institute for Advanced Study is far greater than this book can possibly repay.

*East Lansigg, Michigan*
*October* 1952

# *Introduction*

THE ruins of Mexico are certainly not old by European standards, yet they have about them the air of belonging to a past so irrevocable and strange that, as one looks at a pyramid standing sharp and clear in the lucid sun, one gets the overwhelming feeling that here indeed is the real past, a past so gone and dead that it could have had no connection whatsoever with human activity and memory. Perhaps it is because the Mexican ruins are the work of peoples now almost completely submerged, while the European monuments, for all their age, are yet familiar and living, the result of their continuous human use; they are old, but they are not strange. The number of Mexican excavations is small and they are not always accessible, nor when excavations have been made are they always in a finished state. But occasionally one finds work on a pyramid far enough along so that the interior can be entered. Then one learns that what on the surface appears to be a solid block of stone is in fact a series of layers, one superimposed upon the other, the topmost being merely the last addition by the most recent people to have utilized the structure. Time, which had hitherto seemed static and one-dimensional, now takes on perspective in depth: one sees the first people coming on the place, building on it, worshipping there, sanctifying it by human use, passing under; followed by another people, taking over the site, catching up the note of the past, adding to it something uniquely their own, forgetting the people who had been there before them, but continuing in their own way their predecessors' work; then passing under in their turn, followed by yet another people who also build there and are also submerged, and so up into time. Each is drawn to the site, attracted by its power;

each rejects the past only to reshape it to its own needs and uses; each adds a layer both of masonry and meaning, until the whole structure is permeated with significance. Yet it is not until the innermost core is reached that the meaning of the whole is revealed, and, as one penetrates deeper and deeper into the pyramid, reversing in a few light moments the barely perceptible movements of heavy time, layer upon layer is seen, in one pyramid as many as seven, each differing from yet dependent upon the other, each with a character of its own but which can be fully understood only in relation to the others, until the centre is reached, the core upon which the others have grown up and which binds together and unifies the layers into a single comprehensive structure.

Our response to tragedy is much the same. The more we examine our reaction to tragedy, the more we learn to peel off successive layers of meaning, the more we realize we must penetrate to its central core if we are to respond fully to the structure as a whole. To be sure, Aristotle has told us all we need to know about the mechanism of tragedy: what the pleasure peculiar to tragedy is, and how it is induced in us through the medium of tragedy. But there remains a more fundamental question which Aristotle did not raise, or, if he did, answered too cryptically for us to understand, and that is: why do we take pleasure in the pleasure peculiar to tragedy? Perhaps this is the kind of question by which the restless modern mind probes itself, or perhaps it is the kind of question which Aristotle did not need to raise for the reason that all then knew the answer. Whatever the reason, I think it must be the experience of all who see and read tragedy that, no matter how much Aristotle has told us about it, and he has told us more than anyone else, something essential to our understanding of it is lacking, indeed the most essential element of all, which is: why we take pleasure in the fall of a fellow-man yet feel morally refreshed after we have witnessed and, in a sense, have actually participated in that fall. We feel, as Professor Bowra has sensitively recorded, an emptiness which Aristotle's explanations do not quite fill, for we feel that our response to tragedy has gone much deeper than the *Poetics* has been able to lead us. It stops where we most need guidance; for when we have learned how we respond to tragedy, we still do not know why we respond as we do, and that is what we feel we most want and need to know.

In responding to tragedy, we respond first of all to an art form, but we respond to much more than that alone. Nor is it altogether religion taken in its ordinary sense that we also respond to, though that is likewise present, so much so that Aristotle probably took this component of tragedy, for us a matter of such painful reconstruction, for granted. As an art form which had its origins in religious rites and was an indispensable part of religious practice, tragedy cannot be separated from religion, yet this prohibition did not prevent the post-Sophoclean sceptical mind from enjoying tragedy nor yet the contemporary sceptical mind from enjoying it now, just as it enjoys the Matthew Passion and *Paradise Lost* (nor need it be converted to do so). It is not without significance, however, that, while the sceptical mind after Sophocles and of our own time enjoys tragedy, neither has been able to create it; on the other hand, it is equally significant that the believing mind of the Middle Ages neither enjoyed nor created tragedy as an art form. The faithful mind believes so strongly in myth that it prevents myth from attaining to the objective formality of art; the unbelieving mind so strongly clings to the objective formality of art that it prevents form from being fructified by myth; where either passion or form is wanting, where one dominates over the other, there can be either belief alone or design alone, but not art, which is the balance of the tension between them Tragedy is the product of scepticism and faith together, of faith sceptical enough to question and of scepticism faithful enough to believe. It is the resolution of the tension between scepticism and faith in a balance which is on a plane of conviction higher than each by itself, but arrived at only after the struggle between them as equals is ended, and it is seen that neither is the victor nor yet the vanquished, but that what has taken their place is something new, which, though it partakes of the essence of each, is yet different in kind from them.

I think that the analogy of the pyramid will help us over this critical hump in two important ways, first as regards the technique of art, and second as regards its meaning-content. An artist must of necessity work with contemporary symbols, otherwise he has no means of communicating with his immediate audience which he needs must address; this is the outer layer of the pyramid, the one that first attracts our eye and invites us to make a closer inspection. If he is an artist-journalist only, that is the sole layer he has to offer and in time he becomes a footnote. But if he is a serious artist, he will infuse his immediate and contemporary symbols with permanent and universal meaning; he will attach to them a significance greater than that of his times alone, one which men of other times and other places will be able to translate into their own terms and then appreciate; this is the layer below the surface of the pyramid. And if he is a great artist, he will bring himself, consciously or otherwise, into harmony with patterns of belief so old and so basic that they form the ultimate stuff out of which meaning is derived, and it is to these ultimate patterns of belief that, in the final analysis, we respond, regardless of what other faiths (or faithlessness) to which we may be temporarily attached; this is the inner core of the pyramid, as it is of art and of tragedy.

In this study, I should like to examine only three links in the chain of our response to tragedy, for I have postulated a chain made up of the following links: first, the impact of experience which produces the archetypes of belief; second, the formation of the archetype of rebirth; third, the crystallization of the archetype of rebirth in the myth and ritual of the ancient Near East; fourth, the infusion and transformation of myth and ritual into and in the religions of the ancient world, including Christianity; fifth, the concretization and formalization of the archetype of rebirth into the concept of *felix culpa*, the paradox of the fortunate fall; and finally, the secular utilization of the paradox of the fortunate fall as the substance out of which tragedy, and particularly Shakespearean tragedy, is made. The forging of the first two links in the chain lies hidden so deeply both in the past of man and in his unconsciousness that only the combined labours of the archaeologist and of the psychologist can hope to uncover the process of formation and development. The making of the third, fourth, and fifth links forms the subject-matter of this book; the last link must wait for a study of its own. In terms, then, of this chain of response to tragedy, I hope to show that our reaction to tragedy goes far deeper than at first we might have suspected, that in fact, because it is made up of links in so long a chain, it binds us to a pattern of belief so strong in its grip on the mind of man that in whatever form we encounter it we cannot but respond, and respond deeply, to it. This, I think, is the secret of the hold which tragedy has on us.

My attitude towards the materials which I utilize in this study is not so much textual and philological as it is associative and literary. For this reason, I have employed certain concepts as suggestive, more as analogies and metaphors, rather than as strictly defined and exact. For example, when I use the phrase, 'myth and ritual pattern of the ancient Near East', I do not mean by it an actually existing, rigorously articulated arrangement of beliefs and practices, but rather my own grouping together out of a number of elements those features of the religious thought of the ancient Near East which most nearly approximate and illuminate the paradox of the fortunate fall. I regard this construction as a nexus whose limits are deliberately left undefined and out of which and into which arteries and veins of meaning pour back and forth to animate the living whole. More specifically, I shall be dealing with those myths and rituals which cluster about the theme of the dying and resurrected God, concerning which there appear at present to be two schools of thought. The first holds that the theme is universal through the ancient Near East, so much so that Professor Theodor H. Gaster, following Frazer, treats Tammuz, Osiris, Attis, and Dionysos not so much as separate and sharply differentiated individuals but rather as '. . . so many variations and elaborations of a single central myth—that of the Dying and Reviving God'.[1] The other point of view is exemplified by Professor Henri Frankfort who has undertaken to show that there are many significant differences in the handling of the death and resurrection theme by the various peoples of the ancient Near East. Conceding that it is possible to recount a myth of a dying God which would contain features which would be common to the myths of Egypt, Mesopotamia, and Syria, he argues that Frazer's dying God is a mortal in whom the spirit of fertility is for the moment incarnate, and who dies a violent death. But such a concept, he thinks, is foreign to the myth of the dying God in the ancient Near East; he is not incarnate in a human being and is not killed but dies in the regular round of the seasons; more, there is uncertainty as to whether the dead God will be found and even more whether he will be resurrected; and the community does not passively await his resurrection but rather goes out in frantic search for him, often symbolized in the mourning and search undertaken by his wife and mother. Again, Osiris ranks below the Sun God, nor is he the child of the goddess who saves him; Adonis is not thought of as a creator; Horus does not help Osiris in the same way in which Nabu and Ninurta aided Marduk and Enlil; Osiris is not merely a

[1] Theodor H. Gaster, ' "Baal is Risen . . ." An Ancient Hebrew Passion-Play from Ras Shamra-Ugarit', *Iraq*, VI (1939), p. 111. On the other hand, Professor Gaster would seem to take quite another tack in his review of Ivan Engnell's *Studies in Divine Kingship in the Ancient Near East* in *The Review of Religion*, IX (1945), pp. 267–81. Cf. Cylde Kluckholm, 'Myth and Ritual: A General Survey', *HTR*, XXV (1942), pp. 45–79.

dying God, he is actually a dead God who never returned, as did Tammuz, to the land of the living, and his place was taken there by Horus; there are variations in the relations of these Gods to plant life, to animals, and to water; and finally, there are many disparities between the various cultic practices associated with the Gods. 'The gods as they confront us in the religions of the ancient Near East', Professor Frankfort concludes, 'express profoundly different mentalities.'[1] Professor Frankfort is reacting strongly against the indiscriminate use of the notion of a primitive *urmyth*, and rightly, but perhaps too uncompromisingly so.[2] Nevertheless, to accuse Frazer of failing to see distinctions where they do not occur in fact and of suggesting that he is guilty of the paternity of the *urmyth* is to make us less sensitive to other, and I think, more important values in Frazer's work. Professor Frankfort is not alone in criticizing Frazer, and in the light of the voluminous new information which has been accumulated since his time, it is fair that his deficiencies should be pointed out. But Frazer is not quite the pedant he is made out to be, nor the naive evolutionist as some see him, nor yet the indifferent and rationalistic denigrator of the peoples he spent a lifetime devotedly studying. Frazer saw the difference between the myths of Osiris, Tammuz, Attis, and Adonis, and he indicated them, but he also saw more, and that more is the measure of his achievement: he saw man engaged in a most heroic attempt to work out for himself his place in a hostile universe; he sympathized with that attempt as only one who followed it in all its bitter and frustrating detail alone could; and

[1] Henri Frankfort, *Kingship and the Gods* (Chicago, 1948), p. 294. I have summarized in the last few sentences his argument advanced in the 'Excursus: Tammuz, Adonis, Osiris', ibid., pp. 286–94. Cf. M. E. L. Mallowan, 'Kingship and the Gods: A Review', *Antiquity*, XC (1949), pp. 93–99; and S. G. F. Brandon, 'The Problem of Change in the Ancient World', *Folk-Lore*, LXI (1950), pp. 88–97.

[2] The bluntness of the position taken in the 'Excursus' has been softened in Professor Frankfort's review of Miss Gertrude Levy's *The Gate of Horn*, where he quotes with approval her thesis of '. . . the survival of a body related ceremonial customs, which seem, however greatly their significance may have deepened and widened in the early civilizations upon which our own is founded, to have their sources at the very beginning of discernible human institutions. There they appear, not as haphazard or isolated phenomena, but already organized into a coherent discipline, which may even merit the name of religion.' She admits that there is no certain proof of development from a common source, but goes on to say that '. . . the weight of the whole body of evidence . . . is offered here as the expression of a living unity of belief and practice, which underlies the religious, artistic, and social development of the ancient world before the revolutions of the iron age.' Gertrude Rachel Levy, *The Gate of Horn: A Study of the Religious Conceptions of the Stone Age, and Their Influence upon European Thought* (London, 1948), p. xii. Professor Frankfort's review appears in *JNES*, IX (1950), pp. 48–50.

he evolved out of the mass of his evidence the tragic drama of man making himself over, no less. He saw it as a tragic drama because he could perceive the false starts, the wrong turns, and the bestiality and cruelty of man; he could also see that in the long run the attempt was doomed to failure because the methods were hopelessly wrong, and perhaps even that the aims themselves were bound to be fruitless (the universe does remain indifferent, no matter how frantically we try to re-order it); but it was a tragic drama in another sense too, for out of the struggle he could see that man would learn what he was capable of becoming. For if there is no God at the end of the road, there is something else, perhaps not so awesome but certainly much more human, namely man himself. For these reasons, then, Frazer undertook to put together out of the specifically different the generically alike. The desires and hopes of the men of the ancient Near East were in their ultimate goals too much alike for him to be content with having exhibited their differences. One first analyses differences, but one goes on to seek similarities, the hidden and meaningful ones. As a matter of fact, it is not so much that one proceeds from differences to similarities; rather, one elevates the problem to a higher stage. Without, therefore, concerning ourselves with the problem posed by the assumptions implicit in the theory of the monogenesis of culture, we can, I think, safely accept Professor Frankfort's statement that the development of human culture is a continuous process, and add to it these considerations: that, by and large, similar material conditions provoke similar human responses, that the human mind is reluctant to invent but prefers rather to adapt and re-adapt, that it often appears to reject what it in fact takes over, that each new adaptation is conceived in terms of the unique imprint and stamp of that people, and that the infusion from new people is not so much a mere addition as a distinctive step, and that mainly in the upwards direction.

It would appear that in the history of thought the stock of really important ideas is surprisingly quite small; the mind seems not so much to originate new ideas as to elaborate on the tried and trusted ones; it proliferates variations on the basic themes with astounding fecundity and versatility but it does not bring itself to create new themes if the old can be made to serve; it distrusts originality but admires adaptation; in the excitement of the new it wants the reassurance of the old. Once an idea has demonstrated that it serves a fundamental need and that it is capable of transmission through adaptation, continuous use is made of it, no matter how many transformations it may be made to undergo. This does not mean that ideas have their own being and volition independent of the men who believe in them. If this were so, ideas would never change and would move coldly in a flat, unending, and unvarying motion. But under the stress of new circumstances, men give the old ideas new meanings and fit them to new uses, and in so doing they impress on ideas their own characteristic individualities either as persons or as peoples. Thus the level stream of ideas is, as need dictates, suddenly lifted up and made to water new plains; not only is new wine poured into old bottles but the bottles themselves are always changing shape but retain all the time their function as containers of meaning; change is retained within tradition but tradition is made to live with change. But the motivating force remains, after all, man; he clings to the old but reaches to the new; he believes and he acts.

Second, since we shall find that the myth and ritual pattern of the ancient Near East is a kind of cosmic drama repeated here on earth in the person of the divine king who passes through the same movement from death to resurrection and from chaos to cosmos in a great and fateful struggle, from which, after much suffering, he emerges victorious, thus ensuring the well-being of the community for whom he acts and which acts with him for yet another year, it is necessary to explain in what sense I mean the drama of death and resurrection. I do not of course employ the term 'drama' in its technical, stage sense; rather, I have in mind Frazer's description of the sacred drama made in *The Scapegoat*:

'The intention of these sacred dramas, we may be sure, was neither to amuse nor to instruct an idle audience, and as little were they designed to gratify the actors, to whose baser passions they gave the reins for a time. They were solemn rites which mimicked the doings of divine beings, because man fancied that by such mimicry he was able to arrogate to himself the divine functions and to exercise them for the good of his fellows. The operations of nature, to his thinking, were carried on by mythical personages very like himself; and if he could only assimilate himself to them completely he would be able to wield all their powers. This is probably the original motive of most religious dramas or mysteries among rude peoples. The dramas are played, the mysteries are performed, not to teach the spectators the doctrines of their creed, still less to entertain them, but for the purpose of bringing about those natural effects which they represent in mythical disguise; in a word, they are magical ceremonies and their mode of operation is mimicry or sympathy. We shall probably not err in assuming that many myths, which we now know only as myths, had once their counterpart in magic; in other words, that they used to be acted as a means of producing in fact the events which they describe in figurative language. Ceremonies often die out while myths survive, and thus we are left to infer the dead ceremony from the living myth. . . .

'The actors sought to draw down blessings on the community by mimicking certain powerful superhuman beings and in their assumed character working those beneficent miracles which in the capacity of mere men they would have confessed themselves powerless to effect. In fact the aim of these elementary dramas, which contain in germ the tragedy and comedy of civilized nations, was the acquisition of superhuman power for the public good.'[1]

I do not intend, then, that the terms drawn from the vocabulary of the drama to be taken in their literal and technical sense; the terms refer rather to the performance of stylized ritual actions which mimetically reproduce what they wish actually to achieve. For this reason, I cannot altogether agree with Professor Gaster's brilliant restatements of the Canaanite ritual texts in terms of the actual language of the theatre; to look for act and scene divisions, to compare the incidents and characters of the ritual with similar incidents and characters in Greek drama does, it seems to me, an injustice both to the ritual and to the drama in that it denies the potency of the ritual to achieve its purposes mimetically on the one hand and lowers the drama to the level of the ritual on the other. But the two are decidedly not the same; and if the drama does stem from ritual, nevertheless to look for detailed points of similarity, and often Professor Gaster will cite examples so far removed from pertinence that their relevance is rather difficult to detect,[2] to look for such resemblances seems to me to confuse too many different things. The drama does employ many of the elements taken from the myth and ritual pattern we are about to study, but in so doing, it changes them, and it is this very process of adaptation and change which distin-

[1] James G. Frazer, *The Scapegoat* (London, 1913), pp. 374–5.

[2] Professor Gaster's position is stated in its extreme form in his article, 'New Light on Early Palestine Religion: More Texts from Ras Shamra', *Religions*, XVIII (1937), pp. 28–30. Cf. Professor Gaster's *Thespis* (New York, 1950), pp. 3–5, 73–106.

guishes it from ritual, gives it its distinctive character, and elevates it to the realm of art.

A word must be said concerning the criticism made of Frazer and of the so-called Cambridge school by those American anthropologists who have studied the civilizations of North and Central America. Their argument runs somewhat as follows: that since Frazer and his followers failed to devote sufficient attention to these other civilizations, their generalizations, based on materials drawn from a restricted geographical area, that of the Near East and of the Mediterranean basin, are limited in scope, and that, in particular, the theme of the dying and resurrected God, because it appears to be found only in these areas and does not seem to manifest itself elsewhere, does not have the signal importance which Frazer attached to it. I must confess that I do not see that the conclusion follows from the premise: interesting and significant as the civilizations of North and Central America are in themselves, it is quite clear that they did not, nor could they have had, any effect on the making of the Western mind. If any influence is to be looked for, it must come from the opposite direction, from the fertile Crescent and from the Mediterranean. An attempt has been made to show that the civilizations of Central America did possess the rudiments of the theme of the dying God,[1] but it is not altogether convincing nor is it really necessary, for the good reason that it is precisely because the theme of the dying and resurrected God is found in the ancient Near East and in the Mediterranean area that it was able to exercise its influence on the thought of the Western world, and consequently on the development of tragedy. To deny that the myth and ritual pattern of the ancient Near East existed outside of that area and then to demand that it be shown to exist everywhere is to make conditions which in the very nature of the situation cannot be met.

Finally, I take no stand on the vexing problem of whether myth precedes ritual, or ritual myth, for the reason that I think the problem a purely verbal one which is based on the fallacy of regarding thought as separate from action. I am certain that myth and ritual were not so separated by the peoples who believed in and practised them, nor, for that matter, do we ourselves, in actual practice, divide thought from action; they are indispensable components one of the other; to think is an action and an action is the result of thought. Myth and ritual are then one and the same thing; the difference be-

[1] Gertrude R. Levy, op. cit., pp. 178–95.

tween them is the result only of our particularist way of apprehending the phenomenon as a whole. The thing said and the thing done are one; it is we who divide them for the convenience of analysis.

These caveats out of the way, I think we may turn to our consideration of the paradox of the fortunate fall, and we start first with a brief analysis of its psychology.

## CHAPTER I

# *The Psychology of the Paradox of the Fortunate Fall*

In a paper titled, 'Milton and the Paradox of the Fortunate Fall',[1] Professor Arthur O. Lovejoy designated the thought expressed in lines 473-8 of Book XII of *Paradise Lost*, the paradox of the fortunate fall. It will be recalled that in this passage Adam has just been told by the Archangel Michael what his future will be and how man's fate is to be decided, and this prophecy of the Second Coming and of the Final Judgment so overwhelms him that he exclaims:

> *O Goodness Infinite, Goodness immense*
> *That all this good of evil shall produce*
> *And evil turn to a good . . .*
> *Full of doubt I stand,*
> *Whether I should repent men now of sin*
> *By me done or occasioned, or rejoice*
> *Much more that much more good thereof shall spring—*
> *To God more glory, more good will to men*
> *From God—and over wrath grace shall abound.*

Such a view of the fall may well be termed a paradox because, while on the one hand, the fall of man was indeed the occasion of the most bitter sorrow—'sin by me done', yet on the other hand, without it, the subsequent history of man would be without meaning and purpose, the Incarnation and the Redemption could not take place—'more good thereof shall spring', and man could not look forward

[1] Arthur O. Lovejoy, 'Milton and the Paradox of the Fortunate Fall', *Essays in the History of Ideas* (Baltimore, 1948), pp. 277–95.

to the ultimate goal of creation, the Second Coming and the Final Judgment, when Christ shall reward his faithful and receive them into bliss—'over wrath grace shall abound', events of such cosmic transcendence, that, though they are projected into the future, they alone make possible the conception of a universe as understandable, just, and good: 'thus good of evil shall produce, and evil turn to good.' For only under this divine plan can the good which Paul would do, be achieved, and the evil which he would not, be undone. Thus the fall of man is felt to be simultaneously harrowing and ecstatic, for at the very moment when man is thrown into the deepest despair, at that moment, and at that moment alone, he is made aware of the possibility of realizing the greatest good, and in this way, and only in this way, does good come out of evil. This idea, which comes from the innermost core of Milton's conviction that to be truly man, one must be capable of choice, and more, must be capable of bearing the burden of that choice, this idea, the progression from ignorance through experience to light, which at first glance seems so obvious a logical contradiction because it appears to contravene our own bitter experience of the irrationality and injustice of the world, transcends that experience in a leap which hurtles over the evidence of our senses to the creation of an intelligible pattern of human destiny capable of being held with the most profound conviction. Such a leap seems always to be made by those who, finding the notion of a universe as indifferent to man repugnant to them (and even Lucretius, though he rejected the Gods, could not bear to think of a meaningless universe), wrench experience into shape by forming a universe in which man enjoys, though at a bitter price, a transcendent rapport with himself, with nature, and with God. For Professor Lovejoy's purposes, it was enough for him to demonstrate how traditional and orthodox the paradox of the fortunate fall was by citing pertinent passages from Ambrose, Leo I, Gregory the Great, Augustine, the Easter Even hymn, the *Exultet*, *The Vision of Piers the Plowman*, Wyclif, Pererius, St. Francis de Sales, Du Bartas, and Giles Fletcher, and it was from the Easter Even hymn that he derived the classic expression of the idea as well as its name: '*O certe necessarium Adae peccatum, quod Christi morte deletum est! O felix culpa, quae talem ac tantum meruit habere redemptorem!*'

However, the idea of *felix culpa* has more than historical and theological interest; it possesses the power to attract, for, as the late Theodore Spencer testified, it produced in him an enlargement of experience, though he could afford no explanation of his experience.[1] Now, there are two ways by which the analysis of the paradox of the fortunate fall can be made: first, by the investigation of the psychological implications of the nature of religious contradiction which lies at the root of the paradox, a method suggested by Professor Lovejoy himself, and the second, by a consideration of the historical affinities of the idea. The first method I can only hint at, but some suggestions can be briefly indicated concerning its use and what it can be expected to accomplish. In a certain sense, the psychology of religious contradiction formed the central subject of James's *Varieties of Religious Experience*, for in that book he undertook to lay bare the state of mind of the 'twice-born', as he called them, those '. . . sick souls who must be twice-born in order to be happy', to whom the world is a 'double-storied mystery', which can be resolved only by the passage from one belief to another through conversion. This passage from belief to belief we can find movingly expressed in the Old Testament:

'And I will give them one heart, and I will put a new spirit within you; and I will take the stony heart out of their flesh, and I will give them a heart of flesh: that they may walk in my statutes, and keep mine ordinances, and do them: and they shall be my people, and I will be their God.' (Ezekiel 11, 19-20.)

And again in the New Testament:

'Verily, verily, I say unto you, he that heareth my word, and believeth him that sent me, hath eternal life, and cometh not into judgement, but hath passed out of death into life.' (John 5, 24.)

And in Paul's vivid words:

'But now we have been discharged from the law, having died to that wherein we were holden; so that we serve in newness of the spirit, and not in oldness of the letter.' (Romans 7, 6.)

From death to life, from oldness to newness, these are the classic phrases to express that stirring movement from one state of mind to another, a movement which proceeds from despair to exultation in a victory of the spirit of man over the brute fact of meaningless existence. But the process of conversion need not be limited to re-

[1] Theodore Spencer, Review of Professor Lovejoy's *Essays in the History of Ideas*, *JHI*, IX (1948), pp. 439–46.

ligious conversion alone, as James was quick to see; he meant it to describe the conversion from one belief to another, and even from faith to scepticism as well. In any case, the process of conversion seems to consist of a repeated pattern of behaviour: first, irritation and frustration caused by the feeling that all is irrational, combined with an almost overpowering sense of chaos and meaninglessness leading to despair and instability of mind; then this state gives way when the pieces in the puzzle seem all at once to fit together under the impetus of conversion, and there is an almost overwhelming feeling of exhilaration which comes from the effect of strong conviction, and above all, the feeling of knowledge and power which comes from having ascended from ignorance to light, the recognition of order and design in the world which had hitherto seemed empty of them.[1]

Immediate and striking is the description of his conversion given by Augustine:

'Hastily therefore went I again to that place where Alypius was sitting; for there had I laid the Apostle's book whenas I rose from thence. I snatched it up, I opened it, and in silence I read that chapter which I had first cast mine eyes upon: Not in rioting and drunkenness, not in chambering and wantonness, not in strife and envying: but put ye on the Lord Jesus Christ; and make not provision for the flesh, to fulfil the lusts thereof. No further would I read; nor needed I. For instantly even with the end of this sentence, by a light as it were of confidence now darted into my heart, all the darkness of doubting vanished away.'[2]

Hopkins has written how the power of conversion can turn the stubborn intractability of man against the will of God into the gentle acceptance of his ways:

*Thou art indeed just, Lord, if I contend*
*With thee; but, sir, so what I plead is just,*
*Why do sinners' ways prosper? and why must*
*Disappointment all I endeavour end?*

[1] My friend and colleague, Professor Arthur J. M. Smith, has called my attention to the description of the five stages in mysticism as stated by Evelyn Underhill: (1) Awakening or Conversion; (2) Self-Knowledge or Purgation; (3) Illumination; (4) Surrender, or the Dark Night; and (5) Union in *Mysticism* (London, 1923), pp. 205–6. But, as I believe, the process of conversion and illumination need not be confined to religion alone. See A. D. Nock, *Conversion* (Oxford, 1933), pp. 1–16.

[2] *St. Augustine's Confessions with an English Translation by William Watts,* 1631, ed. W.H.D. Rouse (London, 1912), I, p. 465.

*Wert thou my enemy, O thou my friend,*
*How wouldst thou worse, I wonder, than thou dost*
*Defeat, thwart me? Oh, the sots and thralls of lust*
*Do in spare hours more thrive than I that spend,*
*Sir, life upon thy cause. See, banks and brakes*
*Now, leave how thick! laced they are again*
*With fretty chervil, look, and fresh wind shakes*
*Them; birds build—but not I build; no, but strain,*
*Time's eunuch, and not breed one work that wakes*
*Mine, O thou lord of life, send my roots rain.*

He has done. Such is the power of illumination that it reveals in a flash the divine paradox of creation:

'O the sweet exchange, O the inscrutable creation, O the unexpected benefits, that the wickedness of many should be concealed in the one righteous, and the righteousness of the one should make righteous many wicked!'[1]

James confined his illustrations of conversion to the area of religion, but conversion is a process of conviction found in all fields; and in our time, conversion is probably much more to be experienced in the area of social and political conviction than it is in religion, and the hero of Tolstoi's last novel, fittingly called *Resurrection*, is perhaps a more modern prototype than Augustine, though in both the process of conversion is strikingly the same.

But James did not try to account for conversion, nor did he intend to use the phrase 'sick souls' in any pejorative sense, 'sick' meaning merely the confusion and doubt which confront us all in the presence of the uncertain and the unclear. A possible explanation of the psychology of conversion may be found in Jung who distinguishes three mental levels: (1) consciousness; (2) the personal unconsciousness; and (3) the collective unconsciousness. The last he terms 'a timeless and universal mind', the repository of 'customary and eternally repeated facts' which, once having indelibly stamped their impress on the mind of man, everlastingly retain their potency to affect him. Concretized into permanent images, they become archetypes:

'. . . the formulated resultants of countless typical experiences of

[1] *The Epistle to Diognetus*, ix, 5 in *The Apostolic Fathers*, tr. Kirsopp Lake (London, 1913), II, p. 371.

our ancestors. They are, as it were, the psychic residue of numberless experiences of the same type. . . . Each of these images contains a piece of human psychology and human destiny, a relic of suffering or delight that has happened countless times in our ancestral story, and on the average follows the same course.'[1]

These configurations of images, small in number but basic to the constitution of the mind, account for our reaction to poetry, for these 'basic, age-old patterns of central human experience . . . lie at the root of any poetry (or any other art) possessing special emotional significance.'[2] Now, in her stimulating effort to link the Jungian psychology to the understanding of literature, Miss Maud Bodkin has shown that one such archetype is that of the rebirth pattern in which the conflict of emotional tendencies of opposite character is resolved in two ways simultaneously; through the assertive acts of the individual hero, and, through his death, the surrender of the ego to a greater power, that of the community consciousness. Such a process of rebirth, or of conversion, is made up of two succeeding movements: one downward and inward toward *statis* and death, the other upward and outward toward 'reintegration and life-renewal'.[3]

The problem of determining the origins of these archetypes Miss Bodkin cautiously avoided, but Jung had already attributed them to the racial consciousness, a concept which I suspect he obtained from elaborating on Freud's theory, first suggested in *Totem and Taboo*, and later and more fully, in *Moses and Monotheism*, but with political and racial implications which Freud had carefully kept out. Freud had suggested that the primeval history of mankind is a kind of recapitulation of the psychological history of the individual, and that the two cast a mutual light on each other. Thus there is effected a link, indissoluble and everlasting, between the most impressive experiences of man's past, which have bitten so deeply into the collective consciousness that they have become constituent parts of its very nature, and his contemporary consciousness at any time. 'Early trauma-defence-latency-outbreak of the neurosis-partial return of the suppressed material: this was the formula', Freud wrote in *Moses* and

[1] C. G. Jung, 'On the Relation of Analytical Psychology to Poetic Art', in *Contributions to Analytical Psychology*, tr. H. G. and Cary F. Baynes (London, 1928), p. 246.

[2] Stanley Edgar Hyman, *The Armed Vision* (New York, 1948), p. 143. Cf. also the explanation of the theory of archetypes in Joseph Campbell, *The Hero with a Thousand Faces* (New York, 1949), pp. 17–19.

[3] Maud Bodkin, *Archetypal Patterns of Poetry* (London, 1934), pp. 4, 19–20, 81.

*Monotheism*, 'we drew up for the development of a neurosis.' And he then assumed that what had happened in the life of the individual had happened in the life of the species itself: '. . . mankind as a whole passed through conflicts of a sexual-aggressive nature, which left permanent traces, but which were for the most part warded off and forgotten; later, after a long period of latency, they came to life again and created phenomena similar in structure and tendency to neurotic symptoms.'[1] From the theory of repressed trauma reasserting itself at a later stage of development in a changed form, Freud derived his account of the early history of man. Man in his original state lived in small hordes each dominated by a strong male who was '. . . the master and father of the whole horde, unlimited in his power, which he used brutally'. The sons were deprived of all possessions, including women, and were therefore finally forced to band together to kill the father and eat him. In so doing, they exhibited a characteristic ambivalence: on the one hand, they feared and hated him, and therefore killed him; on the other hand, they respected his power and therefore partook of his body. Recognizing that internecine warfare would lead to endless slaughter, the brothers now created '. . . the first form of a social organization accompanied by a renunciation of instinctual gratifications', that is to say, the taboo of incest and the law of exogamy. And the memory of the father was perpetuated in the creation of the totem which, like the killed and eaten father it commemorated, was both revered and then slaughtered and eaten in the totem feast. In the course of time, the totems were humanized into Gods, '. . . but the memory of that first great act of sacrifice had proved to be indestructible despite all attempts to forget it'. The son tried more and more to put himself in the place of the father but the sense of guilt occasioned by the primeval murder could not be allayed; it had to be expiated: 'A Son of God, innocent himself, had sacrificed himself, and had thereby taken over the guilt of the world. It had to be a Son, for the sin had been murder of the Father.'[2] Thus father and son are reconciled and, at the same time as the son makes his sacrifice, he takes over the rôle of the father.[3]

Here too, according to Freud, is the explanation of tragic guilt: the hero is the primal father and the primal murderer in one, and he

[1] Sigmund Freud, *Moses and Monotheism*, tr. Katherine Jones (London and New York, 1939), p. 126. [2] Ibid., p. 136.

[3] Sigmund Freud, *Totem and Taboo*, tr. by J. Strachey (London, 1950), p. 145.

takes upon himself that primeval guilt so as to free the members of the chorus from its taint:

> 'The crime foisted upon him, namely, presumption and rebellion against a great authority, is the same as that which in the past oppressed the colleagues of the chorus, namely, the band of brothers. Thus the tragic hero, though still against his will, is made the redeemer of the chorus.'[1]

Something of the same idea, though less specific, is found in Professor Gilbert Murray's recognition of '. . . the strange, unanalyzed vibration below the surface' of such plays as the *Agamemnon* or *Electra* or *Hamlet*, '. . . an undercurrent of desires and fears and passions, long slumbering yet eternally familiar, which have for thousands of years lain near the root of our most intimate emotions and been wrought into the fabric of our most magical dramas'.[2]

The mystery of our response to tragedy, a response which over and above such discernible factors as the Aristotelian categories, for example, with which we are accustomed to grapple for the secret of tragedy, is thus given a deeply-rooted psychological basis which in its turn is found buried in the innermost layers of the group consciousness. That there are a basic few patterns in art which in various guises occur and reoccur, is, I think, without question, and Mr. Joseph Campbell has gone so far as to speak of the monomyth, which he describes as follows:

> 'The mythological hero, setting forth from his common-day hut or castle, is lured, carried away, or else voluntarily proceeds, to the threshold of adventure. There he encounters a shadow presence that guards the passage. The hero may defeat or conciliate this power and go alive into the kingdom of the dark (brother-battle, dragon-battle: offering, charm), or be slain by the opponent and descend in death (dismemberment, crucifixion). Beyond the threshold, then, the hero journeys through a world of unfamiliar yet strangely intimate forces, some of which severely threaten him (tests), some of which give magical aid (helpers). When he arrives at the nadir of the mythological round, he undergoes a supreme ordeal and gains his reward.

[1] Ibid., p. 926.

[2] Gilbert Murray, *The Classical Tradition in Poetry* (Oxford, 1927), p. 240. Cf. F. M. Cornford, 'The Unconscious Element in Literature and Philosophy', in *The Unwritten Philosophy and Other Essays*, ed. W. K. C. Guthrie (Cambridge, 1950), pp. 1–13.

The triumph may be represented as the hero's sexual union with the goddess-mother of the world (sacred marriage), his recognition by his father-creator (father atonement), his own divinization (apotheosis), or again—if the powers have remained unfriendly to him—his theft of the boon he came to gain (bride-theft, fire-theft); intrinsically, it is an expansion of consciousness and therewith of being (illumination, transfiguration, freedom). The final work is that of the return. If the powers have blessed the hero, he now sets forth under their protection (emissary); if not, he flees and is pursued (transformation flight, obstacle flight). At the return threshold the transcendental powers must remain behind; the hero re-emerges from the kingdom of dread (return, resurrection), the boon that he brings restores the world (elixir).'[1]

This ideal version of the monomyth is substantiated in many ways by Lord Raglan's study of the myth of the hero, in which, from an analysis of the stories of Oedipus, Theseus, Romulus, Heracles, Perseus, Jason, Bellerophon, Pelops, Asclepios, Dionysos, Apollo, Zeus, Joseph, Moses, Elijah, Watu Gunung, Nyikang, Siegfried, Llew Llawgyffes, Arthur, and Robin Hood, he arrives at a pattern made up of the following incidents, all or most of which occur in the life of the hero:

'1. The hero's mother is a royal virgin;
2. His father is a king, and
3. Often a near relative of his mother, but
4. The circumstances of his conception are unusual, and
5. He is also reputed to be the son of a God.
6. At birth an attempt is made, usually by his father or his maternal grandfather, to kill him, but
7. He is spirited away, and
8. Reared by foster-parents in a far country.
9. We are told nothing of his childhood, but
10. On reaching manhood he returns or goes to his future kingdom.
11. After a victory over the king and/or a giant, dragon or wild beast,
12. He marries a princess, often the daughter of his predecessor, and
13. Becomes king.

[1] Joseph Campbell, op. cit., pp. 245–6.

14. For a time he reigns uneventfully, and
15. Prescribes laws, but
16. Later he loses favour with the Gods and/or his subjects and
17. Is driven from the throne and city, after which
18. He meets with a mysterious death.
19. Often at the top of a hill.
20. His children, if any, do not succeed him.
21. His body is not buried, but nevertheless
22. He has one or more holy sepulchres.'[1]

Lord Raglan rightfully suggests that the considerable number of coincidences points to a ritual pattern as the origin of the myth of the hero and he notes that the three principal incidents in the life of the hero, his birth, his accession to the throne, and his death, correspond to the three principal *rites de passage*, at birth, at initiation, and at death.

But it is not necessary, I think, to subscribe whole-heartedly to the theory of the monomyth (I am afraid Mr. Campbell rather overdoes it) to accept the idea that there are, as I have said, a few basic patterns in art which, more than others, seem to possess much potency and such vitality that in whatever form we encounter them we respond immediately and intensely to them. I do not wish to minimize the differences which exist between the incidents in the lives of the heroes which Mr. Campbell and Lord Raglan tend to gloss over, but before we can deal with the differences, it is necessary first to take into account the similarities, for then we are in a sane and stable position to estimate the crucial matter of value which only the analysis of difference can make, and this is particularly true at the stage of literary development in which not the making of myth, but the use of myth, that is to say, at the conscious literary level, is our concern. Moreover, the emphasis on the monomyth alone fails to bring out with sufficient force the nature of the transformation of the hero; Mr. Campbell seems to see the story in the form of a rounded circle, the going forth, the encounter, and the return with

[1] Lord Raglan, *The Hero* (Oxford, 1937), pp. 178–80. Compare, too, the lengthy 'Annex II to V. C (ii) (a)', titled 'Christus Patiens', in *A Study of History* (Oxford, 1939), VI, pp. 376–439, in which Professor Toynbee uses the comparative method to demonstrate some eighty-seven points of similarity between the life of Christ and the lives of a number of pagan heroes. But his image of the pruner's knife and of the pollarded tree leads him to read history as a kind of relentless drive leading up to the making of Christ, at which point it abruptly stops, so that all subsequent events are but a dull and dispirited falling away from this one moment of great glory.

the boon, but it is precisely the changed character of the hero on his return, a change which is fundamental and indeed dialectical in quality, as from a lower to a higher stage of development and with a corresponding insight and understanding, which gives the myth its power of illumination. From myth to literature there is as great a jump as from experience to myth.[1]

I have suggested that between experience and literature lies myth; in the same way, between myth and tragedy lies the paradox of the fortunate fall, a necessary intermediate step which translates the emotional overtones of myth into the conscious creation of tragedy. First, experience, the repeated primeval traumatic shocks ultimately crystallizing themselves into the archetype of rebirth; then, the myth and ritual mould of the ancient Near East, concretizing the archetype of rebirth into a pattern of behaviour and belief infused with conviction and faith; then, the paradox of the fortunate fall, summing up in brief the essence of the myth and ritual of the ancient Near East, sharper in its formulation, more ideological, yet, at the same time, carrying with it the emotional aura of the myth and ritual pattern; and finally, tragedy, the deliberate work of art, using the paradox of the fortunate fall as its ideological backbone, so to speak, but divergent in kind from the archetype of rebirth, from the myth and ritual of the ancient Near East, and from the paradox of the fortunate fall, yet partaking of the force of each, and adding to them the conscious choice of materials and meaning which distinguishes art from the stuff out of which it is made. However, it is, as I have said, only with the transformation of the myth and ritual of the ancient Near East into the paradox of the fortunate fall that I shall be concerned here. And since we are dealing here with a pattern of thought which penetrates to man's most urgent needs, we can expect that this shape will necessarily undergo successive transformations, for, as man learns more, the more he attempts to retain what he already believes within what he keeps on learning; the pattern persists, but the forms it takes are almost endless in their variety. At the same time, I think we can also note a direction in the transformation of the form, for in its successive adaptations, it seems to move toward a greater refinement of significance; it becomes successively spiritual-

[1] Richard Chase, 'Myth as Literature', *English Institute Essays*, 1947 (New York, 1948), p. 10, seems to me to illustrate the failure to perceive this difference. See the sharp but sensible criticism of Chase's position by Stanley Edgar Hyman, 'Myth, Ritual, and Nonsense', *The Kenyon Review*, XI (1949), pp. 455–75, which also contains a sound examination of Mr. Campbell's book.

ized, so that at the end its origins are almost completely concealed, and we are left with a pattern to which we respond without knowing why it is that we do respond. Thus, by returning to the sources, we revitalize the pattern, and, at the same time, we can look forward, we can see what further transformations it is capable of undergoing.

# CHAPTER II

## *The Origin of the Paradox of the Fortunate Fall in Myth and Ritual*

THE myth and ritual pattern of the ancient Near East, which is at least six thousand years old, centres in a divine king who was killed annually and who was reborn in the person of his successor. In its later development, the king was not killed, but went through an annual symbolic death and a symbolic rebirth or resurrection.[1] Starting out as a magical rite designed to ensure the success of the crops in climates where the outcome of the struggle between water and drought meant literally the difference between life and death, the pattern was gradually transformed into a religious ritual designed this time to promote man's salvation, and finally became an ethical conviction, freed now of both its magical and religious ritual practices, but still retaining in spiritualized and symbolic form its ancient appeal and emotional certitude. Because it begins with the need to survive, the pattern never loses its force, for it is concerned always with survival, whether physical or spiritual. So far as can be ascertained at present, the pattern had a double growth, one along the lines of the ancient civilizations of the Near East, the Sumerian, the Egyptian, the Babylonian, both South and North, the Palestinian, first with the Canaanites and then with the Hebrews, and from thence into Christianity; the other along the lines of the island civilizations of the Aegean, from Crete to the mainland of Greece, from thence to Rome and once more into Christianity, the two streams of development flowing into each other and reinforcing

[1] Lord Raglan, *Death and Rebirth* (London, 1945), p. iii. Cf. Christopher Dawson, *Religion and Culture* (London, 1948), pp. 115–16.

themselves at this crucial juncture. In a sense, however, the idea of the two parallel streams is actually misleading in that it is overcautious; the two currents cannot be separated too sharply, geographically speaking, since the ancient world was as much swept by the winds of doctrine as we are to-day; the same needs gave rise to similar solutions; and there was a steady interchange, both of objects and of ideas, between the various parts of the ancient world.[1]

Despite the differences between the religions of the ancient Near East, as, for example, between those of Egypt and Mesopotamia, and between that of the Hebrews and of all the others, nevertheless they all possess certain significant features of myth and ritual in common. These features, in their turn, stem from the common bond of ritual, characteristic in one form or another, of all together, though, to be sure, none possessed completely all the elements, which varied to some degree from religion to religion. In this single, idealized ritual scheme, the well-being of the community was secured by the regular performance of certain ritual actions in which the king or his equivalent took the leading rôle. Moreover, the king's importance for the community was incalculably increased by the almost universal conviction that the fortunes of the community or state and those of the king were inextricably intermingled; indeed, one may go so far as to say that on the well-being of the king depended the well-being of the community as a whole.[2] Luckily, we need not concern ourselves here with the vexing problem of the origin of the conception of the divine king nor with the even more trying choice between single or multiple origins; we may simply content ourselves with Frazer's theory of the origin of the kingship '. . . in the order of public magicians or medicine-men'.[3] And we may also accept the statement of Mr. Hocart to the effect that the '. . . earliest known religion is a belief in the divinity of kings'.[4]

But it is worth spending a moment or two on Mr. Hocart's idealized version of the coronation ceremonies of the king, particu-

[1] I owe this correction to Dr. Machteld Mellinck, assistant to Professor Hetty Goldman, of the Institute for Advanced Study.

[2] Samuel H. Hooke, 'The Myth and Ritual Pattern in Jewish and Christian Apocalyptic', in *The Labyrinth*, ed. Samuel H. Hooke (London, 1935), pp. 213–14.

[3] James G. Frazer, *The Magic Art and the Evolution of Kings* (London, 1911), I, p. 420. Cf. A. E. Crawley, 'Kings' in *The Encyclopedia of Religion and Ethics*, ed. James Hastings (Edinburgh, 1914), VII, p. 709; and Calvin W. McEwan, *The Oriental Origin of Hellenistic Kingship* (Chicago, 1934), pp. 1–3.

[4] A. M. Hocart, *Kingship* (Oxford, 1927), p. 7. Cf. A. Rugg-Gunn, *Osiris and Odin the Origin of Kingship* (London, 1940).

larly in the light of the idealized life of the hero, as already described by Lord Raglan. A complete set of the parts, he suggests, would include the following:

'A. The theory is that the King (1) dies, (2) is reborn, (3) as a God.
B. By way of preparation he fasts and practises other austerities.
C. (1) Persons not admissible to the sacrifice, such as strangers, sinners, women and children, are kept away and are not allowed to know anything; (2) an armed guard prevents prying eyes.
D. A kind of sabbath is observed; the people are silent and lie quiet as at a death.
E. The King must fight a ritual combat (1) by arms, or (2) by ceremonies, and (3) come out victorious.
F. (1) The King is admonished to rule justly, and (2) promises to do so.
G. He receives communion in one or two kinds.
H. The people indulge at one point in (1) obscenities, or (2) buffoonery.
I. The King is invested with special garments.
J. He is baptized with water,
K. and anointed with oil,
L. when a human victim is killed,
M. and the people rejoice with noise and acclamations,
N. and a feast is given.
O. The King is crowned,
P. puts on shoes,
Q. and receives other regalia, such as a sceptre, a ring, etc.,
R. and sits upon a throne.
S. He takes three ceremonial steps in imitation of the rising sun.
T. At the conclusion of the ceremonies he goes the round of his dominions and receives the homage of the vassals.
U. He receives a new name.
V. The Queen is consecrated with the King.
W. So are the vassals or officials either at the coronation ceremony, or in the course of the King's tour.
X. Those who take part in the rites are dressed up as gods, sometimes with masks,
Y. which may be those of animals, thus identifying the wearer with some kind of beast.

Z. A king may be consecrated several times, going up each time one step in the scale of kingship.'[1]

Thus, on the basis of his investigation of the Fijan, Brahmanic Indian, modern Cambodian, ancient Egyptian, Hebrew, Roman, Byzantine, Abyssinian, and European Christian coronation ceremonies, Mr. Hocart has systematically worked out what may very well have been the parent ritual ceremony: preparation, victory, admonition and promise, clothing, communion, unction, investing with regalia, and procession; and he shows too that the marriage ceremony, the installation of officials, the installation rites of consecration, and the initiation ceremonies, all in varying degrees, parallel the coronation rites of the king; thus, from the equation, the king equals the sun-God, it follows that:

'. . . the rites of a king's consecration mostly bear their own explanation writ large across them: death, fasting and quiescence, battle and victory, oath to preserve law and order whether it be in the calendar, in the ritual, or in civil life, rebirth and lustration in the waters of ocean, crown, shoes and throne, circumambulation, marriage, are all episodes in the career of the sun who, overcome and slain by the powers of darkness, is mourned for, but again battles with his foes, defeats them, and can thus be reborn again to maintain order in the universe, is washed free from the impurities of the womb and is anointed for strength, assumes his disc, and, leaving the earth, ascends the sky, takes possession of the whole world in his circular course, and by his beams unites himself with the earth to produce offspring and crops.'[2]

Corroborating evidence for the spread and existence of the central rôle of the coronation ceremony is found in Tor Irstam's analysis of some sixty-two coronation ceremonies taken mainly from the central belt of Africa; again the idealized ceremony would include:

'1. Ceremonies that symbolized the king's death and rebirth.
2. The king was dressed in special robes.
3. The king received a new name.
4. Entrance dialogue and proclamation.
5. Ritual fight.
6. The king went into retirement for a certain period.
7. Communion.

[1] Ibid., pp. 70–1. [2] Ibid., p. 155.

8. The king was baptized.
9. The king mounted a hill.
10. The king planted a life-tree.
11. Admonitions and promises.
12. The king was anointed with oil.
13. The king put on shoes.
14. The king received certain regalia.
15. The king sat on the throne.
16. The king was crowned.
17. Fires were extinguished and rekindled.
18. The king scattered beans, etc., among the people.
19. Not all were allowed to be present at the most important ceremonies.
20. After the coronation the king travelled round his domain and received homage.
21. Festivities were held.
22. The king was made the butt of the people.
23. Those taking part dressed themselves as gods.
24. Human sacrifices.
25. The king's brothers were killed.
26. Substitute king.
27. The queen was crowned at the same time as the king.'[1]

The description of the Canaanite enthronement ritual made by G. Widengren is similar.[2] Finally, we have Professor Patai's listing of the rites in the installation ritual of the Hebrew kings:
(The numbers refer to Irstam's list above.)

'1. The Hebrew king was conceived of as being reborn at the time of his installation as the son of God.
2. He was dressed in purple royal robes.
4. The prophet, or the person functioning as his anointer, addressed him. The king answered. He was proclaimed as king.
5. A real fight preceded the king's final installation. The king's (ritual) victory over his enemies is often alluded to.

[1] Raphael Patai, 'Hebrew Installation Rites', *HUCA*, XX (1947), pp. 147–8, from Tor Irstam, *The King of Ganda, Studies in the Institutions of Sacral Kingship in Africa* (Stockholm, 1944), p. 26.

[2] *Psalm* 110 *och det sakrala kungadomet i Israel* (Uppsala, 1941), pp. 1–12, as summarized by Ivan Engnell, *Studies in Divine Kingship in the Ancient Near East* (Uppsala, 1943), p.79, footnote 8.

6. After the initial stage the installation ritual was interrupted for the duration of a week.
7. The king received communion by partaking of a sacrificial meal.
8. He was baptized.
9. He mounted a hill, The Bamah, or the 'pillar'.
10. The king set up for himself a memorial pillar.
11. He was admonished by the prophet and promised to follow the divine instructions.
12. The king was anointed with oil.
14. The king received as his regalia a spear, a shield, etc.
15. The king sat on the throne.
16. The king was crowned.
17. A fire rite took place.
18. The king distributed baker's ware among the people.
20. He made the round of his domain.
21. Festivities were held.
22. The king was made the butt of the people.
24. Human sacrifices.
26. Substitute king,

In addition, there are the following features of the ritual of installation of the ancient Hebrew king to which correspondences in African practice can also be found:

'1. The king is chosen by both electors and oracle.
2. A high official (priest, prophet) functions at the election as well as at the installation.
3. Animosity or incompatibility exists between this official and the king.
4. The king must be of unblemished body, healthy, strong and beautiful.
5. The king must not defile himself with a dead body.
6. Ceremonial marriage in a special hut.
7. The king marries the widow of his predecessor.
8. The king rides on a mount.
9. The king hides, is sought and found.
10. The 'shooting of the nations'.
11. Ritual combat omitted in case real fighting goes on.
12. Installation ritual very protracted.

13. Periodical (annual, on New Year's Day) repetition of installation rites.
14. Monthly new moon festivals.
15. The king is the chief priest of his people.'[1]

Thus, on the basis of evidence covering different peoples at different times, we can arrive at the conclusion that in the ancient Near East there existed a pattern of thought and action which gripped the minds and emotions of those who believed in it so strongly that it was made the basis on which they could apprehend and accept the universe in which they lived. It made possible a view of the universe as intelligible and ordered; it made possible man's conviction that he could control that universe for his own purposes; and it placed in his hands the lever whereby he could exercise that control. Millenia of acceptance and faith etched the efficacy of that pattern so deeply into the mind of man that he has always turned to it for consolation and security, adapting and reshaping it to fit his needs as they changed, but retaining it always in one form or another, different in shape, but the same in function. D. H. Lawrence has forcefully described the feeling for life which underlies the myth and ritual pattern; in the chapter on 'The Painted Tombs of Tarquinia' from *Etruscan Places*, he writes vividly about the idea of the vitality of the universe which the Etruscan possessed, and we may well apply it to the other peoples of the ancient world.[2]

For our purposes, then, it is enough to note that at the time from which our earliest evidences date, the ritual pattern emphasized, not so much the actual killing of the king, but rather the symbolic representation of the killing of the king in order to insure the renewal of the community's vitality and welfare. The motives for the actual killing of the king centred about the desire for control over the processes of nature as they affected man, for, as I have said, the king symbolized the corporate well-being of the people. The king was killed to obtain his magical powers, to bring about the restoration in the spring of the dying vegetation parched by the summer heat, to participate in the victory of the sun over winter, to remove the taint

[1] Ibid., pp. 215–17. The 'shooting of the nations' refers to the practice of shooting an arrow in the ritual combat towards each of the four quarters to symbolize the mastery over enemies. See 2 Kings 13, 14–19. When the high priest took over the ritual functions of the king, most of the installation rites were retained.

[2] D. H. Lawrence, *Etruscan Places* (Penguin Books, 1950), pp. 78–81.

of collective guilt by the slaying of the king as a scapegoat, and to retain for the community the potency of kingship by killing the old king before his powers waned and by transferring them to the new and virile king. While the force of these motives did not diminish, nevertheless there was gradually substituted for the actual killing of the king a symbolic act in the form of the killing of a human figure who wore a horned cap intended to symbolize the divine attributes, the slaying of a figure who was half-human and half-beast, the killing of various animals, such as the Zu bird, the bull, and the serpent, and finally, the cutting down of the sacred tree, such as the *Huluppu*-tree, or *Dd*-tree; all these acts served as substitutions for the killing of the king himself, but at the same time they were able to preserve the potency of the original intent. In the latest stages of development, the killing became '. . . purely symbolic and was carried out in mimic representation by masked actors'.[1] But whatever the motives and whatever the stage of symbolism, the killing and the resurrection of the king was the nexus around which the ritual pattern of the ancient Near East grew and flourished, for it was only by the regular and faithful performance of the ritual acts that the prosperity of the community could be safely and surely secured.[2]

From an analysis of the seasonal rituals, particularly in the New Year Festivals, and from the coronation, initiation, and personal rituals of the ancient Near East, it is possible to make a reconstructed model of the basic ritual form. To be sure, no one extant ritual possessed all the elements which constituted the ideal pattern in equal measure, nor could they be expected to, owing to the variety of peoples and the divergences in their modes of procedure. Variations in method and attitude are bound to be discovered from place to place and from time to time, with one or the other of the elements taking precedence over the others, and some may, in the course of

[1] Samuel H. Hooke, *The Origins of Early Semitic Ritual*, The Schweich Lectures of the British Academy, 1935 (London, 1938), pp. 13–15. Cf. W. Robertson Smith, *Lectures on the Religion of the Semites* (London, 1901), pp. 213–440; Edwin O. James, *The Origins of Sacrifice* (London, 1933), pp. 21–100; G. B. Gray, *Sacrifice in the Old Testament* (Oxford, 1925); and W. O. E. Oesterley, *Sacrifice in Ancient Israel* (London, 1937).

[2] It is beyond our concern here to undertake to describe the psychology which prompts such a mode of behaviour; a brilliant exposition of its causative mythopoetic mode of thought which makes possible the belief in myth and ritual will be found in the essay by H. and H. A. Frankfort, 'Myth and Reality', in *The Intellectual Adventure of Ancient Man* (Chicago, 1946), pp. 3–27. Cf. Paul Radin, *Primitive Man as Philosopher* (New York and London, 1927).

time, even drop out or be so transformed as to be scarcely recognizable in terms of its original character and use. But it is this very process of adaptation, shifting in emphasis, and elimination which makes possible the constant use of the myth and ritual pattern by different people in different circumstances; it is this very protean quality which gives it its tremendous vitality and living force. Answering as it does an absolutely fundamental human need, it is therefore essential that it adapt itself to varying conditions, yet at the same time, that it maintain undiminished not so much its form as its potency. This double challenge it meets successfully, for it appears to be a pattern of human thought and action which goes so deep both in the history of man and in his basic psychological composition that his response to it has remained steadfast, no matter in what form he finds it. Essentially, then, the pattern contains these basic elements: (1) the indispensable rôle of the divine king; (2) the combat between the God and an opposing power; (3) the suffering of the God; (4) the death of the God; (5) the resurrection of the God; (6) the symbolic recreation of the myth of creation; (7) the sacred marriage; (8) the triumphal procession; and (9) the settling of destinies.[1]

Of the ritual festivals of the ancient Near East, the New Year Festival was by far the most significant. However, since we celebrate New Year's Day on a fixed date, it is necessary for us to realize that for the peoples of the ancient Near East, the year was not regularly and minutely measured as ours is, nor did the New Year's celebration take place at the same time that ours does; in fact, for the ancients, New Year's Day was celebrated more than once during the year, when each new harvest was made; and when several fruits and grapes ripen at various times, there may be several different New Year Festivals. 'The first dividing up of time', Professor Wensinck tells us, 'was made without any fixed calendar and was based upon the periodic needs and mode of life, on the one hand, and the periodic amenity of nature on the other.'[2] Accordingly, he suggests that the

[1] This list is based on Samuel H. Hooke, 'The Myth and Ritual Pattern of the Ancient East', in *Myth and Ritual*, ed. Samuel H. Hooke (Oxford, 1933), pp. 7–9. Cf. Lord Raglan, *The Hero*, op. cit., pp. 145–77; Edwin O. James, *The Old Testament in the Light of Anthropology* (London, 1935), pp. 47–64; and Edwin O. James, *Comparative Religion* (London, 1938), pp. 73–145. Professor Hooke has five elements in the pattern, numbers 4 and 5 combined into one, and numbers 6, 2, 7 and 8 in my list above. See also T. H. Gaster, *Thespis* (New York, 1950), pp. 34–43.

[2] A. J. Wensinck, 'The Semitic New Year and the Origin of Eschatology', *Acta Orientalia*, I (1923), p. 158.

following festivals be kept in mind when the New Year ritual is under consideration:

| *Autumn* | *Winter* | *Spring* |
|---|---|---|
| Arabian: Hadjdj<br>Jewish:<br>New Year<br>Day of Atonement<br>Feast of Tabernacles | Heathen: Natalis invicti<br>Jewish: Chanukka<br>Christian: Epiphany | Persian: Nawruz<br>Babylonian: Zagmuk<br>Jewish: Easter<br>Christian: Easter[1] |

He then goes on to make a very profound and important point:

'The New Year—or seasonal—festivals are connected with the apparent motion of the sun, with solstices and equinoxes, and it is natural that these momentous occurrences in the skies should be reflected in the ceremonies and liturgies of the season. Not only because human existence, at a certain stage of development, is influenced so strongly by these events, but also because in that stage of development the idea of nature and natural laws has not yet arisen, and their place is taken by a dramatic conception which sees everywhere a strife between divine and demoniac, cosmic and chaotic powers, a struggle in which the sun or sun-god is finally victorious, sol invictus. And even when monotheism had conquered Asia Minor and the cosmic powers were all submitted to one God, it was still voluntary acts of that God which created phenomena each time anew, the deity who not only was, but is the creator, who causes the world to arise and decay according to his will. The succession of ages, as well as of years, seasons and months, yea, even the changes of night into day, must be regarded from this point of view, if we are to understand the relation in which man then stood to the universe. Each sunrise is the triumph of light over darkness, of the God of light over the chaos of night.'[2]

It is this dramatic conception of struggle between opposing forces, in which the symbol of light, life, and good is defeated by the symbol

[1] Ibid., p. 159.

[2] Ibid., p. 160. For the transition from the idea of the universe viewed as a dramatic struggle between light and dark to the conception of the universe as governed by natural law, see Hans Kelsen, *Society and Nature* (London and Chicago, 1943), pp. 1–185.

of darkness, death, and evil, only to emerge victorious with the coming of the New Year, the appearance of Spring after Winter, the falling of the rain after drought, and the sprouting of the young shoots in renewed vegetation; it is this dramatic conception underlying all the phenomena of nature which is the ultimate basis of the ritual pattern which seeks to propitiate the forces of nature, to regularize them, and to gain from them the means of sustenance. The New Year Festival in particular gathers to itself these fructifying powers and by the strict observance of the ritual pattern brings about the success of the crops. In the performance of the ritual, the imagery of light, reflecting the power of the sun, the imagery of the dying and flowering of vegetation, reflecting the planting and harvesting, and the imagery of water, reflecting the bringing of fertility, are united in the myth, the thing said at the ritual, which is the thing done, for the myth, as Professor Malinowski has said: '. . . expresses, enhances, and codifies belief'.[2] The New Year, then, is the time of '. . . new light and the fertile waters which bring forth the new vegetation'; it is the time of new creation, often symbolized in the deluge story, when out of chaos comes cosmos: 'After the chaos of summer and winter God brings forth out of the dead material the living cosmos of vegetation, a constantly repeated creation, a drama in which the cosmic and chaotic powers strive with one another, and which ends with the victory of the creative God.'[2]

In his important studies of the Hebrew festivals, Professor Julian Morgenstern has demonstrated how many of the later New Year Festivals of the ancient Near East possess certain significant features in common; for example, he has shown that the Gileadite festival of Jeptha's daughter, the Syrian New Year's Day Festival of the Seleucidean era, the Syrian New Year's Day Festival of the Roman legions at Durostorum, the festival at Caesare, and St. Barbara Day, the festival of Dusares, and Christmas, though late in form, '. . . are all, not borrowings or developments the one from the other, but rather outgrowths of a common, original Semitic festival of high antiquity, which, marking the end of the old and the beginning of the new year, must have been celebrated at or very near the winter solstice'.[3] The link between the New Year and the harvest is indi-

[1] Bronislaw Malinowski, 'Myth in Primitive Society', in *Magic, Science and Religion and Other Essays*, ed. Robert Redfield (London and Glencoe, Ill., 1948), p. 79.

[2] A. J. Wensinck, op. cit., p. 174.

[3] Julian Morgenstern, 'The Chanukkah Festival and the Calendar of Ancient Israel', *HUCA*, XX (1947), p. 135.

cated by the very name of the autumnal feast of Palestine which was known as the Feast of *Asioh* or Ingathering, and it was held at the 'turning' or *tequphah*, from Exodus 34, 22, or 'going out' or *ceth*, from Exodus 23, 16, of the year.[1] Though he is speaking of a late New Year's Day Festival, Professor Morgenstern's account of it reveals the memorable meaning of the New Year Festival in the myth and ritual pattern of the ancient Near East:

'At the beginning of the festival, in the earliest and most elementary form of its celebration, a human victim seems to have been offered, who, as a voluntary sacrifice and with a smile on his face, died in simulation of the waning and dying sun, and, no doubt, with the confident expectation of sure and speedy resurrection. The festival began, like all other similar ancient Semitic festivals, with ceremonies of fasting and self-humiliation, the casting of earth or ashes upon one's own person and other rites of mourning and wailing for the dead deity, thought to have been slain by his, or her, father, rites in which the women worshippers seem to have borne the leading rôle. But these rites gradually changed, with the progress of the festival, to ceremonies of rejoicing, merry-making and even acts of sexual licence, designed, through their homeopathic magical character, to further the marital union of the parent dieties and the resultant rebirth of the divine child. He was expected to be reborn upon the last, climactic day of the festival. His rebirth, indicated or symbolized by the coming of the first rays of the rising sun upon what was thought to be the day of the winter solstice, marked the beginning of the new year. It was a moment and a ceremony extremely critical in the life of its celebrants; for, of course, should the divine child, the sun of the new year, not be reborn, should clouds overcast the heavens, and the rays of the sun not break through to cheer the anxious multitudes, should it be a day of darkness and not of light, then, not good fortune, but only doom, inadequate crops, hunger and starvation, could befall the people during this new year, and their existence would become most precarious. Accordingly bonfires were kindled in the sanctuaries and streets and at the house entrances, or other, parallel fire ceremonies were performed, designed, through their homeopathic, magical power, to promote the rebirth or revivification of the waning and dying sun.

'This day, which marked the culmination of this great, annual

[1] Norman H. Snaith, *The Jewish New Year Festival* (London, 1947), p. 56.

New Year's Day Festival, was indeed a day of crisis in the life of the people of every Syrian city-state or district, upon which their very survival as a people was thought to hang in the balance.'[1]

With good reason, therefore, could the Alexandrian women sing:

*The Seasons, the Seasons, full slow they go and come,*
*But some sweet thing for all they bring, and so they are welcome home.*

And sincere, too, must have been their concluding prayer:

*Adonis sweet, Adonis dear,*
*Be gracious for another year;*
*Thou'rt welcome to thine own alway,*
*And welcome we'll both cry to-day*
*And next Adonis-tide.*[2]

But by the time Theocritus had so ironically recorded the Adonis song, the impulse behind the myth and ritual pattern of which this is so belated a survivor had already passed on into another more forceful and more spiritualized form.

[1] Julian Morgenstern, op. cit., pp. 135–6. Professor Morgenstern's studies in the calendar and festivals of Israel are very valuable; see the three in *HUCA*, I (1924), pp. 13–78; III (1926), pp. 77–107; and X (1935), pp. 1–148 on the three calendars of ancient Israel, as well as 'A Chapter in the History of the High Priesthood', *AJSL*, LV (1938), pp. 1–24, 183–97, 360–77; 'The Gates of Righteousness', *HUCA*, VI (1929), pp. 1–37; 'The Channukkah Festival and the Calendar of Ancient Israel', *HUCA*, XX (1947), pp. 1–136, XXI (1948), pp. 365–496; 'The New Year for Kings', in the *Gaster Anniversary Volume*, ed. Bruno Schindler and A. Marmorstein (London, 1936), pp. 439–56; Cf. also, in addition to Snaith's *The New Year Festival*, cited above, Oliver S. Rankin, *The Origins of the Festival of Hanukkah* (Edinburgh, 1930); and William A. Heidel, *The Day of Yahweh* (New York, 1929). For the meaning of the fire in the festivals, see James G. Frazer, *Balder the Beautiful*, 2 vols. (London, 1913). For the place of the sacred dance in the festivals, see W. O. E. Oesterley, *The Sacred Dance* (Cambridge, 1923).

[2] Theocritus, XV, 'The Women at the Adonis-Festival', in *The Greek Bucolic Poets*, tr. J. M. Edmonds (London, 1912), pp. 191, 195.

CHAPTER III

# *The Paradox of the Fortunate Fall in the Ancient Near East*

I SHOULD now like to examine in a little greater detail some of the more important elements in the myth and ritual pattern which I have up to now characterized in general terms in an effort to see how the paradox of the fortunate fall ultimately stems from it, and I shall begin with the concept of the king as divine and his central position in the ancient community, but excluding for the moment the thought of the Hebrews. 'God and the king', Professor Gadd tells us, 'are two conceptions so nearly coupled in the oriental mind that the distinction is constantly blurred.'[1] The same point had been made by Frazer:

'All that the people know, or rather imagine, is that somehow they themselves, their cattle, and their crops are mysteriously bound up with their divine king, so that according as he is well or ill the community is healthy or sickly, the flocks and herds thrive or languish with disease, and the fields yield an abundant or a scanty harvest. The worst evil which they can conceive of is the natural death of their ruler, whether he succumb to sickness or old age, for in the opinion of his followers such a death would entail the most disastrous consequences on themselves and their possessions; fatal epidemics would sweep away man and beast, the earth would refuse her increase, nay the very frame of nature itself might be dissolved. To guard against these catastrophes it is necessary to put the king to death while he is still in the full bloom of his divine manhood, in

[1] C. J. Gadd, *Ideas of Divine Rule in the Ancient East*, The Schweich Lectures of the British Academy, 1945 (London, 1948), p. 33. Cf. E. O. James, *The Origins of Religion* (London, 1937), p. 89.

order that his sacred life, transmitted in unabated force to his successor, may renew its youth, and thus by successive transmissions through a perpetual line of vigorous incarnations may remain eternally fresh and young, a pledge and security that men and animals shall in like manner renew their youth by a perpetual succession of generations, and that seedtime and harvest, and summer and winter, and rain and sunshine shall never fail.'[1]

Frazer is here speaking of the time when the actual killing of the king was practised, but we are to concern outselves with a more advanced stage when the death and resurrection of the king was mimetically re-enacted in the portentous festivals; but the single, overpowering purpose behind the myth and ritual pattern of the ancient Near East remained as Frazer has described it, except in so far as in the course of time and under the impact of the differing genius of differing peoples, the pattern underwent successive transformations in the direction of an ever higher and higher spirituality. Frazer has spoken of the abiding need to maintain the succession of generations, and of the summer and winter; his phrases come from Genesis where, after God has decided no longer to smite anything living and will make a covenant with Noah, he resolves: 'While the earth remaineth, seedtime and harvest, and cold and heat, and summer and winter, and day and night shall not cease.' (Genesis 8, 22.) Yet, while the language remains the same as in Frazer's description of the attitude of mind of primitive peoples, the meaning has been changed; the same words are now used to express a far more significant ethical idea, and it shall be a part of our purpose to follow this fascinating process of transformation.

The divinity of the king can be quickly established by a consideration of the theory of kingship found in the various Near Eastern civilizations. Thus, the divinity of the king in Egypt was attested to in numerous ways. For example, he was by birth divine, his father being the sungod Re, so that his divinity was already present in the pre-natal stage; his enthronization from crown prince to king later on was the ceremony which confirmed the rank he already held by virtue of his birth.[2] In the Memphite theology, the living king was equated with Horus and the dead king with Osiris, the fusion bring-

[1] James G. Frazer, *Balder the Beautiful* (London, 1913), I, pp. 1–2.

[2] John A. Wilson in *The Intellectual Adventure of Ancient Man* (Chicago, 1946), p. 72; Ivan Engnell, *Studies in Divine Kingship in the Ancient Near East* (Uppsala, 1943), pp. 4–5; and James G. Frazer, *The Magic Art* (London, 1911), I, pp. 418–20.

ing about a living continuity of God, king, and rule.[1] Moreover, his divinity was expressed both in his names and in his attributes: 'Behold, the son of Re comes, the beloved of Re comes, who was made to come by Horus.'[2] The Pharaoh Mernephtah is addressed in this way:

*Turn thy face unto me, thou rising sun,*
*that illumineth the Two Lands with its beauty!*
*Thou sun of mankind, that banisheth the darkness from Egypt.*
*Thou art like thy father Re, who ariseth in the firmament.*
*Thy beams enter (even) into a cavern, and there is no*
*place that is devoid of thy beauty.*
*Thou art told how it fareth in every land,*
*whilst thou resteth in the Palace.*
*Thou hearest the words of all lands,*
*thou hast myriads of ears.*
*Thine eyes are more bright than the stars of heaven,*
*and thou canst see better than the sun.*
*Even if one speaketh, and the mouth is in a cavern,*
*yet cometh it into thine ear.*
*If aught is done that is hidden, yet will thine eye behold it.*
*Mernephtah, beloved of Amun, lord of grace, who createth breath!*[3]

At the same time, the king was the high priest *par excellence*, and in his triple capacity as God, king, and high priest, was chief officiant at the ceremonies of the great festivals.[4] The king was conceived of as the source of vitality, the giver of life to the people, for the sun-god:

'... appointed him to be shepherd of this land, to keep alive the people and the folk, not sleeping by night as well as by day in seeking out every beneficial act, in looking for possibilities of usefulness.'[5]

The rôle of the king in the festivals we shall consider a little later on, but enough has been shown, I think, to substantiate the point that in Egypt the king was thought of as divine and that his position in the community was of transcendent importance to its well-being.

[1] Henri Frankfort, *Kingship and the Gods* (Chicago, 1948), pp. 32–5. Cf. James H. Breasted, *The Dawn of Conscience* (New York, 1934), pp. 35–42.

[2] Pyr. 1492, tr. by James H. Breasted, *Development of Religion and Thought in Ancient Egypt* (New York and London, 1912), p. 118.

[3] Adolf Erman, *The Literature of the Ancient Egyptians*, tr. A. M. Blackman (London, 1927), p. 280.

[4] A. M. Blackman, 'Myth and Ritual in Ancient Egypt', in *Myth and Ritual*, p. 17. Cf. Samuel H. Hooke (Oxford, 1933).

[5] Cairo 34501, tr. by Professor Wilson in *The Intellectual Adventure*, op. cit., p. 79.

When we turn to the Sumero-Accadian ideology, we find that the king was there, too, considered to be of divine origin. Professor Frankfort has subtly distinguished between the religion of Egypt and that of Mesopotamia by showing how in the Plain of the Two Rivers anxiety and gloom alternated with ecstacy and exultation whereas in Egypt there is a sense of security and continuity; nevertheless, we can also agree with Professor Engnell's formulation that '. . . the king is divine, he is God, and manifests himself as such especially at the New Year Festival'.[1] For kingship began with Anu or Enlil and from thence descended to the king, who maintained it. *The Sumerian King List* begins:

'When the kingship was lowered from heaven the kingship was in Eridu(g).'[2]

Professor Jacobsen, the editor of *The King List*, calls attention to the Sumerian epic edited by Poebel in his *Historical and Grammatical Texts* which deals with the beginning of the world and contains the following passage:

'when the crown of kingship was lowered from heaven, when the the sceptre and the throne of kingship were lowered from heaven[3] . . .

The king is known as the 'true God' and as 'the sun-God of his country'; at the same time, he is identified with the forces of fertility: he is '. . . a cedar rooted by abundant waters', he who '. . . has the water'; he therefore '. . . gives life to men'; and in a royal letter, we read: 'We were dead dogs, the Lord-King gave us life, he placed the plant of life under our nose.'[4] Again, as in Egypt, the king played the leading rôle in the New Year's Festival, as we shall shortly see.

In the Hittite religion, something of the same pattern is to be seen, though much more dimly, since the texts are not as clear. But from the king's epithets and from his iconography, as well as from his rôle in the cult, we can deduce that his position was in the most important respects similar to that of the king in Egypt and Mesopotamia. And when we pass to the Canaanite materials, we find that here too there is considerable evidence for the existence of a cult in which the king-

[1] Ivan Engnell, op. cit., p. 18. Cf. James G. Frazer, *Adonis Attis Osiris* (London, 1914), I, pp. 13–18.

[2] Thorkild Jacobsen, *The Sumerian King List* (Chicago, 1939), p. 71.

[3] Ibid., p. 58.

[4] Ivan Engnell, op. cit., pp. 23, 28–30. Cf. George Widengren, *The Accadian and Hebrew Psalms of Lamentation as Religious Documents* (Stockholm, 1937), pp. 6–11, for other examples.

God is made to fight, to die, to be resurrected, and to be enthroned. The king is called the sun-God; he gives life to his lands; he is the giver of breath. From the Ras Shamra texts, we can with some caution note that the king seems to have the leading rôle in the person of *Ltpn il dpid* in II AB,[1] and it has also been suggested that in the character of Dnil the king and the God have been merged into one.[2] That in Phoenicia the king of Tyre was conceived of as divine we can learn from this passage in Ezekiel:

'Moreover the word of the Lord came unto me, saying, Son of man take up a lamentation for the king of Tyre, and say unto him, Thus saith the LORD GOD: Thou sealest up the sun, full of wisdom, and perfect in beauty. Thou wast in Eden, the garden of God; every precious stone was thy covering, the sardius, the topaz, and the diamond, the beryl, the onyx, and the jasper, the sapphire, the emerald, and the carbuncle, and gold: the workmanship of thy tabrets and of thy pipes was in thee; in the day that thou wast created they were prepared. Thou wast the anointed cherub that covereth: and I set thee, *so that* thou wast upon the holy mountain of God; thou hast walked up and down in the midst of the stones of fire. Thou wast perfect in thy ways from the day that thou wast created, till unrighteousness was found in thee.' (Ezekiel 28, 11–15.)

Professor S. A. Cook has termed the letters of Abimilki of Tyre 'the most striking illustrations of the conception of the divine king' and he quotes from letter CXLVII as follows:

'My lord is the Sun which goeth forth daily over the lands according to the decree of Shamash, his gracious father, (and) which liveth by his good breath and returneth (?) after his setting, which putteth the whole land at rest by the might of (his) hand (?), which giveth his thunder like Addu in heaven and all the land quaketh (?) because of his thunder.'[3]

Finally, as to the position of the king in the cultus, we may recall the designation of Melchizedek, king of Salem, as the priest of God most high who brought forth bread and wine. (Genesis 14, 18.)

Up to now, we have been considering the concept of the divine

[1] S. H. Hooke, *Origins*, op. cit., p. 42.

[2] J. Pedersen, 'Canaanite and Israelite Cultus', *Acta Orientalia*, XVIII (1940), pp. 1–2.

[3] Stanley A. Cook, 'Syria and Palestine in the Light of External Evidence', *Cambridge Ancient History*, ed. J. B. Bury, S. A. Cook, and F. E. Adcock (Cambridge, 1928), II, p. 341. Shamash represents the Egyptian Sun-God with whom the king is identified.

king as a theoretical principle in its static state, so to speak. And, seen from this point of view, the idea of the power of the divine king seemed drained of life and incapable of arousing devotion and faith. But the idea is in its essence not an abstract principle, bloodless and abstract, but rather a live movement of live forces. The divine king does not merely exist; he acts, and in and through his actions secures the well-being of his people. Furthermore, his acts are fraught with the deepest significance; they represent in a real and vivid way man's ceaseless struggle to establish himself in a hostile universe. The king faces the most insurmountable obstacles; he engages in the most desperate of struggles; he is plunged into the bottom-most pits of despair and humiliation; he makes the greatest sacrifice of all, that of himself; and, at the very moment of his final degradation, and, indeed, precisely because he has taken on himself the burden of all and has undergone all that man can suffer, at that moment he bursts forth victorious over his opponents and carries with him to success the fearful aspirations of his people. Seen from this point of view now, the idea of divine kingship takes on an altogether different aspect; it is vibrantly alive, exciting, fundamental, and it goes directly to the very heart of how man can conquer his fate; it dares greatly and by so daring achieves even more greatly. Man is seen as engaged in a cosmic struggle in which he is made to face up to his opponents, that is to say, chaos and evil, without equivocation or the minimizing of their reality and effect; he forces himself to meet, to be temporarily conquered by, and then to vanquish his antagonists, and in the process he wins through to the greatest victory of all: he changes himself. He changes himself by accepting the need for what he has to do and by accepting the responsibility for what he does, in fear and in desperation, to be sure, but in glory too, and he comes to belief and faith only as a result of all that he has gone through: he has learned for himself. He has learned that, in spite of chaos and evil, he can live in an ordered and good world. It is for reasons such as these, then, that the myth and ritual pattern held such an abiding place in the mind of the ancient Near East, a place which never lost its centrality and importance, no matter how much the pattern changed in its details.[1]

[1] Besides the work of Freud, Jung, and Campbell, already mentioned, see, for the psychological implications of the idea of the divine kingship, H. G. Baynes, 'On the Psychological Origins of the Divine Kingship', *Folk-Lore*, XCVIII (1936), pp. 74–104; and Geza Roheim, *Animism, Magic, and the Divine King* (New York, 1930).

Having seen for ourselves the significance of the rôle of the divine king in the myth and ritual pattern of the ancient Near East, and having come to a realization of what solemn weight was attached to his course of action, we are now in a position to follow him as he goes through his sequence of struggle, defeat, and victory, for, as we have noted, we are here dealing with a movement and not a stasis, a movement in which active participation and not contemplation is the key which opens the door to securing the well-being of the community, and this in the face of the most desperate obstacles. The people are identified with the king who in his own person suffers his passion and resurrection, and by and through his suffering secures for the community its safety and security for another year to come. We begin therefore with the first act of the cosmic drama, that of the sacred combat. Thus, Osiris engages in a struggle with Seth; in Plutarch's version of the myth, Osiris is shut in a chest; in the Pyramid texts, he is felled to earth; and in yet another version, he is drowned.[1] To avenge his father's death, caused by Seth's jealousy over Keb's designation of Osiris as successor to his throne, Horus, the son of Osiris and Isis, meets Seth and seriously mutilates him, though he himself loses an eye in the struggle: Thoth, the God of Wisdom, makes the eye whole again by spitting on it and gives it to Horus, who in turn hands it over to Osiris to eat, thus bringing about the God's resurrection:

'Osiris speaks to Horus when he has removed the evil that was in Osiris on his fourth day, and had forgotten what was done to him on his eighth day. Thou hast come forth from the lake of life, purified in the celestial lake, becoming Upwawet. Thy son Horus leads thee, after he has given to thee the Gods who were against thee, and Thoth has brought them to thee. How beautiful are they who saw how satisfied are they who beheld, who saw Horus when he gave life to his father, when he offered satisfaction to Osiris before the western Gods.

'Thy liberation is poured by Isis, Nephthys has purified thee, thy two great and mighty sisters, who have put together thy flesh, who have fastened together thy limbs, who have made thy two eyes to shine (again) in thy head.'[2]

[1] James H. Breasted, *Development*, op. cit., p. 25.

[2] Pyr. Ut. 670, nos. 1976–82, as retored from Ut. 482, tr. James H. Breasted, ibid , pp. 32–3.

In the Memphite Theology, the contention between Horus and Seth is described in the second section; here Geb divides Egypt into two parts, the upper part going to Seth, the lower going to Horus, but then Geb changes his mind: 'It suited Geb ill that the portion of Horus was like that of Seth,' so gave his entire heritage to Horus, 'the son of his son, his eldest (literally, "his opener-of-the-body")'.[1] Again, we read in Egyptian mythology of the daily journey of the sun across the heavens and of the obstacles he must encounter: as the sun moves in his boat, a serpent, who waits to attack the boat and to swallow the sun, had to be defeated.[2] The theme of combat is particularly prominent in Mesopotamian mythology, and in the *Enuma Elish* we witness the titanic struggles between Tiamat and Marduk. After Ea kills Tiamat's consort, Apsu, she undertakes to avenge her husband's murder, but in the conflict which follows, Marduk drives the evil wind into her belly, and, having killed her, he forms of the two parts of her split body heaven and earth.[3] And in the Sumerian myth, called by Professor Kramer, 'Gilgamesh, Enkidu, and the Nether World', two battles take place: one between Enki and Kur, and the other between Gilgamesh and the snake at the foot of the *huluppu*-tree.[4] In addition, there are two more combat themes connected with Kur, in the myths, 'The Feats and Exploits of Ninurta' and 'Inanna and Ebih', but since the interpretation of these myths is still a matter of dispute, I must be content merely with mentioning them.[5] *The Gilgamesh Epic* tells of the great fights between Gilgamesh and Enkidu, between Gilgamesh, Enkidu, and Humbaba, and between Gilgamesh, Enkidu, and the bull demanded of Anu by Ishtar.[6] In the Hittite myth dealing with Illuiankas, the high God-

[1] Henri Frankfort, *Kingship and the Gods*, op. cit., p. 26.

[2] John A. Wilson, in *The Intellectual Adventure*, op. cit., p. 48. Cf. the later myth concerning the serpent Apop, 'whose voice re-echoes in the lower world', who '. . . is thrown into the ocean at the new year's day', and who swallows the sun in the evening, only to disgorge him in the morning; even later, Apop and Seth are finally merged. W. Max Muller, *Egyptian Mythology* (London and Boston, 1923), pp. 27, 107–110.

[3] Alexander Heidel, *The Babylonian Genesis* (Chicago, 1942), pp. 16–32. See the review by Samuel N. Kramer, *JAOS*, LXIII (1943), pp. 69–73.

[4] Samuel N. Kramer, *Sumerian Mythology* (Philadelphia, 1944), pp. 34, 38. Cf. S. N. Kramer, 'Sumerian Literature: A Preliminary Survey of the Oldest Literature in the World', *PAPS*, LXXXV (1942), pp. 293–323.

[5] Ibid., pp. 79–83. For corrections in translation and interpretation, especially relating to the Kur myths, see Thorkild Jacobsen, 'Sumerian Mythology: A Review Article', *JNES*, V (1946), pp. 128–52.

[6] Alexander Heidel, *The Gilgamesh Epic and Old Testament Parallels* (Chicago, 1946), pp. 32, 40–9, 51–5. Cf. S. N. Kramer, 'The Epic of Gilgames and Its Sumerian Sources', *JAOS*, LXIV (1944), pp. 7–23.

weather God is overcome by a dragon and loses his eye, which, however, is recovered by his son who in his turn is slain by his resurrected father who also kills the dragon.[1] In the Hittite myth, the 'Theogony' of Kumarbi, we learn of the fight between Alalu, king of heaven, and the mighty Anu, the first of the Gods, in which Alalu is defeated and goes down to the dark earth. But Kumarbi, in the place of Alalu, fights Anu, and pulls Anu down from the heavens.[2]

Not only is the sacred combat prominent in the myths, but it appears frequently in glyptic art: for example, on a seal from Tell Asmar, a seven-headed dragon or Hydra is shown being slain by two Gods; another shows the fight between Marduk and Tiamat, the latter in the form of a serpent; others show both the bird-man and scorpion-man captured and brought before the God in judgment; finally, there are early Akkadian seals which represent a contest between a human figure with divine attributes engaged in a struggle with a bull, a lion, or other mixed forms.[3] From the Ras Shamra tablets, many scenes of combat can be selected; for example, in the myth of the Hunting of Baal, the old God, El, fights with the young God, Baal, who is forced to encounter the *aququim* (probably derived from the monsters created by Tiamat) who presumably defeated him. And in the myth of Mot and Aleion, the son of Baal, and the God of the sky, winds, and rain, we find, when the extant text begins, that Mot has already killed Aleion who is mourned by his sister Anat and who avenges her brother's death by cleaving Mot with a sickle, grinding him between mill-stones, and casting his remains over the fields. Then, when the heavens rain and the wadies flow with honey, Aleion revives and fights once more with Mot.[4] Since this myth seems to have been the dramatic centre of the Canaanite New Year ritual, fuller consideration of it must remain until we reach its ritual form. A similar combat theme is to be found in the Phoenician myth of Zas (Baal?) and his fight with Ophioneus (Tannin?).

When we turn to the rituals of the ancient Near East, we find the

[1] Ivan Engnell, op. cit., pp. 63–4.

[2] Hans Gustav Guterbock, 'The Hittite Version of the Hurrian Kumarbi Myths: Oriental Forerunners of Hesiod', *AJA*, LII (1948), p. 124. For the larger significance of the myth, see E. A. Speiser, 'An Intrusive Hurro-Hittite Myth', *JAOS*, LXII (1942), pp. 98–102.

[3] Henri Frankfort, *Cylinder Seals* (London, 1939), pp. 197–204; S. H. Hooke, 'The Myth and Ritual Pattern in Jewish and Christian Apocalyptic', in *The Labyrinth*, ed. S. H. Hooke (London, 1935), pp. 224–5. Cf. James G. Frazer, *The Dying God* (London, 1911), pp. 105–12.

[4] Cyrus H. Gordon, *The Loves and Wars of Baal and Anat* (Princeton, 1943), pp. 5–19.

theme of combat plays as prominent a part there as it does in the mythology. In the Spring Festival in honour of the resurrection of Osiris, a festival celebrated on the twenty-sixth of the month of Khoiakh in Memphis, there took place a ceremonial combat between people symbolizing the inhabitants of Buto, which had been the predynastic capital of Lower Egypt, to represent the victory of Horus over the enemies of Osiris. Likewise, on the occasion of the festival in honour of the Memphite God Ptah, the drama re-enacted at that time represents the struggle between Horus and Seth. Another example of ritual combat is to be found in the Coronation Drama, dating from the reign of Sesostris I; in the ninth scene, barley symbolizing Osiris, is trodden by oxen, symbolizing Seth, who cut the barley to pieces on the threshing floor. The text, with its stage directions, reads as follows:

> *It happened that barley was put on the threshing floor.*
> *It happened that male animals were brought to trample it.*
> *That means Horus avenging his father . . .*

Horus speaks to the followers of Seth: 'Do not beat this my father.' (*Stage directions*) Beating Osiris; cutting up the God-barley. Horus speaks to Osiris: 'I have beaten for thee those who have beaten thee.' (*Stage directions.*) The followers of Seth—the bulls. Letopolis. Horus speaks to Osiris: 'His spittle shall not slash thee.' (*Stage directions.*) Seth—the asses. Ascension to heaven. Then, after the *Dd*-pillar has been raised and lowered, a mock fight takes place, and we read:

> *It happened that there was fighting.*
> *That means Horus fighting with Seth.*
> *Geb speaks to Horus and Seth: 'Forget!'*

(*Stage directions.*) Conflict between Horus and Seth. Fighting.

> *Horus speaks to the Children of Horus:*
> *'It is you who must forget.'*

(*Stage directions.*) Conflict between Children of Horus and Followers of Seth. Boxing.[1]

Nor is the theme of combat less frequently found in the rituals of Mesopotamia. In the Babylonian *akitu* festival, which stretched over

[1] Henri Frankfort, *Kingship*, op. cit., pp. 127, 129.

a period of the first eleven days of the new year, on the sixth day, Nebo comes from his temple at Borsippa to Babylon whereupon two bedecked figures, which had been made on the third day, have their heads cut off and are thrown into a fire. Again, from the eighth to the eleventh day, Marduk and his companion Gods resided in the Festival House on whose doors was found a representation of the combat with Tiamat and here it is likely the ritual combat took place.[1] Now, if we take the name of Tammuz to stand for a group of vegetation Gods, we soon see that such names as Abu, Ningizzida, Ninurta, Ningirsu, and Tammuz were not so much proper names for different Gods as, rather, different epithets for the same God whose various aspects were worshipped in different ways in different places.[2] Tammuz, whose Sumerian name *Dumu-zid-abzu* means 'the Faithful Son of the Subterranean (fresh-water) Ocean',[3] is overpowered in many ways: he is drowned by the tempest, and by flood and waves; he is overcome by the heat and in the shrivelling of the flora and fauna; he was sunk down, carried off, and chained; and he languished and died in the waste land.[4] Langdon translates a liturgy of the classical period which shows the identification of Tammuz with the power of fertility:

*'O brother, the verdure where is it taken?*
*Who has taken, who has taken?*
*The plants who has taken?'*
*'My sister, that which is taken I restore to thee.*
*Innini, that which is taken I restore to thee . . .'*
*'O brother, the crushed, where are they gone?*
*Who has garnered, who has garnered?*
*The plants from me who has garnered?'*
*'My sister, that which is garnered I will restore to thee.*
*Innini, that which is garnered I will restore to thee.'*

*'O brother, that which has been garnered, where is it transported?*
*Whom shall I embrace, whom shall I embrace?*
*Thee I would embrace, yea I would embrace.*
*Thee, my husband, I would embrace.'*[5]

[1] C. J. Gadd, 'Babylonian Myth and Ritual', in *Myth and Ritual,* op. cit., pp. 57–8.
[2] Henri Frankfort, 'God and Myths on Sargonid Seals', *Iraq,* I (1934), p. 17.
[3] William F. Albright, *From the Stone Age to Christianity* (Baltimore, 1940), p. 144.
[4] Machteld J. Mellinck, *Hyakinthos* (Utrecht, 1943), p. 80.
[5] Stephen Langdon, *Tammuz and Ishtar* (Oxford, 1914), p. 32.

While the evidence for the mock combat in the west-Semitic materials is at present meagre, when we look for it in the Ras Shamra texts, we find it re-occurring with such frequency that we feel that the Canaanites took delight in the depiction and enactment of struggle almost for its own sake, above the necessity for its use in the ritual pattern.[1] Thus, in VAB, we learn that Anat fights, wading in blood, and destroys 'the sons of the town', 'the people of the seashore', and 'the population of the setting of the sun'.

*At her feet (roll) their heads, like swathes;*
*About her (fall) their (severed) heads, (numerous) as locusts;*
*Like cut fruit left to dry, the severed heads of the ministrants pile high.*
*She girds herself for combat; now reach the (severed) hands up to her kirtle.*
*She bathes her knees in the blood of the attendants,*
*Her skirts in the entrails of the ministrants.*[2]

Again, in column VII of V AB, another ritual combat takes place in which Balu and his enemies fight. In I* AB, a dragon is killed, and there seems as well to be a fight depicted in columns III and IV, and in columns V and VI of I AB, too, where the fight is stopped by the goddess Sapsu who appeals to Mot: 'How canst thou contend against Aliian Balu?'[3] III AB, A, titled by Professor Gaster, 'The Battle of the Rain and the Sea', tells of the struggle between Baal, lord of abundance, and his 'inveterate foeman':

> *So the team charged onward at the gallop,*
> *Whilst Baal became straightway (?) like an eagle;*
> *With his ta(l)ons he smote the shoulder of His Highness of the Sea,*
> *And between the claws the Suffete of the River.*
>
> *Then lo, the fury of the sea subsided;*
> *Lo, the surface thereof flowed but gently,*
> *Lo, the deep thereof coursed out mildly.*[4]

Finally, the theme of combat finds expression in the story of Keret,

[1] Ivan Engnell, op. cit., pp. 101–2, from p. 37 of Hvidberg.

[2] Theodor H. Gaster, '"Baal is Risen . . ." An Ancient Hebrew Passion Play from Ras Shamra-Ugarit', *Iraq*, VI (1939), pp. 133–4.

[3] Ivan Engnell, op. cit., p. 123.

[4] Theodor H. Gaster, 'The Battle of the Rain and the Sea: An Ancient Semitic Nature-Myth', *Iraq*, IV (1937), p. 31. Professor Gaster calls attention to the parallels in Psalm 93 and Habakkuk 3. Cf. Rudolf Wittkower, 'Eagle and Serpent: A Study in the Migration of Symbols', *JWI*, II (1938–9), pp. 293–325; and E. Douglas Van Buren, 'The Dragon in Ancient Mesopotamia', *Orientalia*, n.s., XV (1945), pp. 1–45.

in the Krt text, who, though wounded, survives his wounds and lives on.

But, before the conflict can be resolved, the divine king must suffer and be humiliated, and he must die before he can be reborn, for the trial is not intended to be easy; too much is at stake, and a cheap victory cannot achieve the security of the community; suffering, humiliation, and death are the only coins with which victory can be paid for. In Egypt, the theme of suffering, however, does not occur with the same frequency with which it is found in Mesopotamia.[1] Nevertheless, even in Egypt, the serene optimism of the Old Kingdom, as Breasted calls it, gives way in time to the pessimism of the Feudal Age:

*How prosperous is this good prince!*
*The godly destiny has come to pass,*
*The generations pass away,*
*While others remain*
*Since the time of the ancestors,*
*The Gods who were aforetime,*
*Who rest in their pyramids,*
*Nobles and the glorious departed likewise,*
*Entombed in their pyramids . . .*
*Behold the places thereof;*
*Their walls are dismantled,*
*Their places are no more,*
*As if they had never been.*[2]

The passage calls to mind the note of sadness always implicit in the Golden Age theme, of which we have this striking Sumerian example, perhaps the oldest expression of the theme extant:

*In those days there was no snake, there was no scorpion, there was no* hyena,
*There was no lion, there was no* wild dog, *no wolf,*
*There was no fear, no terror,*
*Man had no rival.*
*In those days the land Shubur (East), the place of plenty, of righteous decrees,*

[1] Henri Frankforf, *Kingship*, op. cit., p. 4.

[2] James H. Breasted, *Dawn*, op. cit., p. 165. Cf. John A. Wilson, in *The Intellectual Adventure*, op. cit., pp. 101–10; and Raffaele Pettazoni, *La Confessione dei Peccati* (Bologna, 1935), II, pp. 1–68.

> *Harmony-tongued* Sumer (*South*), *the great land of the 'decrees of princeship'*,
> *Uri* (*North*), *the land having all that is* needful,
> *The land Martu* (*West*), *resting in security*,
> *The whole universe, the people in* unison!
> *To Enlil in one tongue* gave praise.[1]

Again, the lament of Isis over the body of Osiris:

> *The het-bird comes, the falcon comes; they are Isis and*
> *Nephthys, they come embracing their brother, Osiris . . .*
> *Weep for thy brother, Isis! Weep for thy brother, Nephthys!*
> *Weep for thy brother, Isis sits, her arms upon her head;*
> *Nephthys has seized the tips of her breasts (in mourning) because of her brother.*[2]

recalls the laments of Ishtar for Tammuz:

> *For far removed there is wailing,*
> *Ah me, my child, the far removed,*
> *My Damu, the far removed,*
> *My anointer, the far removed.*
> *For the sacred cedar where the mother bore him,*
> *In Eanna, high and low, there is weeping,*
> *Wailing for the house of the Lord they raise.*
> *The wailing is for the plants, the first lament is, 'they grow not'.*
> *The wailing is for the barley: the ears grow not.*
> *For the habitations and the flocks it is: they produce not.*
> *For the perishing wedded ones, for perishing children it is: the dark-headed people create not.*
> *The wailing is for the great river; it brings the flood no more.*
> *The wailing is for the fields of men; the* gunu *grows no more.*
> *The wailing is for the fish-ponds; the* dasuhur *fish spawn not.*
> *The wailing is for the cane-brake; the fallen stalks grow not.*
> *The wailing is for the forests; the tamarisks grow not.*
> *The wailing is for the highlands; the* masgam *trees grow not.*
> *The wailing is for the garden store-house; honey and wine are produced not.*

[1] S. N. Kramer, op. cit., p. 107. For later examples, see W. F. Albright, 'Primitivism in Ancient Western Asia', in Arthur O. Lovejoy and George Boas, eds., *Primitivism and Related Ideas in Antiquity* (Baltimore, 1935), pp. 421–32.

[2] Pyramid text, 1280–2, translated by Professor Breasted, *Development*, op. cit., p. 27.

*The wailing is for the meadows; the bounty of the garden, the* sihlu *plants grow not.*
*The wailing is for the palace; life unto distant days is not.*[1]

The counsel of despair permeates the end of Gilgamesh's story:

*Gilgamesh said to him, to Utnapishtim the Distant:*
*'Oh, what shall I do, Utnapishtim, (or) where shall I go,*
*As the robber has (already) taken hold of my members?*
*Death is the dwelling in my bedchamber;*
*And wherever I set my feet there is death!'*[2]

But, bitter as this is, it is more than matched by the pessimism of despair which sweeps through the whole of the *Lamentation over the Destruction of Ur*, which begins:

*He has abandoned his stable, his sheepfold (has been delivered) to the wind;*
*The wild ox has abandoned his stable, his sheepfold (has been delivered) to the wind.*
*The lord of all the lands has abandoned (his stable), his sheepfold (has been delivered) to the wind.*
*Enlil has abandoned . . . Nippur, his sheepfold (has been delivered) to the wind.*[3]

Finally, the myths themselves make clear the suffering and humiliation of the God; for example, Marduk is taken a prisoner, tried and beaten; he is then imprisoned in the mountain which symbolizes the underworld and there kept from the sun.[4]

The ritual practices of the ancient Near East abundantly confirm the widespread and deep-rooted theme of the suffering and humiliated God-king. In the Babylonian New Year Festival, during the course of the ceremonies on the fifth of Nisan, the king was stripped of his crown and sceptre by the high priest who also slapped him and pulled his ears; then, on his knees, the king recited the following prayer of repentance:

*I have not sinned, O Lord of the lands, I have not been unregardful of thy Godhead,*
*I have not destroyed Babylon, I have not commanded her ruin,*

[1] Stephen Langdon, op. cit., pp. 10–11.
[2] Alexander Heidel, *The Gilgamesh Epic*, op. cit., p. 90.
[3] Samuel N. Kramer, *Lamentation over the Destruction of Ur* (Chicago, 1940), p. 17.
[4] A. J. Wensinck, 'The Semitic New Year and the Origin of Eschatology', *Acta Orientalia*, I (1923), p. 185. Cf. Raffaele Pettazoni, op. cit., II, 69–139.

*I have not shaken E-sagil, her rites have I not forgotten,*
*I have not smitten the cheek of the people in my charge . . . nor caused their humiliation.*
*I take thought for Babylon, I have not beaten down her walls.*[1]

The king is found worriedly inquiring about hidden sins; for five days sacrifices are made and expiatory rites are performed, all leading to the climax when the king is humiliated in order to be triumphantly reinstated.[2] Similarly, in the enthronement festival of the Hittites, the king was forced to say: 'It is so, I have committed it.'[3] The intensity of the feeling of sin and suffering in the Accadian psalms of lamentation is both striking and moving, and though these psalms are not necessarily spoken by the king, nevertheless, since they could have been recited by either a king or by an individual, we may take them as expressing the sense of sin and suffering which the king himself feels. Such phrases as 'What have I done, O my God and goddess', 'The boundaries of God have I transgressed', 'I have sinned against my goddess', 'Many are my wrongdoings', abound in the lamentation formulas of the psalms.[4] The bitterness of humiliation is painfully felt:

*In the woe of heart, in bitter weeping,*
*In lamentation he sitteth,*
*In painful sighings, distress of heart,*
*In bitter weeping, in bitter lamentation*
*Like a dove he lamenteth, toilsome night and day*
*Until his God, the merciful, like a woman in travail he crieth*
*Sorrowful lamentation to thee he maketh.*
*Unto his God in prayer he humiliateth his face.*
*He weepeth and ceaseth not to lament.*[5]

More, he is plagued by many and terrible evils, by enemies, by revolts, by the loss of friends, by the destruction of his house, by the loss of his potency, by drowning, by being put in the grave, by

[1] C. J. Gadd, 'Babylonian Myth and Ritual', in *Myth and Ritual*, op. cit., pp. 53–4.
[2] G. G. Furlani, 'L'umiliazione del re durante la festa di capodanno a Babele', *SMSR*, IV (1928), pp. 51–6, 105–7.
[3] Ivan Engnell, op. cit., p. 66. Cf. Raffaele Pettazoni, 'Confession of Sins in Hittite Religion', *Gaster Anniversary Volume*, ed. Bruno Schindler and A. Marmorstein (London, 1936), pp. 467–71; and Raffaele Pettazoni, op. cit., (Rome, 1936), III, pp. 139–53.
[4] George Widengren, op. cit., pp. 95–6.
[5] Ibid., p. 101–2, from the *Oxford Editions of Cuneiform Texts*, VI, p. 35. Cf. *OECT*, VI, pp. 29, 63.

diseases of all sorts: 'My hair hath plucked out, the robe hath torn, evil hath . . . bound me.' Therefore he turns to his God:

> *I have cried unto thee, O my Lord, in the midst of the bright heavens,*
> *I bow down, I stand and seek thee.*[1]

No wonder, for his sins have been many and grievous:

> *Rebellious thoughts have I planned, loosened the evil.*
> *What is not welfare I have spoken, all evil thou know(est?)*
> *The food of God, my creator, I have eaten.*
> *I have trampled upon abomination evil I have done.*
> *To thine own wide property I lifted up my face.*
> *To thy precious silver my desire we(nt).*
> *I lifted up my hand touching what should not be touched.*
> *In my impurity I entered into the house (of God (?) )*
> *A strong abomination against thee have I done, I,*
> *What is displeasing unto thee I have offered before thee (?)*
> *In the anger of my heart I have cursed thy divinity.*[2]

How far from and yet how near to Paul we are, we may note in the repeated confession: 'Wrongdoing whether I know it or not have I done,' and 'The sin which I have done, convert into goodness'. Finally, one may listen to a psalm of lamentation recited by Asurbanipal:

> *Why are bound at me*
> *Sickness and evil of my heart?*
> *Tribulation and destruction,*
> *Enmity in the land,*
> *Strife in the house,*
> *Are not removed from my side.*
> *Disturbing and word of evil*
> *constantly draw up in battle-array against me.*
>
> *Illness of heart and illness of body,*
> *have bent my figure*
> *With woe and wail*
> *I make an end to my days.*
>
> *On the day of the city-God,*
> *On the festival day,*
> *I am disturbed.*

[1] Ibid., p. 129. [2] Ibid., p. 149.

*Death and trouble*
*make an end of me.*

*Because of grief and sorrow*
*day and night*
*I lament.*

*I sigh! O God,*
*Give (it) to him who is not fearing (Thee).*
*May I see Thy light.*

*How long, O God,*
*wilt thou do that to me.*
*It is done to me*
*as to one who is not fearing God or Goddess.*[1]

Already we begin to hear Job's cries in this psalm, nor is it alone in its bitterness; the despair which comes to man when he knows not God's inscrutable ways is expressed in the *Ludlul vel Nemeki*, which we shall consider in another connection, and in other psalms: 'As for thee, thy word who comprehendeth it? Who can equal it?' and 'His wisdom is difficult, the people do not understand,' and finally:

*Who comprehends the will of the Gods in heaven?*
*The counsel of God full of knowledge who understands it?*
*What infirm men have comprehended the way of God?*[2]

The humiliation of the king is repeatedly found in the Canaanite ritual texts: for example, in V AB, Mot declares that Balu has been expelled from his throne, his diadem dragged off, and his ear pulled. Again, BH seems to hint at some form of expiatory ritual, and the prayer in *Dnil*:

*Wouldst thou bless him, O Bull-El, my Father,*
*wouldst thou show him grace, O Creator of creatures?*
*And may a son of his be in the 'house',*
*a root in the midst of his palace.*
*One that raises the stele of his* il ib *in the shrine,*
*one that makes* ztr *to him in the earth,*
*that brings his incense down to the dust,*
*that guards his holy place,*

[1] Ibid., pp. 222–3. [2] Ibid., p. 184.

*that makes* tbk *with the tablets of his* nis (?)
*that expels him who revolts against him;*
*a holder of his hand in drunkenness,*
*his arm in satiety of wine;*
*one that nourishes with his offering (?) the house of Balu,*
[*that provides (or the like)*] . . . *the house of El,*
*a plasterer of his roof on the day of . . .*
*a washer of his clothes on the day of . . .*[1]

is interpreted by Professor Engnell as a passage of suffering in the cult, though the meaning of the prayer is open to other interpretations. But much more straightforward is III D, column I, of *Dnil*:

*They strike him twice on the pate,*
*three times on the ear.*
*They spill his blood as when shedding*
*as at a slaughter they surely bring him on his knees,*
*so that like wind goes out his soul,*
*like a breath his spirit,*
*like smoke (from his body?),*[2]

and, later, the king is abjured to '. . . shed his tears like quarter-shekels'. Enough has been shown, I think, to indicate the place of the theme of humiliation and suffering in the myth and ritual pattern of the ancient Near East, and we may conclude with Frazer's explanation of the idea of suffering:

'If we ask why a dying God should be chosen to take upon himself and carry away the sins and sorrows of the people, it may be suggested that in the practice of using the divinity as a scapegoat we have a combination of two customs which were at one time distinct and independent. On the one hand we have seen that it has been customary to kill the human or animal God in order to save his divine life from being weakened by the inroads of age. On the other hand we have seen that it has been customary to have a general expulsion of evils and sins once a year. Now, if it occurred to people to combine these two customs, the result would be the employment of the dying God as a scapegoat. He was killed, not originally to take away sin, but to save the divine life from the degeneracy of old age; but, since he had to be killed at any rate, people may have thought that they might as well seize the opportunity to lay upon him the burden of

[1] Ivan Engnell, op. cit., p. 136. [2] Ibid., p. 139.

their sufferings and sins, in order that he might bear it away with him to the unknown world beyond the grave.'[1]

From the suffering and humiliation of the God to his death is the next inevitable step. Here, of course, the evidence is very considerable, for the outcome of the combat was in almost every case the death of the God. Osiris is defeated by Seth, and is imprisoned in the earth. Tammuz, too, dies in all his many forms, as do Attis, Adonis, and Aleion-Baal. And they die because at bottom they are nature Gods in whom are incarnate the forces of regular fructification. Thus, Osiris was identified with the life-giving waters of the Nile: 'Thou art indeed the Nile, great on the fields at the beginning of the seasons; Gods and men live by the moisture that is in thee.'[2] He was also identified with the soil: 'The soil is on thy arm, its corners are upon thee as far as the four pillars of the sky. When thou movest, the earth trembles. . . . As for thee, the Nile comes forth from the sweat of thy hands.'[3] And he was also identified with the vegetation: 'I live as "Grain", I grow as "Grain" . . . I am barley.'[4] 'One grown great in the submerged grain' is what the mother-Goddess calls Tammuz,[5] and in an incantation he is referred to as: 'Creating the seed of cattle, lord of the stalls.'[6] And these descriptions are found in his iconography on the Sargonid seals: one shows the God producing corn, another has him holding an ear of corn.[7] Baal, too, is described as the 'Lord of Green Things', while the Hittite Tessup is called the 'Lord of the Camp'. But there is no need to belabour the evidence for a theme which is so well known as the death of the God in Near Eastern mythology.[8]

Ritual practice repeats the element of the death of the God in many instances. Thus, in the Osirian festival of Khoiakh, a hollow gold effigy of Osiris was filled with barley and sand, wrapped in rushes, and placed in a stone trough which was watered and placed in the sun until the twenty-second of the month, when it was sent on a voyage in the temple pool, and on the twenty-fourth day of the

[1] James G. Frazer, *The Scapegoat*, op. cit., p. 227.
[2] James H. Breasted, *Development*, op. cit., p. 18.
[3] Ibid., p. 21.
[4] Ibid., p. 23.
[5] S. Langdon, op. cit., p. 15.
[6] Ibid., p. 35. For other epithets, see Machteld J. Mellinck, op. cit., pp. 81–2.
[7] H. Frankfort, *Cylinder Seals*, op. cit., pp. 110–16. Cf. James G. Frazer, *Adonis Attis Osiris*, op. cit., I, pp. 227–34.
[8] James G. Frazer, *Adonis Attis Osiris*, op. cit., I, p. 6.

month was transferred to the House of Sokar.[1] Again, in Babylonian ritual, some time during the eighth and eleventh days of Nisan, the God Bel meets his death at the hands of Tiamat, and in a commentary explaining the ritual acts of the people during the New Year Festival, we learn that, when it is said that Marduk is imprisoned in the mountain, it means the death of the God, and a cylinder seal shows the liberated God emerging from the mountain. The people of the city frantically search for the God, saying: 'Where is he held captive?' until Nabu overcomes the opponents of Marduk and frees the God.[2] I* AB, the Death of Baal, clearly indicates the death of the God in Canaanite ritual:

> *Forthwith* Ltpn il dpid
> *descends from the throne.*
> *He goes down from step to step,*
> *He sits on the earth.*
> *He pours the sheaf of woe on his head,*
> *the dust of wallowing on his pate,*
> lps *he tears asunder the girdle,*
> *the* gr *of stone he throws,* (*away*)
> *the image of wood.*
> *He tears away side-whiskers and chin-beard,*
> *he cuts off the stick of his organ.*
> *he ploughs* (*his body*) *like a garden of autumn fruit,*
> *like a valley he demolishes the heights.*
> *He lifts his voice and cries:*
> *'Balu is dead!*
> *Where are the people of bn Dagan,*
> *where the crowd of Balu's temple?*
> *I will descend into the earth.'*[3]

Dnil is mourned over by weeping women until seven years have passed, and Keret, too, weeps over the death of the God:

> *And* (*when*) *he falls asleep at his crying*
> *the humming of the sleep fatigues him,*
> *and he lies there* (*in the*) *sighing and* (*overflows with tears—or the like*),
> (*then*) *in his dream Il descends,*

[1] A. M. Blackman, 'Myth and Ritual in Ancient Egypt', in *Myth and Ritual*, op. cit., pp. 19–20. Cf. James G. Frazer, *Adonis Attis Osiris*, op. cit., II, 84–8.
[2] H. Frankfort, *Kingship*, op. cit., pp. 321–5.
[3] Ivan Engnell, op. cit., pp. 119–20.

*In his vision the Father of Man.*
*And he brings near, as Karit wished, hundreds (?),*
*(while) Numan galim Il (Il's servant), the king is crying,*
*the Bull, his father, wishes him sovereignty (? or: 'generations'?),*
*yea, the Father of Man. . .*[1]

IV AB seems to show the death of Balu, as does SS, 'The Gracious Gods', in which, as Professor Gaster has shown, the image of the pruned vine symbolizes the slain God:

*As lord and master sate he enthroned*
*In his one hand was the sceptre of childlessness,*
*In his other that of widowhood;*
*yet see, they now prune him* who *prune the vine,*
*smite him who smite the vine,*
*make his rotten grapes to fall as from a vine.*[2]

I will not add to the evidence on this point since it may be said that, whenever the theme of humiliation and suffering occurs, and with it attendant lamentations, the implication that the God is dead follows from it, and we have already cited enough instances from the myth and ritual pattern of the ancient Near East on the theme of suffering to demonstrate how abiding and pervasive it was, and consequently with it the theme of the death of the God. For the God must die, and if at first he dies because he merely represents the flowering and decay of the vegetation, he soon takes on to himself much more than mere representative action. He dies that the people might live; through him they vicariously expiate their sins and pay their penance; in his suffering they suffer; and in his death is their life. In time, the dying God becomes a God of redemption, and in his own person undergoes the searing experiences of combat, suffering, and death.

But, if the God suffers and dies, he is also reborn, and perhaps of all the elements in the myth and ritual pattern of the ancient Near East, this is the most significant and far-reaching both in its function and effects. For, without the absolutely indispensable element of resurrection, the pattern could have no useful meaning, the well-being of the community could not be secured, and only chaos and despair would reign supreme. That small moment before the God

[1] Ibid., pp. 151–2.
[2] Theodor H. Gaster, 'A Canaanite Ritual Drama: The Spring Festival at Ugarit', *JAOS*, LXVI (1946), p. 49.

revived filled the hearts of men with the most wrenching anguish, for they knew that the struggle was not easy nor the stakes small, and they knew above all that there was always the fearful possibility that the God might not in fact be resurrected. One senses in the myths and rituals this quiet, fateful moment when all the world seems to stand still in terrible anticipation of the outcome of the theophany of the God. Carlyle called it, not quite accurately, the centre of indifference, but Beethoven caught it in all its silent terror when in the passage for the basses in the Fifth Symphony just after the chaotic tumult of the third movement we stand immobile, unable to go backward or forward, waiting but not really being sure that the note of triumph which announces the final exulting movement will actually be sounded, and this is a passage which is heard often in differing forms in the last quartets as well. But the God does revive, the vegetation reappears, the waters flow again, the sun rises once more, spring comes again, and man renews his hopes for the coming year; the victory of the God symbolizes man's conquest for the coming year of all the forces which stand threatening and ready to overwhelm him. Even in the very moment of joy, however, he remembers the struggle and suffering of the God; the enemies are not defeated so much as held off for the time being, and it remained for the Hebrews to show man how he could snatch victory out of the very mouth of defeat by looking to the protection of the one force greater than the forces which ringed him round, a force which, paradoxically enough, was not in nature but in an idea.

We may recall that Osiris met his death in a number of ways, by being felled, by inclosure, and by drowning. Isis then seeks him far and wide; in one version of the myth we read:

'Isis and Nephthys saw him. . . . Horus commanded Isis and Nephthys in Busiris, that they seize upon Osiris, and that they prevent him from drowning. They turned round the head (of Osiris) . . . and they brought him to the land.'[1]

In some cases we find that after Anubis had reunited the scattered parts of Osiris's body and had wrapped it in bandages for burial, Isis revived him by '. . . making a shadow with her pinions and causing a wind with her winds' and in this way '. . . raising the weary limbs' of the dead Osiris, and in the Heliopolitan form of the myth, Osiris is revived by being washed. Again, we know that the sun-God is re-

[1] James H. Breasted, *Development*, op. cit., pp. 26–7.

born in the shape of the divine beetle Khepri when he proceeds from the Netherworld and settles in the Morning Boat and appears between the thighs of Nut, the sky.[1] The dead king is abjured to rise as did Osiris: 'Arise and see Arise and Near'; 'Pepi ascends to Heaven'; Unas '. . . rises at the eastern side of Heaven. Renewed in thy time, rejuvenated at thy hour.'[2] One more illustration from Egyptian mythology must suffice, and this comes from a text dealing with the royal dead in which Atum and the dead king are virtually equated; one stanza reads as follows:

*Thou risest and settest; thou goest down with Re,*
*sinking in the dust with Nedy.*
*Thou risest and settest; thou risest up with Re and*
*ascendest with the Great Reed Float.*
*Thou risest and settest; thou goest down with Nephthys,*
*sinking in the dusk with the Evening Boat of the Sun.*
*Thou risest and settest; thou risest up with Isis,*
*ascending with the Morning Boat of the Sun.*[3]

The resurrection of the God in Babylonian myth is movingly recorded in a Tammuz liturgy:

*In Erech its brick-walls reposed; upon Erech a faithful eye he cast.*
*The figs grew large; in the plains the trees thrived (?)*
*There the valiant in (his) boat descended, from Hades hastened.*
*The holy husband of the heavenly queen in a boat descended, from Hades hastened.*
*Where grass was not, there grass is eaten.*
*Where water was not, water is drunk.*
*Where the cattle-sheds were not, cattle-sheds are built.*[4]

The identity of the God with the renewed vitality of burgeoning nature is made clear, for, when he is born again, the grass grows, water is drunk, and the cattle live; man can once more face the new year with courage and hope. But the Tammuz liturgies are late; much earlier is the lovely Sumerian myth called 'Inanna's Descent to the Nether World', just now available in its original form, thanks to the learning and skill of Professors Chiera and Kramer. The poem

[1] H. Frankfort, *Kingship*, op. cit., p. 156.
[2] Ibid., pp. 116, 118.
[3] Ibid., p. 121.
[4] Stephen Langdon, op. cit., p. 21.

begins when the great goddess sets her mind to go from the great above to the great below:

*My lady abandoned heaven, abandoned earth,*
*To the nether world she descended,*
*Inanna abandoned heaven, abandoned earth,*
*To the nether world she descended,*
*Abandoned lordship, abandoned ladyship,*
*To the nether world she descended.*

Taking with her the seven decrees, that is, the crown upon her head, radiance on her countenance, the rod of lapis lazuli in her hand, sparkling stones on her breast, a gold ring in her hand, a breastplate about her breast, and ointment on her face, she walked to the nether world with her messenger, Ninshubur, whom she instructs that, should she fail to return, the messenger should appeal for her deliverance from Enlil, and, if he refuses, to appeal to Nanna, and, as a last resort, to Enki, saying:

*O father Enki, let not thy daughter be* put to death *in the nether world,*
*Let not thy good metal be* ground up *into the dust of the nether world,*
*Let not thy good lapis lazuli be* broken up *into the stone of the stone-worker,*
*Let not thy* boxwood *be* cut up *into the wood of the wood-worker,*
*Let not the maid Inanna be* put to death *in the nether world.*

Inanna arrives at the lapis lazuli palace of the nether world, where she announces herself as 'Queen of heaven, the place where the sun rises'. She falsely states that she has come to the land of no return to witness the funeral rites of the husband of her elder sister and is admitted by instruction of her elder sister, Ereshkigal. But, as she passes through the seven gates, one by one her divine decrees are stripped by her:

*Extraordinarily, O Inanna, have the decrees of the nether world been perfected,*
*O Inanna,* do not question *the rites of the nether world,*

until she is stripped naked and brought before the judgment of the seven Anuunaki, who fasten upon her the eyes of death:

The sick woman *was turned into a* corpse,
*The* corpse *was hung from a* stake.

After three days and three nights had passed, Ninshubur appeals to Enlil and to Nanna in vain, but Enki, lamenting: 'I am troubled,' fashions from dirt the *kurgarru* and the *kalaturru*, giving to the first the food of life and to the other the water of life, and instructs Ninshubur to sprinkle on the corpse sixty times the food of life and sixty times the water of life, and 'Verily Inanna will arise'. This done, Inanna does arise, and the dead hasten ahead of her, and thus the poem as it is extant at this date ends.[1] Though, in this case, the resurrected God is in the shape of a female figure, the ancient Near East did not make the sharp sexual differentiation which we do, and the myth is an exciting and beautiful version of the dead and resurrected vegetation God.

In the Canaanite 'Baal is Risen', Anat, after finding the dead Baal, embraces him:

> *Yea, she embraces him . . .*
> *And covers him with a garment . . .*
> *Then* rises *her song and her exultation* (?)
> . . . *her youthful exultation* (?):
> *Sweetly issues the voice from her mouth:*
> *'The valley which erst was an highway of Death*
> *Is turned to a valley of Life Triumphant!'*
> *Thereupon she goes up into the . . .*
> *Yea, unto the . . . and the Hill of the North,*
> *Which lies in that pleasant place, the valley of life Triumphant!*
> *Then unto Baal she utters her voice:*
> *'Glad tidings, every God! Glad tidings every baal!*
> *And glad tidings, every scion* (?) *of Dagan!*
> *For now is a due steer indeed to be born for Baal,*
> *And a wild ox for Him Who Rides upon the Clouds!'*
> *Baal Puissant rejoices* (*thereat*), . . .[2]

The Hill of the North to which Anat goes is but one example of the many references to the primeval hill or sacred mountain which are to be found in the myth and ritual pattern of the ancient Near East. In the Egyptian cosmogony, life first manifested itself on the primeval hill which arose out of Nun, the abyss, and in time it came to be thought that the sun temple of Heliopolis itself stood on this very spot, though each temple also partook of the life-giving power

[1] Samuel N. Kramer, *Sumerian Mythology*, op. cit., pp. 88–96.
[2] Theodor H. Gaster, ' "Baal is Risen",' op. cit., p. 130.

of the sacred hill, and the royal tombs, too, were made in the shape of the hill to insure the rebirth of the king by virtue of the life force inherent in the hill upon which the tomb was modelled. We recall, too, the mountain from which Marduk is liberated, and it is probable that the ziggurat was the symbol for this mountain.[1]

The ritual practices of the Near East repeat in symbolic form the mythical element of the resurrection of the dead God. On the thirtieth of the month of Khoiakh, the *Dd*-column was raised to symbolize the resurrection of Osiris; at the same time, this festival commemorated the accession of a famous king, probably Menes. Moreover, the day was considered to be the ideal one for the accession of a king, as well as being the day selected for the celebration of the king's jubilee, the Sed-festival. And, since it was in addition to all these, the New Year's Day as well, it is not hard to understand what high significance was attached to it, so that there are, in fact, many layers of meaning in the symbolic act when Osiris was revived and his son Horus was triumphantly installed. The *Dd*-column is found in its mythical form in the sycamore which grew up around and enveloped the body of Osiris after he was found by the two sisters, and in a Pyramid text, the king Pepi goes to the Field of Offerings where the swallows, who are the Imperishable Stars, give him '. . . this tree of life, whereof they live, that ye (Pepi and the Morning Star) may at the same time live thereof'.[2] The essential meaning of the raising of the *Dd*-tree has been well pointed out by Professor Blackman.[3] On many of the Mesopotamian cylinder seals which Professor Frankfort has studied with such penetration, the sacred tree is frequently depicted, and often in conjunction with the God in the winged disc, which in itself is a symbol for the sky; the fusion of the three elements creates an interchange between the God, the king, and the sacred tree which, as Professor Hooke has suggested, points to the tree as the symbol of the life-giving functions of the king.[4]

[1] For the sacred mountain in Egypt and Mesopotamia, see Gertrude R. Levy, *The Gate of Horn* (London, 1948), pp. 168–70, 173–5.

[2] James H. Breasted, *Religion*, op. cit., p. 134, Pyr. 1209–16.

[3] A. M. Blackman, in *Myth and Ritual*, op. cit., pp. 24–5. See James G. Frazer, *The Dying God*, op. cit., pp. 211–12, for the meaning behind the resurrected God, and *Adonis Attis Osiris*, op. cit., II, 15, 86–91, 108–12, 153–7, for Egyptian ritual.

[4] Henri Frankfort, *Cylinder Seals*, op. cit., pp. 204–16; S. H. Hooke, 'The Myth and Ritual Pattern in Jewish and Christian Apocalyptic', in *The Labyrinth*, op. cit., p. 226. In addition, see Hélène Danthine, *Le palmier-dattier et les arbres sacrés dans l'iconographie de l'Asie Occidentale ancienne*, 2 vols., (Paris, 1937); and Nell Perrot, *Les représentations de l'arbre scaré sur les monuments de Mesopotamie et d'Elam* (Paris, 1937).

Similarly, and not surprisingly, water symbolized the life-giving function of the king. Not only is Tammuz represented in one liturgy as having been born in the sacred cedar, but he is also known as the lord of the flood who suffers death in the raging flood:

> *The shining ocean to thy destiny has taken thee.*
> *It has transported, the flood transported, the flood transported, the flood seized thee into Hades.*[1]

Often the God was shown with streams of water pouring from his body or from a vase which he holds.[2] In Egyptian ritual, we find that water was drawn from a sacred pool to be used in the daily lustration of the king at dawn to represent the daily rebirth of the sun-God and the same practice was followed in the course of the coronation of the king and, since the Gods and men live by the moisture that is in Osiris, it was thought that the dead were revivified by the fluid which came out of Osiris. We may recall, too, that Inanna is sprinkled sixty times with the water of life before she can be restored to life. Baal is described as withholding the early rain, and after his defeat:

> *for seven years Balu withholds,*
> *for eight the Rider of the Clouds.*
> *There will be no dew, no showers,*
> *no surging up of the Deep,*
> *no sweetness of the voice of Balu,*
> *because torn is the garment of* Dnil mt rpi,
> *the robe of* Gzr mt hrnmi.[3]

Therefore, so that he '. . . will surely bestow the favour of *gentle rain from the clouds*', the Gods pour libations:

> *'Here is the holy cup,' saith the Consort, addressing him:*
> *'Here is the goblet,' saith Asherat.*
> *Another takes a thousand jars*
> *And mixes ten thousand measures of wine.*[4]

'Not only is each New Year a memorial of the creation', Professor Wensinck tells us, 'but it is a repetition of it, and the creation itself

[1] Stephen Langdon, op. cit., p. 15.
[2] Many examples have been collected by E. Douglas van Buren, *The Flowing Vase and the God with the Streams* (Berlin, 1933).
[3] Ivan Engnell, op. cit., p. 140.
[4] Theodor H. Gaster, ' "Baal is Risen",' op. cit., p. 132.

is regarded as a kind of New Year.'[1] The recital of the myth of creation therefore possessed a virtue which went far beyond that of mere narrative; the recitation of the triumph of creation over chaos was in itself the guarantee of that triumph, and the description of the process of creation was the means whereby the order and regularity of the world, without which man could not possibly survive, could be achieved in the course of the ritual practices which were, in fact, designed for this very purpose of bringing about the control over nature for the coming year which men so fervently desired and needed. The recitation of the myth of creation in the ritual was, as it were, a play within a play, and served almost the same purpose: to bring about mimetically *in parvo* the benefits of the vaster pattern of actual creation. Moreover, the act of creation was indissolubly connected with the resurrection, for, as the God dies, so is he reborn in a fresh and new act of creation; again, we meet with a parallel symbolism in which layers of meaning are enfolded. And it is precisely because of this intense desire for control that we find so many versions of the creation; it is as if the very multiplicity itself would enable man to be sure that out of the many at least one would surely serve. 'The Egyptians', Professor Wilson remarks succinctly, 'accepted various myths and discarded none of them.'[2] According to one myth, then, life was thought to have issued forth from the primordial waters of the underworld, called Nun, from which the sun daily arose and from whose waters the river Nile drew its floods. But Nun was associated with other creatures who inhabited, or, more properly constituted chaos itself: his wife, Naunet, the primeval space who later became the sky which lay over the Netherworld; Huh, the primordial formlessness, and his wife, Hauhet; Kuk, the darkness, and his consort, Kauket; and Amun, or Amon, 'the hidden', and his wife, Amaunet, who are the air and wind. Then, on the Isle of Flames, the Eight made the sun-God to arise out of the waters, and, with this work, their function ceased. Atum in his turn headed the supreme council of the Gods, whose centre was the temple of the sun at Heliopolis; this was the Ennead, which composed Shu and Tefenet, air and moisture; their children, Geb and Nut, or earth and sky; and their children, Osiris and Isis, Seth and Nephythys; and the whole concept established a bridge, to use Professor Frankfort's felicitous phrase, between nature and man through the institution of the king-

[1] A. J. Wensinck, op. cit., p. 169.
[2] John A. Wilson, *Intellectual Adventure*, op. cit., p. 50.

ship. But the sun-God was conceived as having made the creation out of himself:

*When I had formed, then (only) the forms were formed.*
*All the forms were formed after my forming.*
*Numerous are the forms from that which proceeded from my mouth.*
*The heaven had not been formed,*
*The earth had not been formed,*
*The ground had not been created*
*(For?) the reptiles in that place.*

Atum then tells us that he raised himself out of the inertness of the abyss and, thinking wisely in his heart, copulated with himself:

*What I ejected was Shu,*
*What I spat out was Tefenet.*
*My father, the abyss, sent them.*
*My eye followed them through ages of ages (?)*
*As (they) separated from me.*

But Shu and Tefenet returned his eye to him after he had replaced it with a resplendent eye; and he wept, and from his tears came men.[1] In the Turin Papyri, the sun-God is described as:

*. . . the divine God who arose by himself,*
*Who made the heaven, the earth, the air of life, and the fire,*
*The Gods, the men, the wild animals, and the flocks,*
*The reptiles, the birds, and the fish,*
*The king of men and of Gods together . . .*[2]

Indeed, the Book of the Dead has it that the sun-God created the Ennead by giving names to eight parts of his body and 'thus arose these Gods who are in his following'. But much more sophisticated and subtle is the cosmogony of the Memphite theology where the creation is placed in the heart and tongue, that is, in the mind of Ptah the Great:

'When the eyes see, the ears hear, and the nose breathes, they transmit to the heart. It is he (the heart) who brings forth every issue, and it is the tongue which repeats the thoughts of the heart. He fashioned all Gods, even Atum and his ennead. Every divine word

[1] W. Max Muller, op. cit., pp. 68–9.
[2] Ibid., p. 80.

came into existence by the thought of the heart and the commandment of the tongue. It was he who made the kas and (created) the qualities; who made all food, all offerings, by this word; who made that which is loved and that which is hated. It was he who gave life to the peaceful and death to the guilty.'

Then, having made every work, every handicraft, and the movement of every limb:

'There came the saying that Atum, who created the Gods, stated concerning Ptah-Tatenen: "He is the fashioner of the Gods, he, from whom all things went forth, even offerings, and food and divine offerings and every good thing! And Thoth perceived that his strength was greater than all Gods. Then Ptah was satisfied, after he had made all things and every divine word." '[1]

Nor did Ptah rest at this point, for he fashioned the Gods, made the cities, and settled the names; more, he installed the Gods in their holy places, made their offerings to flourish, and '. . . made likenesses of their bodies to the satisfaction of their hearts'. Small wonder, therefore, that Professor Breasted is reminded of the words of the Creator in Genesis and asks: 'Is there not here the primeval germ of the later Alexandrian doctrine of the "Logos"?'

The introduction to the Sumerian poem, titled by Professor Kramer, 'Gilgamesh, Enkidu, and the Nether World', contains a remarkable description of the creation of the universe as conceived of by the Sumerians. This reads:

*After Heaven had been moved away from earth,*
*After earth had been separated from heaven,*
*After the name of man had been fixed;*
*After An had carried off heaven,*
*After Enlil had carried off earth,*
*After Ereshkigal had been carried off into Kur as its prize;*
*After he had set sail, after he had set sail,*
*After the father for Kur had set sail,*
*After Enki for Kur had set sail;*
*Against the king the small ones it (Kur) hurled,*
*Against Enki, the large ones it hurled;*
*Its small ones, stones of the hand,*
*Its large ones, stones of . . . reeds,*

[1] James H. Breasted, *Development*, op. cit., pp. 44–5.

*The keel of the boat of Enki,*
*In battle, like the attacking storm, overwhelm;*
*Against the king, the water at the head of the boat,*
*Like a wolf devours,*
*Against Enki, the water at the rear of the boat,*
*Like a lion strikes down.*[1]

Thus we learn that, prior to creation, heaven and earth were one and even then some of the Gods were already in existence; when heaven and earth were separated, the heaven-God, An, took the heaven and the air-God, Enlil, took the earth. From the primeval sea, came the cosmic mountain, and the separation of heaven from earth was accomplished by Enlil:

*The lord, that which is appropriate verily caused to appear,*
*The lord whose decisions are unalterable,*
*Enlil, who brings up the seed of the land from the earth,*
Took care *to move away heaven from earth,*
*Took care to move away earth from heaven.*[2]

By the time of the *Enuma Elish*, these crude conceptions had been refined into a connected and stirring narrative which begins:

*When above the heaven had not (yet) been named,*
*(And) below the earth had not (yet) been called by a name;*
*(When) only Apsu primeval, their begetter, (existed),*
*(And) mother Tiamat, who gave birth to them all;*
*(When) their waters (still) mingled together,*
*(And) no dry land had been formed (and) not (even) a marsh could be seen;*
*When none of the Gods had been brought into being,*
*(When) they had not (yet) been called by (their) names, and (their) destinies had not (yet) been fixed:*
*Then were the Gods created in the midst of them.*[3]

In this watery chaos, as Professor Jacobsen calls it, two Gods, Lahmu and Lahamu are begotten by Apsu, the sweet waters, and Tiamat, the sea, and from them in turn came Anshar and Kishar, the one the circle which went around the sky and was male, and the other the

[1] Samuel N. Kramer, *Sumerian Mythology*, op. cit., pp. 37–8.
[2] Ibid., p. 52.
[3] Alexander Heidel, *The Babylonian Genesis*, op. cit., pp. 7–8. Other Babylonian creation stories will be found on pages 49–64 of his edition.

circle which went around the earth and was female. From Anshar and Kishar was born Anu, God of the sky who gave rise to Nudimmut or Ea or Enki, lord of the earth, but an earlier version of the creation has it that from Anshar and Kishar came the sky and earth which were in time wrenched apart by the wind. The *Enuma Elish* continues with the description of the divine companions restlessly surging back and forth in Tiamat's belly and she complains to them and threatens them with extinction. But the wise Ea or Enki casts a spell on Apsu and kills him in his sleep, and thus chaos is demonstrated to be dominated by the Gods. As to the element of creation in the Ras Shamra texts, very little can so far be discerned: we know that the head of the Canaanite Panthenon was the God El whose consort was the Goddess Asherat, 'She Who Treads the Sea'. El dwelt in the 'Source of the Two Deeps' from which 'he causes the rivers to flow', and in the myth SS, he seduces two women, who give birth to Shahar, the Dawn, and Shalim, the Perfect One, the two 'beautiful and gracious Gods'.[1]

As to the presence of the myth of creation and its recitation in the ritual practices, we shall content ourselves with a few illustrations. We have already seen that in Egypt the coronation was thought of as a new creation, particularly since the king was so closely identified with the rising sun. Thus, in the Memphite theology, the closing portion narrates how Osiris became earth in the Royal Castle on the north side of this land, while his son, Horus, appeared as king of Upper Egypt and as king of Lower Egypt in the arms of his father, Osiris, and in the presence of the Gods. And the myth of creation is enacted in the course of the other festivals in the symbolic actions which we have already described. In Babylon, in the course of the New Year Festival, the creation epic was recited in its entirety by the high priest on the fourth day of the festival, late in the evening, as he stood before the image of Marduk, and it is significant that the next day was the Day of Atonement. In the Hittite annual festival, in the *purullias*, the epic of creation was included as part of the ritual.

Creation, therefore, means the making and the renewal of life, the actual process of creation and recreation being symbolized in the act of the sacred marriage. Through his connection with the Goddess-queen, the divine God-king creates new life and thus ensures its continued vitality for the coming year. Having passed through the agonies of death and resurrection, he now signifies his victory by

[1] William F. Albright, *Stone Age*, op. cit., pp. 175–6.

the act of creation; he demonstrates yet continued potency. Here is the moment of triumph too for the Goddess-queen, for hitherto her rôle has been somewhat subordinate to that of the God-king, though we remember that it was Isis's faithful search for the lost Osiris and her bringing him to life which effected his resurrection; similarly, Inanna dares the terrors of the nether world, the land of no return, to search for her lost lover; Ishtar, too, long in sorrow wailed for her husband who slept; nor can we forget Anat wallowing in the blood of her enemies. Now the Goddess-queen, having searched for and found her lost father-brother-son, having breathed life into his body, becomes the wife-mother. The mystery of fertility and birth goes back to the earliest stages of man's history and we need only recall that the first-known plastic representations of the human form are the small female statuettes made by the people of the Gravettian culture; these female figures are represented as apparently pregnant, and, though the face and arms are scarcely treated, the womb, the breasts, the hips, and the buttocks are emphasized to the full; and and by the time of the Mesolithic age, there is already in existence a fertility cult.[1] The sacred marriage is frequently celebrated in the myths of the ancient Near East. After Isis raised the weary limbs of Osiris, she received '. . . his seed, bringing forth an heir, nursing the child in solitude, whose place is not known, introducing him when his arm grew strong in the Great Hall'.[2] Again, in Sumerian mythology, the marriage of the gods is often described; for example, in the myth, 'The Begetting of Nanna', the God Enlil is enticed by Ninlil on the advice of her mother:

'*At the pure river, O maid, at the pure river wash thyself,*
*O Ninlil, walk along the bank of the Idnunbirdu,*
*The bright-eyed, the lord, the bright-eyed,*
*The "great mountain", father Enlil, the bright-eyed, will see thee.*
*The Shepherd . . . who decrees the fates, the bright-eyed, will see thee,*
*He will . . . , he will kiss thee.*'[3]

As a result, Ninlil is impregnated with 'the water' of Enlil and bears the moon-God Nanna. But Enlil leaves from Nippur, after having given notice to the 'man of the gate' not to tell Ninlil of his where-

[1] C. F. C. Hawkes, *The Prehistoric Foundations of Europe* (London, 1940), pp. 38–9, 84. Cf. George Thomson, *Studies in Ancient Greek Society,* (London, 1949), pp. 47–8, for a discussion of these and later examples, and Gertrude R. Levy, op. cit., pp. 54–63.

[2] James H. Breasted, *Development,* op. cit., p. 28. Cf. Pyr. 632.

[3] Samuel N. Kramer, *Sumerian Mythology*, op. cit., p. 44.

abouts. When she comes, the man of the gate refuses to tell, but when she insists that she is Enlil's queen, he reveals himself to be Enlil in disguise and the following dialogue and action ensue:

NINLIL: True, Enlil is thy king, but I am thy queen.
ENLIL: If now thou art my queen, let my hand touch thy . . .
NINLIL: The 'water' of thy king, the bright 'water' is in my heart,
The 'water' of Nanna, the bright 'water' is in my heart.
ENLIL: The 'water' of my king, let it go toward heaven, let it go toward earth,
Let my 'water' like the 'water' of my king, go toward earth.

*Enlil*, as *the man of the gate, lay down in the* . . . ,
*He kissed her, he cohabited with her,*
*Having kissed her, having cohabited with her,*
*The 'water' of . . . Meslamtaea he* caused to flow over (*her*) *heart.*[1]

Then, once more in disguise as the 'man of the river of the nether world, the man-devouring river', Enlil impregnates Ninlil to conceive Ninazu; and still a third time, as the 'man of the boat' he begets a third diety on Ninlil. Somewhat similar is the myth called 'The Affairs of the Water-God' in which Enki has relations with Ninhursag, possibly mother earth, ultimately to produce Uttu, the Goddess of the plants in this wise: first, Enki causes to flow the water of the heart upon Ninhursag who gives birth to Ninsar who in turn is impregnated by her father Enki and gives birth to Ninkur; Ninkur, too, has connection with Enki and thus Uttu is born. Both these myths show quite clearly the connection between the sacred marriage and the flowering of the plants and the bringing forth of the life-giving sweet waters. Later on, in Mesopotamia, we find on the cylinder inscription B of Gudea an account of the marriage of the God Ningirsu with the Goddess Bau, the daughter of heaven, who entered between his black arms and from their union comes prosperity to Lagash. Nor was this the only one: we know of the sacred marriage of Nannar and Ningal at Ur and at Larsa; of Enlil and Ninlil at Nippur; Innin and her consort at Uruk; Innin and Lugalbanda at Asnun-nak; Ishtar and Dumuzi at Badtibira; Ishtar and her consort at Isin, Mari, and Zabala; Enki and Ninki at Eridu; Enki and Nintur at Dilmun; Ninhursag

[1] Ibid., pp. 45–6.

and Assergi at Kes and Adab; Ninhursag and the God X, son of Anu, at Umma; Samas and Aia at Sippar; Uras and Ninegal at Dilbat; Marduk and Sarpanitum at Babylon; Nabu and Tasmetum at Borsippa and Kalah; Ishtar and her consort at Arbela and Is; Anu and Antum at Uruk; and Assur and his consort at Assur.[1] Dr. Van Buren has provided a fascinating account of the details of the sacred marriage: the consort came to the marriage in either a chariot richly bedecked or a boat with a square sail; upon landing, a procession was formed to the temple; the bridegroom brought costly gifts; the bride was carefully prepared for the wedding, being washed, anointed, and made up with cosmetics, and she was dressed magnificently, and adorned with jewels; the bridegroom was imprisoned and then clothed anew with a garment of ears of corn, and the Goddess was given a palm-branch to hold; the entrances to the temple were festooned with palm trees; the bridegroom when he approached the bride held a rose and a perfect ear of corn in his hands; the actual union took place in the *gigunu*, built of sweet-smelling cedar wood and richly decorated and adorned with sprays of fresh greenery on a magnificent nuptial couch; after the consummation of the marriage, the Gods were enthroned, the joyful news was announced to the people, who gave thanks, and a great feast took place.[2] 'To guard the life-breath of all lands', as the purpose of the marriage was conceived of in Mesopotamia, is a theme which is repeated in other Accadian texts and on the cylinder seals, and I will content myself with the following lovely passage from *The Gilgamesh Epic*:

> *He washed his long hair (and) polished his weapons.*
> *The hair of his head he threw back over his shoulders.*
> *He threw off his soiled clothes (and) put on clean ones.*
> *He clothes himself with* asitu-*garments and fastened (them) with an* aguhhu.
> *When Gilgamesh put on his tiara,*
> *Great Ishtar lifted (her) eyes to the beauty of Gilgamesh.*
> *'Come, Gilgamesh, be thou my consort.*
> *Grant me thy fruit as a gift.*
> *Be thou my husband and I will be thy wife!*
> *I will cause to be harnessed for thee a chariot of lapis lazuli and gold,*

[1] E. Douglas Van Buren, 'The Sacred Marriage in Early Times in Mesopotamia', *Orientalia*, n.s., XIII (1944), pp. 2–3.
[2] Ibid., pp. 6–34.

*Whose wheels are gold and whose horns are . . .*
*Storm-demons (for) great mules thou shalt hitch (to it).*
*Amid the fragrance of cedar thou shalt enter our house.*
*(And) when thou enterest our house,*
*Threshold (and) dais shall kiss thy feet.*
*Before thee shall bow down kings, rulers, (and) princes.*[1]

In this late and bitter form of the story, Gilgamesh, instead of becoming her husband, enumerates her evil deeds: 'For Tammuz, thy youthful husband, Thou hast decreed wailing year after year,' and she bursts into a rage and demands that her father Anu create for her the bull of heaven that he may destroy Gilgamesh, but Enkidu kills the bull and Ishtar curses Gilgamesh: 'Woe unto Gilgamesh, who has besmirched me and has killed the bull of heaven.' The sacred marriage also appears in Canaanite mythology where I* AB tells how Aleion-Baal loves a heifer to whom is born a child named Mes or Mos and II AB describes either El or Ltpn-Eldpd inviting Asherat to a banquet where he announces the marriage of Bull-El and Asherat. SS is more specific:

*He stoops, he kisses their lips,*
*Behold, their lips are sweet,*
*sweet as ripe grape(s).*
*(By) kissing and conceiving,*
*by embrace (and) passion*
*they (twain are brou)ght to labour,*
*(and) they bear Dawn and Sunset.*[2]

In the Dnil myth, the fruits of the marriage are celebrated: Dnil gives the Gods offerings to eat and drink for six days, and on the seventh, beseeches them to give him a son; the Gods tell him in his dream that his wife will conceive, and he raises his voice and shouts:

*Now I may sit and repose,*
*And my soul shall repose in my breast.*
*For a son shall be born unto me like (unto) my brethren,*
*And an offspring like (unto) my kin:*
*To raise a shrine of my ancestral Gods in the sanctuary;*
*To bury me with my kinfolk [in the earth;*

[1] Alexander Heidel, *The Gilgamesh Epic*, op. cit., pp. 49–50.
[2] Theodor H. Gaster, 'A Canaanite Ritual Drama', op. cit., p. 54.

*To make my incense go forth] from the ground.*
*To guard my path;*
*To expel the inciter of my contempt;*
*To drive out him who provokes my rebellion.*
*To take my hand in drunkenness,*
*To carry off when I be sated with wine.*
*To consume my share in the temple,*
*To eat my portion in the house of God.*
*To plaster my roof on a day of (much) mud,*
*To wash my garments on a day of (much) rain.*[1]

Particularly interesting is the list of duties an obedient son was expected to perform, and Professor Obermann has carefully compared them with the relevant passages in the Old Testament. Finally, in III K, the marriage of king Keret is celebrated.[2] Thus, as Frazer tells us, we find that '. . . a great Mother Goddess, the personification of all the reproductive energies of nature, was worshipped under different names but with a substantial similarity of myth and ritual by many peoples of Western Asia; that associated with her was a lover, or rather a series of lovers, divine yet mortal, with whom she mated year by year, their commerce being deemed essential to the propagation of animals each in their several kind . . . thereby ensuring

[1] Julian Obermann, 'How Daniel was Blessed with a Son :An Incubation Scene in Ugaritic', Supplement to *JAOS*, LXVI (1946), p. 7.

[2] Charles Virolleaud, 'Le mariage du Roi Kéret (III K). Poème de Ras-Shamra', *Syria*, XXIII (1942–3), pp. 146–7, 153. All the Ras-Shamra original texts, with translations into French and comments, were published by Professor Virolleaud from the tablets discovered by Claude F. A. Schaeffer (see his *The Cuneiform Texts of Ras Shamra-Ugarit*, The Schweich Lectures of the British Academy 1936, London, 1939, for a summary) in *Syria* as follows: 'Un poème phénicien de Ras-Shamra. La lutte de Môt, fils de dieux et d'Alein, fils de Baal', XII (1931), pp. 193–224, 350–7; 'Un nouveau chant du poème d'Alein-Baal', XIII (1932), pp. 113–63; 'La naissance des dieux gracieux et beaux. Poème phénicien de Ras Shamra', XIV (1933), pp. 128–51; 'Nouveau fragment du poème de Môt et d'Aleyn-Baal', XV (1934), pp. 226–43; 'La mort de Baal, Poème de Ras-Shamra (I* AB)', XV (1934), pp. 305–36; 'La Révolte de Koser contre Baal. Poème de Ras Shamra (III AB, A)', XVI (1935), pp. 29–45; 'Les Chasses de Baal. Poème de Ras Shamra', XVI (1935), pp. 247–66; 'Hymne phénicien au Dieu Nikal et aux déesses Kosarot, provenant de Ras Shamra', XVII (1936), pp. 209–28. 'Anat et la Génisse. Poème de Ras Shamra (IV AB)', XVII (1936), pp. 150–73; 'La déesse Anat. Poème de Ras Shamra (V AB)', XVII (1936), pp. 335–45, XVIII (1937), VAB, B, pp. 85–102, V AB, C, pp. 256–70; 'Les Rephaim. Fragments de poèmes de Ras Shamra', XXII (1941), pp. 1–30; 'Le Roi Kéret et son fils (II K). Poème de Ras Shamra', XXII (1941), pp. 105–36, 197–217, XXIII (1942–3), pp. 1–20; and the article cited above, pp. 137–42. Around these texts has grown a very considerable literature, much of which is cited in Ivan Engnell, op. cit., *passim*.

the fruitfulness of the ground and the increase of man and beast.'[1]

Not surprisingly, the evidence concerning the presence of the sacred marriage in the Near Eastern rituals is rather full. The sacred marriage was enacted in the course of two Eygptian festivals, that at Edfu and the other at the Theban Festival of Opet. In the first, the image of the Goddess Hathor went by ship to Edfu where she visited her consort Horus in whose company she remained for fourteen days; on the fourth day of the festival, the young Horus was conceived by the Goddess. In the Theban Festival, a procession consisting of Amun and Mut, the king and queen, and priests and other officials, went by barge to the temple at Luxor where the high priestess of the God who was the queen, and therefore equated with Hathor, the wife of the sun-God, performed the nuptial rites with the king in the rôle of Amun. Frazer has described the carvings and paintings of the divine procreation on the walls of the temples at Deir el Bahari and Luxor in which the nativity has been depicted in fifteen vivid scenes, and I quote his version of the accompanying text:

'Thus saith Ammon-Ra, king of the Gods, lord of Karnak, he who rules over Thebes, when he took the form of his male, the King of Upper and Nether Egypt, Thothmes I (or Thothmes IV), giver of life. He found the queen then when she lay in the glory of her palace. She awoke at the fragrance of the God, and marvelled at it. Straightway his Majesty went towards her, took possession of her, placed his heart in her, and showed himself to her in his divine form. And upon his coming she was uplifted at the sight of his beauty, the love of the God ran through all her limbs, and the smell of the God and his breath were full of the perfumes of Pounit. And thus saith the royal spouse, the royal mother Ahmasi (or Moutemouaa), in presence of the majesty of this glorious God, Ammon, lord of Karnak, lord of Thebes, "Twice great are thy souls! It is noble to behold thy countenance when thou joinest thyself to my majesty in all grace! Thy dew impregnates all my limbs." Then, when the majesty of the God had accomplished all his desire with her, Ammon, the lord of the two lands, said to her: "*She who is joined to Ammon, the first of the nobles*, verily such shall be the name of the daughter who shall open thy

[1] James G. Frazer, *Adonis Attis Osiris*, op. cit., I, 39. See Robert Briffault, *The Mothers* (London, 1927), III, pp. 37–45; George Thomson, op. cit., pp. 159–61; Jane Harrison, *Themis* (Cambridge 1912); and C. G. Jung and C. Kerenyi, *Introduction to a Science of Mythology*, tr. R. F. C. Hull (London, 1951).

womb, since such is the course of the words that came forth from thy mouth. She shall reign in righteousness in all the earth, for my soul is hers, my heart is hers, my will is hers, my crown is hers, truly that she may rule over the two lands, that she may guide the souls of all living." '[1]

In the Babylonian New Year's Festival, the sacred marriage was consummated on the night of the twelfth of Nisan, but in the month of Ayar the divine marriage of Nabu and Tasmet was celebrated on the second to the sixth days, and that of Tammuz and Ishtar on the seventh to seventeenth days.[2] Such ceremonies are described in two letters in the *Royal Correspondence of the Assyrian Empire*. The first, from Nabushumiddina to the Crown Prince Ashurbanipal, reads in part:

'On the third day of the month Iyyar the couch of Nabu will be prepared in the city of Calah. Nabu will enter the bed-chamber. On the fourth day will occur the return of Nabu. . . . The God will go forth into the chamber of the palace, from the chamber of the palace he will go to the park. A sacrifice will be made there. The charioteer of the Gods will come *from* the stable of the Gods. He will take the God forth and cause him to pass in procession, he will (then) bring him back (to the temple). He will proceed in stately manner. Of the accompanying people, whatever their sacrifice is they will offer it.'[3]

The other letter, from Nergalsharrani to King Esarhaddon, reads in part:

'On the morrow of the fourth day, toward evening, Nabu and Tashmetum shall enter into the bed-chamber. On the fifth day the food (?) of the king they shall give (them) to eat. The (temple) overseer shall take his seat. The head of a lion and a torch (?) they shall bring to the palace. From the fifth day to the tenth day *the deities* will remain in their bed-chamber, and the overseer will continue (likewise). On the eleventh *day* Nabu shall go forth. He shall free his feet. He shall go to the park. Wild oxen he will slay, (then) he will go up and dwell in his abode. *He will be gracious to the king*.'[4]

[1] James G. Frazer, *The Magic Art and the Evolution of Kings* (London, 1911), II, p. 132. Cf. the translation of this passage by Professor Blackman in *Myth and Ritual*, op. cit., p. 36. A brief survey of the ritual of the sacred marriage is found in Johs. Pedersen, *Israel: Its Life and Culture* (Oxford, 1947), IV, pp. 737–46.

[2] S. Langdon, *Babylonian Menologies and the Semitic Calendars*, The Schweich Lectures of the British Academy, 1933 (London, 1935), pp. 112–13.

[3] Leroy Waterman, tr. *Royal Correspondence of the Assyrian Empire* (Ann Arbor (Mich.), 1930), I, p. 47.

[4] Ibid., p. 255.

In the Hittite festival of the enthronement of the king in spring, it is presumed that the sacred marriage took place in a tent ceremony, *za-lam-gar*.[1] In the Canaanite rituals, the enactment of the sacred marriage is repeatedly performed. In the west-Semitic texts from Mari-Tell Hariri, the king and the goddess are described in their nuptial ceremonies.[2]

I have already described the marriage scene in the 'Birth of the Gracious Gods'; another occurs in the account of the marriage rites of Nikal and Kosarot.[3]

Possibly one more marriage ritual is depicted in Krt:

'And he (*Krt*) returned messengers to him, (saying), "What do I care for silver and yellow gold, which this place loves, or a young male slave, three horses, a chariot from the stable(s) of the Son of Maid (Astarte)? Give *Mtt-hry*, fair of descent whose beauty is like the beauty of Anat, whose charm is like the charm of Astarte, whose pupils (?) are blossoms of lapis lazuli, whose lashes are bowls of *trml*. Let her be girt with . . . , that I may bask (?) in the glances of her eyes. (For she is the one) of whom El in my vision gave me good tidings, (of whom) the Father of Mankind (in my vision gave me good tidings). And (she shall) bear seed to Krt and a child to the Servant of El." '[4]

The element of the sacred procession in the myth and ritual practice of the ancient Near East is perhaps best seen in the ritual, for the reason that it provided one of the most important means for linking the celebrants with the life-giving functions of the king as he performed his cultic duties. The procession, and with it the sacred dance, afforded the people an opportunity for personal participation in the mystery of rebirth; by their own actions, they took part in and partook of the very essence of the process by which the well-being of the community was in the very act of being maintained.[5] Frazer

[1] Albrecht Goetze and E. H. Sturtevant, *The Hittite Ritual of Tunnawi* (New Haven, Conn., 1938), p. 98.

[2] Ivan Engnell, op. cit., pp. 77, 90, and William F. Albright, *Stone Age*, op. cit., pp. 111–12.

[3] Cyrus H. Gordon, 'A Marriage of the Gods in Canaanite Mythology', *BASOR*, LXV (1937), pp. 31–2.

[4] William F. Albright, 'New Canaanite Historical and Mythological Data', *BASOR*, LXIII (1936), p. 31.

[5] For the importance of the rôle of the community as a whole in the myth and ritual of the ancient Near East, see Theodor H. Gaster, 'Divine Kingship in the Ancient Near East: A Review Article', *Review of Religion*, IX (1945), pp. 270–1.

has pointed out that one of the original purposes of the procession was to stimulate the growth of vegetation in the spring; in the course of time, the action became stylized and the primary intent turned dim in the minds of the performers, but the sense of personal participation, the feeling of active contribution to an ardently desired end remained.[1] Similarly, too, with the dances and the fertility rites which were associated with the festivals: they were intended to reproduce by group action mimetically, and therefore to effect, the rebirth of nature. How intimately connected the procession was with the divine marriage has been demonstrated by Frazer in the well-known passage in which he describes the Hittite sculptures carved on the rocks at Boghaz-Keui in north-western Cappadocia.[2] In the Egyptian festival of Sokar, celebrated at Memphis, Sokar, the funerary God of Memphis, was identified with Osiris, and was carried round the walls of the city in a procession in which the king and his people took part. Likewise, in the course of the Harvest Festival of Min, the ceremonies began with a procession in which the king was carried to the temple of Min and thence, preceded by the sacred white bull of Min, in which the God resided, to a field where he symbolically reaped a sheaf of spelt. Here, again, the intimate relationship between the procession and fertility is seen, for the bull was one of the earliest of all symbols for the generative force of nature, and in Egypt bull-worship was one of the oldest elements of the religious cult. Osiris was frequently referred to as 'The Bull of Heaven' and he was incarnated in the moon-bull Apis, the association of the moon and fertility again being one of the oldest beliefs of mankind. Similarly was the king identified with the bull, so that the procession in which he went with the bull to cut the spelt signified the God-bull-king in the ritual act of insuring the success of the harvest and revivifying the fertility of nature.[3] Finally, the procession in the ritual of the Osiris cult at Abydos was its central feature, as we learn from the memorial stone of Ikhernofret, an officer of Sesostris, in which he writes:

[1] James G. Frazer, *The Scapegoat*, op. cit., p. 251.

[2] James G. Frazer, *Adonis Attis Osiris*, op. cit., I, pp. 128–42.

[3] The significance of the bull has been demonstrated by Frazer; cf. Robert Briffault, op. cit., pp. 191–5, where the bull is shown to have a double meaning, as the emblem of fertilizing power and as his identification with the moon; for the cattle cults of Egypt, see Henri Frankfort, *Kingship*, op. cit., pp. 162–80, and pp. 185–90, for a detailed description of the Harvest Festival of Min.

'1. I celebrated the "Procession of Upwawet" when he proceeded to champion his father (Osiris).
2. I repulsed those who were hostile to the Neshmet barque, and I overthrew the enemies of Osiris.
3. I celebrated the "Great Procession", following the God in his footsteps.
4. I sailed the divine barque, while Thoth . . . the voyage.
5. I equipped the barque (called) "Shining in Truth", of the Lord of Abydos, with a chapel; I put on his beautiful regalia when he went forth to the district of Peker.
6. I led the way of the God to his tomb in Peker.
7. I championed Wennofer (Osiris) on "That Day of the Great Battle"; I overthrew all the enemies upon the shore of Nedyt.
8. I caused him to proceed into the barque (called) 'The Great'; it bore his beauty; I gladdened the heart of the eastern highlands; I [put] jubilation in the western highlands, when they saw the beauty of the Neshmet barque. It landed at Abydos and they brought [Osiris, First of the Westerners, Lord] of Abydos to his palace.'[1]

Professor Breasted calls this the outline of a passion play in which 'the royal destiny of Osiris and his triumph over death, thus vividly portrayed in dramatic form, rapidly disseminated among the people that this destiny once probably reserved for the king, might be shared by all'.[2] The implication would thus seem to be that in their identification with the God, the people too will enjoy the passage from death through rebirth to life.

In the Babylonian *akitu* festival, the triumphal procession to the Bit Akitu took place on the ninth of Nisan, followed on the night of the tenth by the divine marriage. However, this procession, which went down the Sacred Way at Babylon, with the king taking the hand of Bel to lead him to the wagon on which he travelled, is more closely associated with the ritual combat, for it led to the Festival House whose doors showed the combat between the hero-God and Tiamat.[3] In the course of the procession Marduk was spoken to by the high priest as follows:

[1] James H. Breasted, *Development,* op. cit., p. 289. Cf. the translation of the same passage by Professor Frankfort, *Kingship*, op. cit., pp. 203–4.

[2] James H. Breasted, ibid., p. 290.

[3] C. J. Gadd, in *Myth and Ritual*, op. cit., pp. 57–8, and Henri Frankfort, *Kingship,* op. cit., p. 318.

*Lord of all the corners of the earth, King of the Gods . . .*
*Who beareth the kingship, who graspeth dominion . . .*
*Who marcheth through the heavens, who formed the earth,*
*Who measured the waters of the sea, who planted vegetation.*[1]

Here the intimate relationship between the creation, the rebirth of the vegetation, and the procession is clearly depicted. A procession was one of the parts of the ritual of the *nuntarias* festival, the winter form of the annual Hittite festival. Thus the procession, by virtue of its integral relationship with the creation and with fertility, was an important element in the myth and ritual pattern of the ancient Near East. And even more important, it provided, almost more than the other elements in the pattern, the opportunity for the people as a whole to participate in the ceremonies which were of such crucial moment to them. By taking part in the search for the God, in the dance, in the licence rites often associated with the festivals, and in the procession, they were able to identify themselves most intimately in the process of rebirth, which they strove so mightily to bring into being. The rituals were not intended for spectators alone; indeed, this is one of the most decisive differences between ritual and drama, in that the latter demands a division, physically reinforced by the nature of the stage, between actors and spectators, their union being emotionally and intellectually apprehended only at a distance, so to speak, and certainly not physically, as in the ritual where the participation of the celebrants was an indispensable necessity for the success of the ritual. In the account which he gives of the history of the dance, Lucian, speaking through the person of Lycinus, significantly states that '. . . those who let out the mysteries in conversation was commonly said to "dance them out" '.[2] And in the eleventh book of *The Golden Ass*, Apuleius vividly describes the procession in honour of the Goddess Isis: 'I saw the streets replenished with people, going in a religious sort, and in great triumph. All things that day seemed to be joyful, as well as all manner of beasts and the very houses, as also even the day itself seemed to rejoice.' He describes too the contentment of the fruitful trees, which smile because of their new buds, and then goes on to characterize, with some slyness, the dress and appearance of the marchers in the procession, the man of arms, the hunter, the rich man, the magistrate, the

[1] W. O. E. Oesterley, in *Myth and Ritual*, op. cit., p. 135.
[2] *Lucian*, tr. A. M. Harmon (Cambridge, Mass., 1936), V, 229.

philosopher, the fisherman, women and men of high and low degree, all together constituting '. . . the peculiar pomp of the saving Goddess triumphantly march[ing] forward'. And in the very midst of the procession, Apuleius, through the intervention of the great priest, is restored to his human shape by eating the garland of roses held out to him; and the people then rejoice, saying: 'Behold him who is in this day transformed into a man by the puissance of the sovereign Goddess; verily he is blessed and most blessed that by the innocency of his former life hath merited so great grace from heaven, and as it were by a new generation is reserved straightway to the obsequy of religion.' In ironic yet also symbolic form, then, Apuleius clearly demonstrates the powers inherent in the procession as a central element in the mysteries for, as his friends said later of him, he was '. . . as a man raised from death to life'.[1] The dance, the procession, and the other communal actions, all of these enabled the people to participate in their own persons in achieving the ends they so ardently desired to bring about. Indeed, we know that the actions of all the performers, both king and people alike, were expected to conform to rigorously enforced formulae, for the slightest deviations could seriously endanger, could, in fact, negate altogether the efficacy of the ritual. We know, for example, that in the course of the Day of Atonement ceremonies in the Hebrew temple, when the high priest entered the Holy of Holies, and, incidentally, this was the only time during the year that he did so, so important were these ceremonies on the tenth of Tishri, the people outside waited most anxiously lest he be wanting in the proper performances of the services and thus fail to bring them the forgiveness they sought with such anguished prayer and penitence. For these reasons, then, the procession was an essential part of the ritual practices of the ancient Near East.

If the resurrection of the God was the emotional climax of the myth and ritual pattern of the ancient Near East, then the fixing of the destinies was its intellectual climax, and, indeed, its very highest point. For it was at this moment in the action that the fate of the community was settled for the coming year and it was toward this climax, so fraught with all the hopes and fears of men, that the whole of the pattern pointed undeviatingly. In the settling of destinies was subsumed all the other elements in the myth and ritual pattern, for it

[1] Apuleius, *The Golden Ass*, tr. R. W. Adlington, rev. S. Gasalee (London, 1915), pp. 551–71.

provided the goal and thereby infused meaning into them; it was then that men knew whether the passion of the God had been in vain or not, whether his tortured struggles, his death, and his rebirth, their dances, their rites, and their processions, and all the vast expense and labour of body and spirit would bring them at last to the end they so fervently needed and desired. Once more, just as they waited in desperate terror for the God to be reborn, so now they went through the silent fear of the small moment, poised between despair and salvation, anxiously awaiting the fateful outcome. For without the settling of destinies, the creation would be a meaningless act, the combat fought in vain, the divine marriage a sterile thing; chaos would conquer, and the indifferent reaches of the universe out of which man and his world had been torn would once more engulf him, this time forever in its endless wastes. At the same time, the settling of destinies was bound up, as it would necessarily have to be, with the quest for justice in all its forms and applications, for without the idea of just rule the destinies could not possibly be fixed, since the arbitrariness of unjust rule, its opposite, would be no more than the reflection of the disordered chaos out of which the world was so painfully created and against which man had so ceaselessly to war. In order for the idea of the settling of destinies to take root, it was therefore necessary that it be given the soil of just rule to flourish in, and indeed the settling of destinies may be thought of as the flowering of justice, the idea that neither the universe nor the Gods nor kings nor men are exempt from order, regularity, form, and, consequently, justice.

When we turn to Egyptian thought, we remember that, after the defeat of Seth by Horus, Seth enters charges against Osiris before the tribunal of the Gods at Heliopolis, but the Gods in their judgment vindicate Osiris who, they hold, is justified through that which he has done and he is commanded by the two truths to rise again; and the Gods are satisfied with this verdict, and Osiris receives the kingdom. We recall, too, the rôle of Ptah as the maker of destiny, he who fashioned the Gods, made the kas, and gave life to the peaceful and death to the guilty; indeed, in Abydos, Ptah is designated '. . . he who created Maat'. Here is foreshadowed the idea that all of creation must serve a just God whose rule is based on a universal application of ordered justice. The same idea is dimly adumbrated in utterance 257 of the Pyramid texts where we read:

' "There is strife in heaven, we see a new thing", say they, the primordial Gods.

'The Ennead of Horus is dazzled (?), the Lords of Forms are in terror of him. The entire Double Ennead serveth him, and he sitteth on the throne of the Lord of All.

'He seizeth the sky, he cleaveth its metal. He is led along the road to Khepre, he setteth alive in the west, the dwellers in the nether world follow him, and he riseth renewed in the east.

'He that adjudged the quarrel cometh to him, making obeisance. The Gods are afraid of him, for he is older than the Great One. He it is that hath power over his seat. He layeth hold on Command, Eternity is brought to him. Discernment is placed for him at his feet.

'Cry aloud to him in joy, he hath captured the horizon.'[1]

The text is admittedly obscure, but I think that in it can be faintly detected the notion that the rule of the ultimate God is based on his impartial rule of justice. Concomitant with this development, we find that kings and men wish to be approved for the good which they have done, and in such phrases as 'I clothed him who was naked therein', 'Never did I do anything evil toward any person', 'I was a doer of that which pleased all men', and 'There is no evil which king Pepi has done', we find this yearning clearly expressed.[2] Gradually, then, there emerged a conception of justice to which kings and men alike bowed, for it was the reflection in the sphere of men of the cosmic justice which lay behind the whole of creation and thereby ordered it. Thus, when Sesostris I built in the temple of Heliopolis, he wrote:

'It is excellent (?) to work for him that hath made me, and to content the God with what he hath given. *I am alike* his son and protector; he hath commanded me to conquer what he hath conquered. . . . It is to gain eternity, if one doeth for him that which is good, and no king dieth that is mentioned because of his possessions. . . .

'And the chamberlains of the king spake and answered before their God: "Commanding Utterance (?) is in thy mouth, and Discernment is behind thee." '[3]

In *The Instruction of Ptahhotep*, there occurs this passage in the later version:

[1] Adolf Erman, op. cit., pp. 4–5.
[2] James H. Breasted, *Development*, op. cit., pp. 168, 172.
[3] Adolf Erman, op. cit., p. 51.

'If thou art a leader and givest command to the multitude, strive after every excellence, until there be no fault in thy nature. Truth is good and its worth is lasting, and it hath not been disturbed since the day of its creator, whereas he that transgresseth its ordinances is punished. It lieth as a (right) path in front of him that knoweth nothing. Wrongdoing (?) hath never yet brought its venture to port. Evil indeed winneth wealth, but the strength of truth is that it endureth, and the (upright) man saith: "It is the property of my father." '[1]

Something of the same tone is to be found in *The Instruction of King Amenemhet* and *The Instruction for King Merikere*, and in the latter we read:

'The soul goeth to the place which it knoweth, and strayeth not from its paths of yesterday. (Wherefore) make fair thine house of the West, and stately thy place in the necropolis, even as one that is just, as one that hath done right. That it is, whereon their heart reposeth. . . .

'Well tended are men, the cattle of God. He made heaven and earth according to their desire. He allayed the thirst (?) for water. He made the air that their nostrils may live. They are His images, that they have proceeded from His limbs. He ariseth in heaven according to their desire. He made for them plants and cattle, fowls and fishes, in order to nourish them. *But He also punisheth:* He slew His enemies, and punished His children, because of that which they devised when they were hostile.'[2]

Here, at last, we are confronted with the problem of the evil in man: God created him in His own image, He made the earth for his enjoyment, yet he wrought evil against Him. The direct confrontation of evil by man is the bitter subject of *The Dispute with His Soul of One Who is Tired of Life*, a remarkable document in which the man laments:

*Lo, my name is abhorred,*
*Lo, more than the odour of carrion*
*On days in summer, when the sky is hot.*

To whom can he speak? Brothers are evil, men are covetous, good is disregarded in every place, men rob, none remembers the past, a

[1] Ibid., p. 57. [2] Ibid., p. 83.

man is treated as an enemy in spite of a right disposition, none is righteous, none is peaceable:

> *To whom do I speak to-day?*
> *The sin that smiteth the land,*
> *It hath no end.*

Therefore:

> *Death is before me to-day*
> *As when a sick man becometh whole,*
> *As when one walketh abroad after sickness.*

But he has this great consolation:

> *Why he that is yonder will be*
> *One that . . . as a living God,*
> *And will inflict punishment for sin on him that doeth it.*[1]

Professor Breasted has well termed this '. . . the earliest utterance of the unjustly afflicted,' and he defines its importance by saying: 'It is a distinct mark in the long development of self-consciousness, the slow process which culminated in the emergence of the individual as a moral force, an individual appealing to conscience as an ultimate authority.'[2]

But now another element in the development of the idea of justice enters in; as men forget the past, as they forego the honest, simple practices of their forefathers and abandon the straight way for the corruptions of the flesh and spirit, we begin to hear laments for the times past; the present is contrasted with the past to its great disadvantage, and, most striking, we hear the call for one who will lead the people from their present ways of evil back to the virtues of the past. Thus the powerful nostalgia of primitivism is added to the making of the moral sense, for a standard of behaviour has been created: let us be as men once were, decent and good. Such a standard affords a most effective measuring stick against which the present can be judged and found wanting, and it enables men to look forward by looking backward, and over all, the trumpet sound of prophetic Messianism is heard. *The Admonitions of a Prophet* depicts by means of the most harrowing details the decay of the land: a man goes to plough with his shield, women are barren, the heart is violent, the

[1] Ibid., pp. 86–92.

[2] James H. Breasted, *Development*, op. cit., p. 198. Professor Wilson concurs in this judgment in *The Intellectual Adventure*, op. cit., p. 103.

highborn are full of lamentations but the poor are full of joy (to the prophet, the reversal of social position is one of the most revealing and terrifying signs of a world gone wrong), the son of the highborn man is no longer recognized, laughter has perished, the children of princes are dashed against the walls, the corn is perished everywhere, and the land is despoiled of the kingship by a few senseless people. The whole social order is subverted in the failure of the king to live up to his solemn obligations. The prophet bids men to recall how once they lived and acted, how fumigation is made, water offered, natron chewed, flag-staffs erected, and how the regulations are observed; so it was done in the past when men lived well and rightly. Now the prophet strongly calls on the king to be what indeed he ought to be:

'It is said: he is the herdsman of all men. No evil is in his heart. His herd is diminished, and (yet) he hath spent all the day in order to tend them. . . . Ah, but had he perceived their nature in the first generation; then would he have smitten down evil; he would have stretched forth the arm against it, and destroyed the seed thereof and their inheritance. . . . Where is he to-day? Doth he sleep then? Behold, his might is not seen. . . .

'Command, Perception, and Truth are with thee, but it is confusion that thou puttest throughout the land, together with the noise of them that contend.'

And the prophet concludes with a description of how well men can live if the king but exercises his power justly as he ought to: it is good when the net is drawn in and the birds are made fast, he says, it is good when the hands of men build pyramids and dig ponds, and it is good when rejoicing is in men's mouths.[1] Though the prophet looks on his times and finds them corrupt because the king is corrupt, yet he looks forward to a time when a great king will restore the land to its pristine goodness: 'Behold, his might is not seen', and with Professor Breasted, it is irresistible to add, 'as yet'. Equally bitter are *The Complaint of Khekheperre-Sonbu* and *The Prophecy of Neferrohu*, but the latter, after showing us the land in lamentation and distress, rises in spite of them to a vision of the future:

'A king shall come from the south, called Ameni, the son of a woman of Nubia, and born in Upper Egypt (?). He shall receive the

[1] Adolf Erman, op. cit., pp. 94–108.

white crown, and wear the red crown; he shall unite the Two Powerful Ones and shall delight the Two Lords with what they love. . . .

'Be glad ye people of his time! The son of man (of high degree) will make himself a name for all eternity. They that would work mischief and devise hostility, they have subdued their mouthings for fear of him.

'The Asiatics shall fall before his carnage, and the Libyans shall fall before his flame. The foes succumb to his onset, and the rebels to his might. The royal serpent that is on his forehead, it pacifieth for him the rebels. . . .

'And Right shall come again into its place, and Iniquity, that is cast forth. He will rejoice who shall behold this, and who shall then serve the king.'[1]

With *The Complaints of the Peasant*, the idea of justice, or maat, emerges sharp and distinct: in this story, the peasant from the salt-field, Khunanap, goes down into Egypt, where he is robbed by Dehutinekt, the son of Iseri, who belongs to the vassals of the high steward Rensi. Seeking justice, for his course has been, as he says, a good one, the peasant appeals for the restoration of his property to Rensi, whom he calls the father of the orphan, the husband of the widow, the brother of her that is put away, the apron of him that is motherless. He abjures Rensi to sail over the lake of truth with a fair wind, to put evil aside, and to do justice. 'Wilt thou not be a man of eternity?' he asks: 'Is it not wrong, forsooth, a balance that tilteth, a plummet that deflecteth, a guardian of the laws who is become one that vacillateth (?)?' And he appeals to him: 'Ward off the robber! Protect the poor man! Became not a torrent against the petitioner! Take heed to the approach of eternity. Will so to be, even as it is said: "To do right is breath for the nose." Mete out punishment to him that should be punished. . . . Answer not good with evil, put not one thing in place of another.' He warns him that men suffer a fall because of greed, for the rapacious fails in his affair. Finally, as his prayers are still not answered, the peasant reaches out to a thrilling conception of a universal and equal justice:

'Do according unto truth for the Lord of Truth, whose truth is the truth (indeed). . . . Good is it, when thou art good, yea good is it, when thou art good.

[1] Ibid., p. 115.

' "But truth [Professor Breasted translates here justice, *maat*, for the two meanings interpenetrate each other] endureth unto the everlasting, and it descendeth with him that doeth it into the nether world. When he is buried and the earth is joined with him, his name is not obliterated upon earth, but he is remembered for goodness."

That is what is laid down in the word of God. . . .

'. . . for this goodly speech cometh forth from the mouth of Re himself: "Speak truth [*maat*], do according to truth [*maat*]; for that is great and mighty, and endureth." '[1]

And this noble vision of an ethical standard to which both kings and men must measure up passes over to the worship of Osiris, who says: 'I perish not, I enter as truth, I support truth, I am lord of truth, I go forth as truth, . . . I enter in as truth'; and again: 'I am Osiris, the God who does righteousness, I live in it.'[2] In a hymn to Osiris, we read:

'The firmament and its stars hearken unto him, and the great portals open to him; to whom men shout for joy in the southern sky. The imperishable stars are under his authority, and the never-wearying ones are his place of abode.'[3]

Similarly, the sun-God is addressed in much the same manner:

*A mother, profitable to Gods and men,*
*A craftsman of experience, . . .*
*Valiant herdsman who drives his cattle,*
*Their refuge and giver of their sustenance. . . .*[4]

Other hymns to the sun-God develop the theme of the union of justice, God, the king, and the people; in one, we learn:

*How manifold are thy works!*
*They are hidden from before (us).*
*O sole God, whose powers no other possesseth.*
*Thou didst create the earth according to thy heart*
*While thou wast alone:*
*Men, all cattle large and small,*
*All that are upon the earth,*
*That go about upon their feet;*
*All that are on high,*

[1] Ibid., pp. 116–31. [2] James H. Breasted, *Development*, op. cit., p. 255.
[3] Adolf Erman, op. cit., p. 142. [4] James H. Breasted, *Development*, op. cit., p. 316.

*That fly with their wings,*
*The foreign countries, Syria and Kush,*
*The land of Egypt;*
*Thou settest every man in his place,*
*Thou suppliest their necessities,*
*Every one has his possessions,*
*And his days are reckoned.*
*The tongues are divers in speech,*
*Their forms likewise and their skins are distinguished.*
*(For) thou makest different the strangers.*

'How excellent are thy designs, O Lord of eternity!' one hymn declares, and still another says: 'The world is in thy hand' for 'Men live through thee' and 'All flowers live and what grows in the soil is made to grow because thou dawnest'.[1] Thus are we led to *The Great Hymn to Amun* where these ideas receive their most lofty expression. In this hymn, Amun is addressed as 'Greatest of heaven, eldest of earth, lord of what existeth. . . . Unique in his nature . . . among the Gods, . . . Lord of Truth, father of the Gods, who made mankind, and created beasts'. He hears the prayer of the prisoner and is kindly of heart when one calls on him. He is '. . . the Sole One, who made all that is, The One and Only, who made what existeth'. The Gods themselves cry out:

'O king, chiefest of the Gods! We revere thy might, because thou createdst us. *We shout for joy to thee*, because thou fashionedst us. We offer thee praise, because thou weariedst thyself with us.'

And men echo this praise:

'Praise to thee, who madest all that is, lord of Truth, father of the Gods, who madest men, and createdst beasts, lord of grain, who makest the sustenance of the wild beasts of the wilderness.'[2]

A penitential hymn to Re calls on the God: 'Punish me not for many sins. I am one that knoweth not himself (?). I am a witless man.' For God is just, and though: 'Thou lofty one, whose course is not known how mysterious is thy being!' yet: 'Thou art a lord in whom men may make their boast, a potent, everlasting God that giveth judgment, that presideth over the Court of Law, that establisheth Truth, and assaileth Iniquity.'[3] Slowly, and with pain and struggle, the

[1] Ibid., pp. 324–31.
[2] Adolf Erman, op. cit., pp. 283–8.
[3] Ibid., pp. 303–7.

Egyptians were in this way able to work out a concept of a divine justice immanent in creation to which all creation bowed and the goal of man was to live in accord with its precepts.[1]

The concept of the settling of destinies in Sumerian myth is found in the myth of Enki and Sumer:

*O Sumer, great land,* of *the* lands *of the universe,*
*Filled with steadfast brightness, the people from sunrise to sunset obedient to the divine decrees,*
*Thy decrees are exalted decrees, unreachable,*
*Thy heart is profound, unfathomable,*
*Thy . . . is like heaven, untouchable . . .*

*The Anunnaki, the great Gods,*
*In thy midst have taken up their dwelling place,*
*In thy large* groves *they consume (their) food.*

*O house of Sumer, may thy stables be many, may thy cows multiply,*
*May thy sheepfolds be many, may thy sheep be myriad,*
*May thy . . . stand,*
*May thy steadfast . . . lift hand to heaven,*
*May the Anunnaki decree the fates in thy midst.*

*To Ur he came,*
*Enki, king of the abyss, decrees the fate:*
*'O city, well-supplied, washed by much water, firm standing*
*Shrine of abundance of the land, knees opened, green like the "mountain",*
Hashur-*forest, wide shade, . . . heroic,*
*Thy perfected decrees he has directed,*
*The great mountain, Enlil, in the universe has uttered thy exalted name;*
*O thou city whose fates have been decreed by Enki,*
*O thou shrine Ur, neck to heaven mayest thou rise.'*

*The lord called to the steadfast field, he caused it to produce much grain,*
*Enki made it bring forth its small and large beans, . . .*
*The . . . grains he heaped up for the granary,*
*Enki added granary to granary,*
*With Enlil he increases abundance in the land; . . .*[2]

[1] Anyone who attempts to trace the development of moral ideas in Egypt must be wholly indebted to Professor Breasted, as I have been. I have used the *Development* rather than the later *Dawn of Conscience*, because, with Professor Wilson, I think it unsurpassed by the *Dawn*.

[2] Samuel N. Kramer, *Sumerian Mythology*, op. cit., pp. 59–61.

Other possible allusions to the settling of destinies may be recognized in the myths 'Enlil Chooses the Farmer-God', 'The Creation of the Pickaxe', and 'Cattle and Grain'; however, the myth, 'The Journey of the Water-God to Nippur' does seem to present a more straightforward account of the settling of destinies, since it tells how Enki, the lord of the abyss, after the water of creation had been decreed, Enki, the lord who decrees the fates, built his house of silver and lapis lazuli in Eridu where the Gods feast and Enlil blesses it, saying: 'The abyss, the shrine of the goodness of Enki, befitting the divine decrees.'[1] The building of the house of God in Eridu may be taken as the symbol of his determining the destiny of that city and the people in it. In the myth of 'The Transfer of the Arts of Civilization from Eridu to Erech', we learn how Inanna takes from Enki '. . . lordship, . . . godship, the tiara exalted and enduring, the throne of kingship. . . . The exalted sceptre, *staffs*, the exalted shrine, shepherdship, kingship' and over one hundred divine decrees including truth, the 'standard', heroship and power, straightforwardness, rejoicing of the heart, crafts, wisdom and understanding, counsel, judgment and decision, as well as evil things too and gives them to Erech.[2]

Professor Jacobsen insists quite correctly that in Mesopotamia the idea of the universe was founded on the concept of authority, but even in this authority there exists the notion of the divine justice in the cosmos; for example, Anu, the power of the sky, is described as follows:

*Wielder of the sceptre, the ring, and the* palu *who callest to kingship,*
*Sovereign of the Gods, whose word prevails in the ordained assembly of the great Gods,*
*Lord of the glorious crown, astounding though thine enchantment,*
*Rider of great storms, who occupies the dais of sovereignty, wondrously regal—*
*To the pronouncements of thy holy mouth are the Igigi attentive;*
*In fear before thee move the Anunnaki,*
*Like storm-swept reeds bow to thy orders all the Gods.*[3]

Similarly is the God Enlil addressed as 'Great Lord, ruler of Gods in heaven, Counsellor of Gods on earth, judicious prince'; and Enki

[1] Ibid., pp. 62–3.
[2] Ibid., pp. 65–6.
[3] Thorkild Jacobsen, in *The Intellectual Adventure*, op. cit., p. 140; translated by Mrs. Frankfort.

is thought of as having been empowered by Anu to 'guide and form' and 'to fix . . . the fates of North and South' with his 'righteous decision and pronouncement' which causes deserted cities to be re-inhabited. But it is in the later *Enuma Elish* that the idea of the settling of destinies is given its fullest expression. We recall that before Marduk undertook to fight against Tiamat, he demanded the sole right of the settling of destinies:

*If I am to be your champion,*
*To vanquish Tiamat and to keep you alive,*
*Summon a meeting, make my lot unsurpassable (and) proclaim (it).*
*When ye are joyfully seated together in the Assembly Hall.*
*May I through the utterance of my mouth determine the destinies, instead of you.*
*Whatever I create shall remain unaltered,*
*The command of my lips shall not return (void), it shall not be changed.*[1]

And the Gods, carefree and exalted, decree for him the destiny:

*Thou art (the most) honoured among the great gods,*
*Thy destiny is beyond compare, thy command is (like) Anu('s).*
*O Marduk, thou art (the most) honoured among the great gods,*
*Thy destiny is beyond compare, thy command is like Anu('s).*
*From this day onward thy command shall not be changed.*
*To exalt and to abase—this (power) shall be (in) thy hand!*
*Established shall be the word of thy mouth, incontestable thy command!*
*No one among the gods shall encroach upon thy prerogative.*
*Maintenance is the requirement of the sanctuaries of the gods;*
*(And so) the place of their shrines shall be established in thy place.*
*To thee have we given kingship over the whole universe.*[2]

But the goal of the settling of destiny in Mesopotamia was not to be so easily reached; far from it, for the Mesopotamian lived in a state of uneasy anxiety in that, while he constantly reached out to the gods in supplication for their beneficence, he was not at all certain of their favours or of their intentions. This feeling of fear and frustration permeates the whole of the melancholy *The Gilgamesh Epic*. Though Gilgamesh is two-thirds God and one-third man, and though he proposes bravely and nobly to destroy all the evil in the land, constantly he hears the warning of the elders:

[1] Alexander Heidel, *The Babylonian Genesis*, op. cit., p. 23.
[2] Ibid., pp. 26–7.

*Thou art young, O Gilgamesh, and thy heart has carried thee away*
*Thou dost not know what thou proposest to do.*[1]

Indeed, his courage is the courage of desperation, and he is motivated mainly by the desire for posthumous fame:

[*Let*] *the combat* [*not diminish(?)*] *thy courage; forget death and* [. . .].
[. . .] *a man ready for action* (?) *and circumspect.*
[*He who*] *goes* [*before*] *protects his person, may he* (*also*) *safeguard the companion.*
[*When*] *they fall, they have established a name for themselves.*[2]

But even this does not avail him; Enkidu succumbs to the curse. As his friend Enkidu lies dying, he curses the prostitute who taught him to eat bread fit for divinity and who clothed him with a magnificent garment: 'The street shall be thy dwelling-place. The shade of the wall shall be thine abode.' He has a dream in which he is overpowered by death, who leads him to the house of darkness:

. . . *from which he who enters never goes forth;*
*On the road whose path does not lead back;*
*To the house whose occupants are bereft of light;*
(*Where*) *they are clad like birds, with garments of wings;*
(*Where*) *they see no light, and dwell in darkness.*
*In the h*[*ouse of dus*]*t, which I entered,*
*I loo*[*ked at the kings* (?)], *and* (*behold!*) *the crowns had been deposited.*
. . . [. . .] *those who* (*used to wear*) *crowns, who from the days of old had ruled the land*, . . .[3]

Gilgamesh sorrows over his friend: 'When I die, shall I not be like Enkidu? Sorrow has entered my heart. I am afraid of death and roam over the desert.' He then goes to Mashu, the mountain which reaches down to the underworld where the darkness is dense, in sorrow and pain, in cold and heat, in sighing and weeping, through impenetrable darkness. There he meets Siduri, the barmaid, to whom he pours out his grief, and she tells him:

*Gilgamesh, whither runnest thou?*
*The life which thou seekest thou wilt not find;*
(*For*) *when the gods created mankind,*

[1] Alexander Heidel, *The Gilgamesh Epic*, op. cit., p. 37.
[2] Ibid., p. 45.
[3] Ibid., pp. 60–1.

*They allotted death to mankind,*
*(But) life they retained in their keeping.*[1]

She counsels him to be merry day and night, to keep his belly full, and to cherish his wife and child: this is the lot of mankind. But how can he be content, Gilgamesh asks, when the fate of mankind has overtaken his friend and he himself has become afraid of death? 'Shall I not like unto him lie down and not rise for ever?' is the question he asks Utnapishtim the Distant who answers him:

*Do we build a house (to stand) for ever? Do we seal (a document to be in force) for ever?*
*Do brothers divide (their inheritance to last) for ever?*
*Does hatred remain in [the land] for ever?*
*Does the river raise (and) ca[rry] the flood for ever?*

. . . . . .

*Does its face see the face of the sun (for ever),*
*From the days of old there is no [permanence].*
*The sleeping (?) and the dead, how alike [they are]!*
*Do they not (both) draw the picture of death?*

. . . . . .

*The Anunnaki, the great gods, ga[ther together];*
*Mammetum, the creatures of destiny, de[crees] with them the destinies.*
*Life and death they allot;*
*The days of death they do not reveal.*[2]

But Utnapishtim resolves to reveal to Gilgamesh a hidden thing, a secret of the Gods; once the Gods resolved to bring a deluge on the city Shurippak and Utnapishtim was warned to build an ark to escape the flood and to secure the safety of his family and the game of the field. The storm blew so hard that even the Gods were terrified; for six days it raged until, on the seventh, the tempest subdued in its onslaught. He opened a window and light fell upon his face; he looked upon the sea, and all was silence; and the tears ran down over his face. For six days, the ark held fast on Mount Nisir and on the seventh he sent forth a dove and a swallow which found no resting-place but the raven went away, saw that the waters had abated, and did not return. Thereupon Utnapishtim did service to the Gods and, though Enlil complained that man had escaped his

[1] Ibid., p. 70. [2] Ibid., p. 79.

vengeance, Ea tells him: 'How, O how couldst thou without reflection bring on (this) deluge? On the sinner lay his sin; on the transgressor lay his transgression.' Whereupon Enlil took Utnapishtim by the hand, touched his forehead and that of his wife as they kneeled before him, and blessed them:

> *Hitherto Utnapishtim has been but a man:*
> *But now Utnapishtim and his wife shall be like unto us Gods.*[1]

Still Gilgamesh wails:

> [*Oh, what*] *shall I do, Utnapishtim*, (*or*) *where shall I go,*
> *As the robber has* (*already*) *taken hold of my* [*member*]*s?*
> *Death is dwelling* [*in*] *my bedchamber;*
> *And where* [*I*] *set* [*my feet*] *there is death!'*[2]

Utnapishtim takes pity on him and reveals still another secret of the Gods: he tells Gilgamesh to seek a plant like a thorn and, if he obtains it, he will find new life, but the poem ends without his finding it. Yet, though the mood of pessimism prevails throughout it, we are left with three hopeful signs: the raven which goes out after the storm has passed, the blessing of Enlil, and the rose of life.

It is in this double mood of despair and hope that the Mesopotamian appealed to his God to settle his destiny; in the prayer of Ashurnasirpal I to Ishtar of Nineveh, this duality is clearly revealed:

> *The matter which has befallen me*, [*even the sorrows*] *in words I will rehearse,*
> *Unto the creatress of peoples*, [*her to whom*] *praise belongs,*
> *Unto her who sits in Emasmas* [*divine Ishtar*] *who has extolled my name,*
> *Unto the queen of the Gods by whose hand the laws of* the Gods *are fulfilled,*
> *Unto the lady of Nineveh*, sister *of the lofty* Gods,
> *Unto the daughter of Sin, twin sister of Shamash, who rules over all kings,*
> *Unto her who renders decision, goddess of all things,*
> *Unto the lady of heaven and earth who receives supplication,*
> *Unto her who hears petition, who entertains prayer,*
> *Unto the compassionate goddess who loves righteousness,*
> *Ishtar the queen, whom all that is confused oppresses,*
> *The woes as many as I see I will weep of before thee.*
> *To my sorrowful discourse may thy ear be given.*
> *At my painful account may thy soul be appeased.*
> *Behold me, O lady, that by thy repentance the heart of thy servant may be strong.*

[1] Ibid., p. 88. [2] Ibid., p. 90.

He goes on to tell of his good deeds and acts of devotion:

*Although I have no sin and committed no disgrace,*
*Yet ever am I cast down in sorrow*
*I am distressed and rest I have not.*

Therefore he pleads with her:

*I am Asurnasirpal the distressed, who fears thee,*
*Who seizes the shawl of thy divinity, praying unto the royal person,*
*Look upon me for I would implore thy divinity.*
*Since thou art enraged, have mercy upon me, may thy soul be appeased.*
*May grace strengthen thy heart toward me.*
*Cause my sickness to depart and remove my sin.*
*By thy command, O queen, may repose fall upon me,*
*The priest-king, thy favority who is changeless ever.*
*Have mercy toward him and his misery cut off.*[1]

The problem of evil is stated even more sharply in the *Ludlul Vel Nemequi*, 'I will praise the lord of wisdom'. The hero of this poem had led a righteous life: he heeded only prayer and supplication, he worshipped the Gods and adored the king, yet diseases cover his body and no God comes to his aid; he, the good man, is treated as the evil man ought to be treated by the Gods. What answers are there? one is that what seems wrong to man is right to God: 'What to one's heart seems bad, is good before one's God.' The other attains to a cosmic perspective:

*Who came to life yesterday, died to-day.*
*In but a moment man is cast into gloom, suddenly crushed.*
*One moment he will sing for joy,*
*And in an instant he will wail—a mourner.*
*Between morning and nightfall men's mood may change:*
*When they are hungry they become like corpses,*
*When they are full they will rival their God,*
*When things go well they will prate of rising up to heaven,*
*And when in trouble, rant about descending into Hades.*[2]

But Marduk restores him to health and good fortune; the way of God to man is thus justified. For God is just; a hymn to Samash reads:

[1] Stephen Langdon, *Tammuz and Ishtar*, op. cit., pp. 65–9.
[2] Thorkild Jacobsen, in *The Intellectual Adventure*, op. cit., p. 215. Translated by Mrs. Frankfort. Cf. W. F. Albright, *Stone Age*, op. cit., p. 253.

*Who is planning sin, his horn thou destroyest*
*The man thinking of bribery, his ground is changed.*
*Thou wicked judge thou causest to see imprisonment.*
*The man receiving bribes; not guiding aright, thou causest to bear punishment.*
*The man not receiving bribes interceding for the weak*
*Is pleasing unto Samas, he maketh the life long.*
*The wise judge who hath judged a righteous judgment*
*He completeth the palace, a princely dwelling is his home.*[1]

Over and over again, the hymns praise God as lord of the destinies, preserver of the people, keeper of truth and justice, forgiver of sins, helper of the oppressed, destroyer of the wicked, the protector of all: 'Thou judgest the cause of men with justice and righteousness.' Therefore the suppliant asks: 'Judge my judgment, decide my decision.' For he knows that the Gods will grant his prayers:

*Hearing the prayer, giving life,*
*with whom is reconciliation speedily,*
*Marduk, hearing the prayer, giving life,*
*with whom is reconciliation speedily.*[2]

The concept of rectitude which the Mesopotamians developed in terms of parallel between divine and human justice is perhaps best illustrated in the Code of Hammurabi, which begins:

'When Anu, the supreme, the king of the Anunnaki, and Bel, the lord of heaven and earth, who fixes the destiny of the universe, had allotted the multitudes of mankind to Merodach, the first-born of Ea, the divine master of Law, they made him great among the Igigi; they proclaimed his august name in Babylon, exalted in the lands, they established for him within it an eternal kingdom whose foundations, like heaven and earth, shall endure.

'Then Anu and Bel delighted the flesh of mankind by calling me, the renowned prince, the God-fearing Hammurabi, to establish justice in the earth, to destroy the base and the wicked, and to hold back the strong from oppressing the feeble: shine like the Sun-God upon the black-haired men, and to illuminate the land.'[3]

Then, having promulgated his code, Hammurabi concludes by

[1] George Widengren, op. cit., p. 50.
[2] Ibid., p. 280.
[3] Chilperic Edwards, *The Hammurabi Code* (London, 1904), p. 23.

stating that his justice confers upon the land a sure guidance and a gracious rule, for he has not withdrawn himself from his people, but has given them places of peace. As Shepherd of Salvation, whose sceptre is just, he calls on his successor to follow his rule and, if he should fail, he pronounces the most terrible curses upon him:

'May the great Gods of heaven and earth, the Anunnaki in their totality, the circuit of his temple of E Babbara; may they all curse him with deadly curses, his reign, his land, his officers, his people, and his soldiers.'[1]

Thus, in the thought of Mesopotamia, the idea of the settling of destinies was, as in Egyptian thought, linked with the idea of divine justice, and the end of man's life was conceived of as the establishment of a rapport in justice and goodness between himself and God.[2]

By virtue of its central importance and because of its dramatic impact, the theme of the settling of destinies provided the climax of the ritual practices of the ancient Near East, particularly since it could be staged with such effective solemnity. Of the Egyptian Book of the Dead, Professor Breasted has these suggestive remarks to make:

'That which saves the Book of the Dead itself from being exclusively a magical *vade mecum* for use in the hereafter is its elaboration of the ancient idea of the moral judgment, and its evident appreciation of the burden of conscience. The relation with God had become something more than merely the faithful observance of external rites. It had become to some extent a matter of the heart and character.'[3]

It is, therefore, in the Book of the Dead that the scene of judgment reaches its most detailed and striking expression, both in the text itself and in the vignettes which lavishly illustrated it. Three different versions of the judgment are found in one of the longest of the chapters, CXXV. The first deals with what is said when the deceased

[1] Ibid., p. 80.

[2] When the Babylonian materials were first made available, it was natural that Hebrew thought should be closely interpreted in terms of it. However, with the uncovering of other cultures, a much wider perspective is now possible, and Babylonian thought is recognized as but one, and not the only, contributing factor to the development of Hebrew ideas.

[3] James H. Breasted, *Development*, op. cit., p. 297. The development of the Book of the Dead from the mortuary texts and the Coffin Texts is traced by Professor Breasted, pp. 292–97; actually, there is no single Book of the Dead, but there is such agreement among the mortuary papyri that they have been numbered by chapters.

reaches the Hall of Truth, is purged from the evil he has done, and '. . . beholds the face of the God'. The deceased speaks to the God: 'Behold, I come to thee, I bring to thee righteousness and I expel for thee sin. I have committed no sin against people. . . . I have not done evil in the place of truth. I knew no wrong. I did no evil thing. . . . I did not do that which the God abominates.'[1] This is followed by a list of specific sins which the deceased avers he did not commit. Then the second scene of judgment takes place. Here Osiris sits as judge of the dead, assisted by forty-two horrific Gods, each of whom is addressed in turn by the deceased's disavowal of a particular sin. This recital is known as the 'Negative Confession', which is made up of two parts, one earlier than the other, and which together include between them, as Professor Albright says, '. . . practically every important type of transgression against religious obligations and the rights of others'.[2] The deceased concludes with a statement of confidence in his case and an appeal that the Gods enter no complaint against him before the Great God. The third scene of judgment is the most impressive, for in it Osiris is shown, enthroned at one end of the judgment hall with Isis and Nephthys behind him, while on one side of the hall are the Ennead, headed by the Sun-God. In the centre of the hall stand the balances of Re with which he weighs the truth; the actual manipulation of the balances is by Anubis, while behind him stands Thoth with writing materials ready to record the results. Other divine figures in the scene are the 'Devouress', 'Destiny', Renenet and Meskhenet, the two goddesses of birth, 'Taste', 'Intelligence', and sometimes 'Truth, daughter of Re'. The verdict is announced for the Ennead by Thoth, their envoy, who reports that no sin of the deceased has been found; therefore, he is not to be given to the 'Devouress' and instead is fed with the bread that comes forth before Osiris. The deceased is now led by Horus to Osiris who, upon hearing favourable report, receives him, after he has knelt, given his offerings, and repeats that there is no sin in his body. Despite the subsequent popularization and vulgarization of the declaration of innocence by which it became a charm sold by the priesthood with the name of the purchaser inscribed on a blank left for that purpose, nevertheless, the scenes of judgment remain an awesome monument to a very early attempt of man to depict the settling of destinies.

In the Babylonian *akitu* festival, two determinations of destiny

[1] Ibid., pp. 297–8.
[2] William F. Albright, *Stone Age*, op. cit., p. 171.

take place, the first on the eighth of Nisan when Marduk is given power of all the Gods together, and the second on the eleventh of Nisan, when the destiny of the community for the coming year is settled. The first corresponds to the scene in the Epic of Creation which has already been quoted; the second deals with the judgment of man and the beginning of the New Year, for, as we have already seen, every New Year is a day of judgment.[1] At the same time, Nisan was the month when the Sun-God, having defeated the darkness of winter, begins anew his ascent. It was also the month that Enlil called together the Gods to determine the fate of man for the ensuing year; the Sumerians called it *iti bar-zag-gar*, 'month of him that sits in the sanctuary'. Finally, Nisan is the month when: 'The king is lifted up, the king is installed,' as the commentary on Nisan runs, for the king was deprived for a day of his divine rights and then received them again from the high priest of Enlil or Marduk. Thus, 'the eternal fate, the fate of life', was written in the course of the ritual depicting the settling of destinies.[2] Professor Hooke has well summed up the meaning of the fixing of destinies in the ritual when he writes:

'. . . this ceremony was the end to which all the New Year Ritual tended. It was, in a literal sense, the making of a New Year, the removal of the guilt and defilement of the old year, and the ensuring of security and prosperity for the coming year. By this ceremony was secured the due functioning of all things, sun, moon, stars, and seasons in their appointed order. Here lies the ritual meaning of the Creation, there is a new creation year by year, as the result of these ceremonies.'[3]

We turn now to a consideration of the theme of the settling of the destinies in the Canaanite ritual texts. In IV AB, the coming of the God is announced and he is depicted as ready to bestow his grace on his people:

[1] A. J. Wensinck, op. cit., p. 182.

[2] Stephen Langdon, *Babylonian Menologies*, op. cit., pp. 67–9.

[3] S. H. Hooke, *Origins*, op. cit., pp. 18–19. For quite another interpretation of the fixing of the fate, see Norman H. Snaith, op. cit., pp. 213–14, 217–18, where the first fixing of the fate is considered to be the possession of *mana*, that is, *shimtu*, through the possession of the tablets of destiny, the earliest meaning, and the second, later meaning, referring to the practice of astrology. That astrological aspects entered into the settling of destinies there seems to be little doubt; we have already seen them in the Eygptian conceptions; but they are far from exhausting the idea as a whole.

'. . . . . .

But thou, *O Virgin Anat*,
Do thou wing *away o'er the hills*,
*That the heavenly beings may know* the news,
*And the* ho*st of the stars* be aware
*That the rainfall is now about* to descend,
That *Baal Puiss*ant is alive,
That *He Who Rides the Clouds* still exists!
*Now is the* God Had (ad) about to vi*sit the peoples*,
Ba*al is about to return to the earth!*
*Now will the dead* be quickened,
For that salvation comes *thro' this Lord of Green Things!*
*He will surely bestow the favour of* gentle rain from the clouds,
Liberal showers *will he furnish!*'
*Then the* Virgin *Anat* takes up word;
*Yea*, Y-b-m-t-L-e-m-m *exclaims:*
'Now is the God Had(ad) about to visit *the peoples*,
Baal is about to retu*rn to the earth!*
He will bestow his grace *on that which is now but a remnant*,
Men's fields and h*omes* will alike rejoice!
Behold, I will take in *my hand*,
In *my* right hand brings as tribute
Mountain-go*ats* by the thousand,
Wild *oxen* by the tens of thousands!'[1]

The identification of the settling of the destinies with the promotion of fertility by the bringing of the rain is clearly revealed in this text. IV AB concludes with a passage already quoted in which Anat embraces and clothes Baal, announces that: 'The valley which erst was an Highway of Death Is Turned into a valley of Life Triumphant!', and goes up into the Hill of the North. The Mountain of the North is designated by the messenger of the God as Baal's goal in V AB, C, as well:

'Like a young man-servant and a pledged slave prostrate thyself at the feet of Anath and pay homage, bowing down honour her. And say to the virgin, Anath, announce to the progenitress of the peoples the order of the mighty-one, Baal, the command of him who is called "I prevail over the battle-axes of those who meet me in the land of battle(s)", "Put mandrakes (?) into an *prt*; pour a libation into

[1] Theodor H. Gaster, ' "Baal is Risen, . . ." ', op. cit., pp. 125–6.

the earth, an . . . into the fields . . . to me; let thy feet run to me, let thy legs strike toward me! For I have a command and I will announce it to thee, I have an order and I will report it to thee. The trees have spoken and the stones have whispered; the heavens have murmured to the earth. I shall create the thunderbolt in order that the heavens may know, that men may know the command, and that the inhabitants of the earth may understand. I shall make (the thunderbolt) ready and I shall preserve (?) it, even I, in my mountain, I, the God of the north—, in the holy (place), in the mount of my heritage, in the beautiful (place), in the hill of power.'[1]

What the command of Baal consists of is reported in V AB where his message is one of hope to his people:

> *This is the word of Him Who is Puissant in Valour: . . .*
> *'I have a message to tell unto thee,*
> *A word to recount (unto thee);*
> *'Tis the message of stock and the whisper of stone,*
> *A message I fain mankind would mark,*
> *And the multitudes of the earth duly note,*
> *'Tis the sigh of the heavens among with the earth,*
> *The seas along with the stars,*
> *Yea, and the levin-bolt too; 'tis a message I fain the heavens would mark;*
> *'Come, we will seek him together, ye and I,*
> *'Mid my valleys yonder do ye look out (for him)!*
> *'Mid pastures green, mid the valley of mine estate!'*[2]

In II AB, the dream of El Dped foretells the coming of an era of peace and plenty:

'In a dream, . . . El Dped, heard the words (?), "Good tidings, O my son whom I have begotten, the heavens will rain down oil, and the beds of torrents will cause honey to flow, and I know that Aleyan the lord lives and that Zebul, lord of the earth, exists. . . . The . . . , El Dped, rejoiced, his feet he placed on a foot-stool (??), and he put away grief and smiled. He lifted up his voice and said, "I will sit down and rest, and my breath of life (i.e. soul) shall rest in my breast, for Aleyan the lord lives, Zebul, lord of the earth, exists." '[3]

[1] William F. Albright, 'Recent Progress in North-Canaanite Research', *BASOR*, LXX (1938), pp. 19–20.

[2] Theodor H. Gaster, ' "Baal is Risen, . . ." ', op. cit., p. 141.

[3] William F. Albright, 'New Light on Early Canaanite Language and Literature', *BASOR*, XLVI (1932), p. 18.

Columns IV–V of II AB relate how Baal is told to go to the heights of the north where he shall pay homage to El, and then we hear Athirat say: 'El, the wise one, has bestowed on thee wisdom, together with eternal life and good fortune. Our king has bestowed (them) on thee, O Aleyan Baal, our judge (magistrate)—and there is none above him.'[1]

When a house is built for Baal, a house of cedar and brick, in which is made a sanctuary of silver and gold, and into which Baal goes and is enthroned, there he says:

> *I alone am he that is king over the Gods,*
> *yea, that nourishes Gods and men,*
> *satisfies the multitudes of the earth.*[2]

The vision of the future as an era of flowing abundance is repeated in I AB when, after the rite of the last sheaf is performed by Anat with Mot, Aleyan Baal is resurrected and the promise is made that:

> *Heaven will rain down fatness,*
> *the bed(s) of the torrent(s) cause honey to flow.*[3]

If, following Professor Engnell, we take Dnil as the representation of the divine king, we see him in one scene of judgment in which he judges the cause of the widow and administers justice to the orphan, while Column VI speaks of the granting of immortal life and the promise of the new birth to humanity.[4] Finally in the Poem of Keret there is once more repeated the theme of the vision in a dream; as sighs spoil his sleep, Keret dreams: 'And in his vision El brings down good tidings to him; the Father of Mankind (brings down good tidings to him) and ——.'[5] Keret thus obtains the promise of a son, that is, a new birth, a promise which is fulfilled in his marriage with *Mtt-hry* '(For she is the one) of whom El in my vision gave me good tidings, (of whom) The Father of Mankind (in my wisdom gave me good tidings). And (she shall) bear seed to *Krt* and a child to the servant of El.'[6] The theme of the settling of destinies in the

[1] William F. Albright, 'More Light on the Canaanite Epic of Aleyan Baal and Mot', *BASOR*, L (1933), p. 15.
[2] Ivan Engnell, op. cit., p. 117.
[3] Ibid., p. 122.
[4] Ibid., pp. 137–8.
[5] William F. Albright, 'New Canaanite Historical and Mythological Data', *BASOR*, LXIII (1936), p. 28.
[6] Ibid., p. 31.

Canaanite ritual texts is characterized by its distinctive emphasis on the very close association of the concept of new birth with the themes of creation and the sacred marriage.

We have followed in some detail the development of those aspects of the religious thought and practice of the ancient Near East which together constituted a pattern of myth and ritual whose efficacy was of such force as to gain the deepest assent and most faithful credence of the peoples who believed and practised it. It seems most probable that these beliefs and rituals, of such distant antiquity to us, were already very old by the time they were put into the forms with which we have dealt with them here. For our materials have been derived, for the greater part, from written record, which must of necessity represent a late stage in the development of the pattern. Accordingly, we must conclude that the pattern is one of man's oldest beliefs, and, in view of his persistent and repeated use of it, it must be one which has given him comfort and security, the assurance that, by reproducing mimetically the basic rhythms of nature he sees and feels around and in him, he can bring himself in harmony with them and thereby with their makers or maker, and perhaps can even secure some degree of control over them and so convert them to his gain. We have noticed, too, that the pattern which, at first, is an expression of man's lowest nature tends more and more with time toward refinement and spiritualization; as man slowly acquires a social and moral sense, the pattern gradually divests itself of its grosser associations, but not so much by expunging them as by transforming them symbolically to a higher level of ethical significance. Above all, the myth and ritual pattern is alive: it has the capacity to change, to adapt itself, and to raise itself, so that, if to its ability to answer a fundamental need of man we add its ability to adapt itself, we can understand, I think, why man has had such a long and frequent recourse to it, from the time before written records to, in changed form, our own.

## CHAPTER IV

# *The Myth and Ritual Pattern in the Mediterranean Area*

BEFORE we can turn to the next stage in the spiritualization of the myth and ritual pattern of the ancient Near East, we must first make a very brief survey of its parallel development in the Aegean area. Indeed, as I have already indicated, to think in terms of parallel growth is to do an injustice to the similarities of thought in the various ideologies in the area extending from the valley of the two rivers westward to the Aegean. Surely Professor Persson goes too far, both in ideas and geography, when he speaks of an Afrasian culture;[1] nevertheless, we can see that, despite all the many diversities between the peoples of the most ancient Near East —and these are, of course, fundamental—there are, in the main, certain likenesses in the ways in which they thought and acted; in which they built, created, and wrote; in the kind of problems they faced and the solutions they brought to them; and in their political ideologies, religious ideas, and forms of worship. One of the reasons for the tendency towards homogenity was the similarity in the ways in which they sustained themselves economically; Professor Childe has pointed out that the historic civilizations of the Mediterranean basin, Hither Asia, and India were built upon cereals, particularly wheat and barley; and to the cultivation of these basic crops was added the breeding of animals, horned cattle, sheep, goats, and swine, and later, fowls, for food. The result of this change from an economy based on food-gathering to one based on food-producing

[1] Axel W. Persson, *The Religion of Greece in Prehistoric Times* (Berkeley (Cal.), 1942), p. 1.

was enormous: man had now to settle down in relatively limited areas where food could be steadily produced; he could undertake to breed selectively; he had some degree of control over his food supply; he could accumulate a surplus and thus engage in trade; he could devise instruments to assist him in his tasks, such as the axe or adze, pottery of several kinds, textiles; and with the development of these tools there came into existence a great body of craft lore. The consequence of these momentous changes in the ways in which man lived was that, in time, he was able to live in cities and thereby engage in the most complex of human activities, such as trade, industry, statecraft, and the intellectual pursuits; now came the clearing away of sites where cities could be built so that they would be ensured a regular water and food supply and to do this required both capital and labour; at the same time, with control over the instruments of production there came a corresponding control over the affairs of men; the diet was enlarged to include dates, figs, olives, and other fruits of the grove and orchard; the invention of the brick made possible large-scale building; the working of copper in particular, and the growth of metallurgy in general, the use of the wheel in transport and in industry, and the fundamental improvements in the means of communication all left a permanent and profound effect on the ways of life of the ancient Near East.[1] Another stimulus towards intellectual unity was the intensity and range of trade both in objects and ideas. Dependent as we are on the use of coal, electricity, and gasoline for our transportation and communication, it is difficult for us to realize how much can be accomplished by wheel and sail if to these are added, as they unquestionably were, curiosity, ingenuity, and, above all, daring. The excavations point up the tremendous exchange of artifacts between the peoples of the ancient Near East, and if they carried on the trade in material things with such avidity, there is no reason to suppose that the exchange of ideas was on a lesser scale.[2] Given, therefore, such similarities in material and cultural development, it is not then so surprising that the problems which were faced were pretty much the same and, more important, that the solutions which could be achieved should likewise be of fairly the same sort and relatively on the same level of accomplishment.

[1] I have been following V. Gordon Childe, *Man Makes Himself* (London, 1948), pp. 66–138.

[2] For a survey of the extent of trade, see V. Gordon Childe, *New Light on the Most Ancient East* (London and New York, 1934), pp. 283–301. Cf. Helene J. Kantor, 'The Aegean and the Orient in the Second Millenium B.C.', *AJA*, LI (1947), pp. 1–103.

The evidence for the Mediterranean treatment of the myth and ritual pattern is detailed and varied, and I propose to do no more than to mention some of the major strands in its composition and to indicate briefly the nature of but a few of these strands. Among the more important components are: (1) the Cretan mother goddess; (2) the Cretan origin of the Greek Gods and of Greek mythology; (3) the ritual origins both of tragedy and comedy; (4) the Greek mystery religions, particularly those of Eleusis, Dionysos, and Orpheus; (5) the Greek hero cults; (6) the Hellenistic mystery religions, such as the Hermetica and the Egypto-Hellenistic, the Syro-Hellenistic, and the Perso-Hellenistic mystery religions; (7) various other pagan concepts, such as the idea of miraculous birth, the influence of the fourth eclogue, the emperor as world saviour, and the myth of the returning emperor; and (8) the Hellenization of late Jewish thought. Confusing as these currents of doctrine and practice are in detail, their larger import is, I think, clear. By the time of the rise of Christianity, the Mediterranean world was pulsating with beliefs, which, however they might differ in details, tended towards one general form, that of salvation through rebirth.

Diodorus Siculus says of the Cretans that their claim was that '. . . the greater number of the gods . . . had their origin, so their myths relate, in their land',[1] and, while the boast is somewhat exaggerated, the Cretans did pass on to the Hellenic world the concept of a great Nature Goddess and her male partner. At the very outset, we note a difference between the treatment of the myth and ritual pattern by the peoples of the Near East and those of the Aegean area, for the latter placed their strongest stress on the Great Mother rather than on the God. In the Minoan period, representations of the God are few in number compared to those of the Goddess.[2] The great Goddess was known under a variety of names, as Rhea, Britomartis, Dictynna, and Aphaia, and from her representations, we can see that she was thought of as the Goddess of fertility, the divine mother, the protectress of animals, and also as the warrior Goddess. The boy God, in his turn, is shown as worshipping his mother, his name being Zan, Zeus, or Zagreos.[3] Now, it is this boy God who dies, is mourned, and is restored to life, and on the gold

[1] *Diodorus of Sicily*, tr. C. H. Oldfather (London, 1939), p. 269.

[2] L. R. Farnell, 'Cretan Influence in Greek Religion', in *Essays in Aegean Archaeology Presented to Sir Arthur Evans*, ed. S. Casson (Oxford, 1927), pp. 10–14.

[3] Sir Arthur Evans, *The Palace of Minos at Knossos* (London, 1930), III, pp. 436–76; IV, Part II, pp. 468–83; Robert Briffault, *The Mothers* (London, 1927), III, pp. 118–20.

rings from Mycenae, his cycle has been depicted. Professor Persson has arranged them into a vegetation cycle consisting of winter, spring, summer, and harvest-time: rings 1–4 deal with the mourning ceremonies connected with a burial in which dying vegetation is portrayed, but also signs are given that the dead shall rise; rings 3–5 depict dances and the giving of gifts to attract the favourable attention of the divinities; ring 6 shows the force of sun magic which in ring 20 has resurrected the God; rings 7–14 represent various forms of thanksgiving at the return of spring, when lilies begin to sprout, the rains come, and the shrines are decorated with green branches; rings 17–19 depict the bull games, with the bull as the symbol of the reproductive forces of nature; in rings 20–24 full summer has arrived, the Great Goddess is worshipped, and the male God has returned; rings 25–28 show the Goddess of Fertility in her divine boat disappearing over the sea and then returning when the vegetation is reborn.[1] The relations of the Minoan Great Goddess with the goddesses of the ancient Near East are at once apparent: Cybele, Anat, Ishtar, and Isis, while correspondingly, the boy-God calls to mind Attis, Baal, Adonis, and Osiris. But in the Minoan period, the Great Goddess overshadowed the boy-God.[2] Modern research has thus confirmed the brilliant description of the Great Goddess, whose hair was flowing and curling, and from whose garland blades of corn were set out, which Apuleius made of her:

'I am she that is the natural mother of all things, mistress and governess of all the elements, the initial progeny of worlds, chief of the powers divine, queen of all that are in hell, the principal of them that dwell in heaven, manifested alone and under one form of all the Gods and Goddesses. At my will the planets of the sky, the wholesome winds of the seas, and the lamentable silences of hell be disposed; my name, my divinity, is adored throughout all the world, in divers manners, in variable customs, and by many names. For

[1] Axel W. Persson, op. cit., pp. 25–104.

[2] Ibid., p. 122. I am aware that Professor Persson takes an extreme position; more moderate accounts will be found in Lewis R. Farnell, *The Cults of the Greek States* (Oxford, 1907), II, pp. 289–306; Martin P. Nilsson, *A History of Greek Religion*, tr. F. J. Fielden (Oxford, 1925), pp. 30–4; Gustave Glotz, *The Aegean Civilization*, tr. M. R. Dobie and E. M. Riley (London and New York, 1925), pp. 243–54; Martin P. Nilsson, *The Minoan-Mycenaean Religion and Its Survival in Greek Religion* (London, 1927), pp. 461–513; Machteld J. Mellinck, *Hyakinthos* (Utrecht, 1943), pp. 70–117; Gertrude R. Levy, *The Gate of Horn* (London, 1948), pp. 213–41; and Martin P. Nilsson, *The Mycenaean Origin of Greek Mythology* (Berkeley (Cal.), 1932).

the Phrygians that are the first of all men call me the Mother of the Gods at Pessinus; the Athenians, which are sprung from their own soil, Cecropian Minerva, the Cyprians, which are girt about the sea, Paphian Venus; the Cretans which bear arrows, Dictynnian Diana; the Sicilians, which speak three tongues, infernal Prosperine; the Eleusians their ancient Goddess Ceres; some Juno, other Bellona, other Hecate, other Rhamnusia, and principally both sort of the Ethiopians which dwell in the Orient and are enlightened by the morning rays of the sun, and the Egyptians, which are excellent in all kind of ancient doctrine, and by their proper ceremonies accustom to worship me, do call me by my true name, Queen Isis.'[1]

The influence of the Cretans on the pantheon of the later Greeks is indicated by the list of the major and lesser divinities which, in one degree or another, stem from the Mother Goddess and her son; among the goddesses may be counted Aphaia, Aphrodite, Ariadne, Aridela, Artemis, Britomartis, Dictynna, Demeter, Eileithria, Ephesia, Helen, Kore, Persephone, and Rhea; among the Gods, Dionysos, Erichthonious, Eros, Glaukos, Hyakinthos, Kronos, and Cretan Zeus.

Turning again to Diodorus Siculus, we find him saying of the Cretans:

'They also assert that the honours accorded to the Gods and their sacrifices and the initiatory rites observed in connection with the mysteries were handed down from Crete to the rest of men, and to support this they advance the following most weighty argument, as they conceive it: The initiatory rite which is celebrated by the Athenians in Eleusis, the most famous, one may venture, of them all, and that of Samothrace, and the one practised in Thrace among the Cicones, whence Orpheus came who introduced them—these are all handed down in the form of a mystery, whereas at Cnosus in Crete it has been the custom from ancient times that these initiatory rites should be handed down to all openly, and what is handed down among other peoples as not to be divulged, this the Cretans conceal from no one who may wish to inform himself upon such matters.'

He then repeats the Cretan claims concerning their primacy in the matter of the origination of the Gods:

[1] Apuleius, *The Golden Ass*, tr. R. W. Adlington, rev. S. Gasalee, (London, 1915), pp. 545–7. Another genealogy, much more fanciful, is given by Robert Graves in his *The White Goddess*.

'Indeed, the majority of the Gods, the Cretans say, had their beginning in Crete and set out from there to visit many regions of the inhabited world, conferring benefactions upon the races of men and distributing among each of them the advantage which resulted from the discoveries they had made.'[1]

Miss Jane Harrison has, I think, confirmed the Cretan claim. She has shown how, from the festival of the Anthesteria to that of the Thargelia and thence to that of the Thesmophoria, held respectively in the spring, summer, and autumn, there is a kind of development, or at least an unfolding in the methods and intent of the purification rites, which were the prime function of the festivals: in the first, fertility is promoted by the purgation of evil influences; the second uses the ceremonial of the pharmakos; and to the third the idea of consecration is added; there is thus a progression in the direction of successive spiritualization. When upon these elements was now imposed the Dionysiac belief in enthusiasm, that is, the notion that man could pass from the human to the divine, and the Orphic conception that the complete union of man with the divine could be effected by means of the Omophagia by the eating of the God, by the Sacred Marriage, and by the Sacred Birth, the mysteries were able to provide their devotees with the means whereby man, 'the son of Earth and starry Heaven, who has suffered the Suffering', could become 'God from Man'.[2]

To the myth and ritual pattern of the ancient Near East, the mysteries made one significant addition. Though, as we have seen, the rituals possessed important features in common, yet their efficacy was limited to those who belonged to the group for which they were performed. The fear of the outsider and of the stranger was still very strong; conversely, the sense of identification with the group, or the city, or the people, was equally strong, but it was a stringent identification which did not admit others into it. Only with the Hebrews is there a suggestion that the non-initiate has as much right to salvation as does the initiate, and even in Hebrew thought the theme of universalism is not very forcefully sounded; the heart of flesh which Yahweh will give remains, after all, a Hebrew heart; the servant suffers for the Hebrews; and on the Day of Judg-

[1] *Diodorus of Sicily*, op. cit., III, pp. 307–9.

[2] Jane Harrison, *Prolegomena to the Study of Greek Religion* (Cambridge, 1908), pp. 574, 583.

ment it is the Hebrews who are judged by the Son of Man. In justice to the presence of the theme of universalism in Hebrew thought, however, mention must be made of Jeremiah where, referring to his evil neighbours, the Lord says: 'And it shall come to pass, if they will diligently learn the ways of my people to swear by my name, As the LORD liveth; even as they taught my people to swear by Baal: then shall they be built up in the midst of my people.' (Jeremiah 12, 16). We recall, too, that in Deutero-Isaiah the Egyptians and the Sabeans shall fall down before the Lord, saying: 'Surely God is in thee; and there is none else, there is no God.' (Isaiah 45, 14.) The same idea is repeated in Malachi: 'For from the rising of the sun even unto the going down of the same my name is great among the Gentiles; and in every place incense is offered unto my name, and a pure offering: for my name is great among the Gentiles, saith the LORD of hosts.' (Malachi 1, 11.) Despite this evidence, however, the concept of universalism, while indeed present in Hebrew thought, is not strong. But the mysteries opened the way for all who would undergo initiation to share in the great process of regeneration, and the barriers of nation, race, and class were, first, under the influence of the mysteries and, later, in the wake of Stoic cosmopolitanism, broken down under the impact of the demand which came from all sides for *soteria*, salvation.[1] The numbers and varieties of the mysteries are almost overwhelming in their profusion, the most important, not including the numerous local cults, being the cults of Orpheus, Dionysos, Pythagoras, the Eleusinian, the Samothracian Kabiri, the Great Mother and Attis, the Egyptian Serapis and Isis, the Syrian Baal and Adonis, the Persian Mithra, the Gnostics, the Phrygian Sabazios, the *Dea Syria*, and the theosophical Hermeticists, some of which enjoyed the devotion of their followers for almost two thousand years;[2] and mention should also be made of the hero-cults, of which that of 'the saviour of the whole world', Asclepios, was the most far-reaching in its effects.[3] Such long popularity and such faithful devotion constitute more than adequate proof that the mysteries provided to the ancients, at least, an answer satisfactory to

[1] Franz Cumont, *The Oriental Religions in Roman Paganism* (London and Chicago, 1911), pp. 27–8; E. O. James, *Christian Myth and Ritual* (London, 1933), pp. 36–7.

[2] S. Angus, *The Religious Quests of the Graeco-Roman World* (London and New York, 1929), p. 77; Harold R. Willoughby, *Pagan Regeneration* (Chicago, 1929), pp. 29–30.

[3] See Walter A. Jayne, *The Healing Gods of Ancient Civilizations* (New Haven, (Conn.), 1925); and Emma J. and Ludwig Edelstein, *Asclepius*, 2 vols. (Baltimore, 1948), particularly II, pp. 132–8.

them, to their persistent cries for salvation. To be sure, not all were convinced of the worth of the mysteries; we recall, for example, Plato's scathing words in *The Republic:*

'And they produce a host of books written by Musaeus and Orpheus, who were children of the Moon and the Muses—that is what they say—according to which they perform their ritual, and persuade not only individuals, but whole cities, that expiations and atonements for sin may be made by sacrifices and amusements which fill a vacant hour, and are equally at the service of the living and the dead; the latter sort they call mysteries, and they redeem us from the pains of hell, but if we neglect them no one knows what awaits us.'[1]

But against this denunciation we must place Pindar's words of praise for the Eleusinian Mysteries:

'Blessed is he who hath seen these things before he goeth beneath the earth, for he understandeth the end of mortal life, and the beginning (of a new life) given of God.'[2]

And again, in a dithyramb probably composed for the Great Dionysia celebrated at the beginning of spring, Pindar in lovely images praises the mysteries:

'Haste to the dance and send your glorious favour, ye Olympian Gods, who, in holy Athens, are marching to the densely crowded incense-breathing centre of the city, and to its richly adorned and glorious mart, there to receive garlands bound with violets, and songs culled in the spring-time. And look upon me, who, with joyance of songs, am once more sped by Zeus into the presence of the ivy-crowned god, whom we mortals call Eromius and Eriboas, to celebrate the progeny of sires supreme and Cadmean mothers.

'Clearly seen are the bright symbols of sacred rites, whensoever, at the opening of the chamber of the purple-robed Hours, the fragrant Spring bringeth the nectar-breathing plants. Then, oh then, are flung on the immortal earth the lovely tresses of violets, and roses are entwined in the hair; then ring the voices of song to the sound of flutes; then ring the dances in honour of diadem-wreathed Semele.'[3]

And if Demosthenes ridiculed his opponent Aeschines by charging

[1] *The Dialogues of Plato*, tr. B. Jowett (Oxford, 1892), III, p. 44.
[2] *The Odes of Pindar*, tr. Sir John Sandys (London, 1915), pp. 591–93.
[3] Ibid., pp. 553–5.

him with participation in the mysteries, dressed in the fawn-skin and crowned with fennel and poplar leaves, shouting: 'I have shunned evil; I have found good!' and taking as pay for his services sops and cakes, and if Livy exposed the scandals of the Dionysian brotherhoods, we have the choral ode in *The Frogs:*

> *Now wheel your sacred dances through the glade with flowers bedight*
> *All ye who are partakers of the holy festal rite;*
> *And I will with the women and the holy maidens go*
> *Where they keep the nightly vigil, an auspicious light to show.*
>
> *Now haste we to the roses,*
> *And the meadows full of posies,*
> *Now haste we to the meadows,*
> *In our own way,*
> *In choral dances blending,*
> *In dances never ending,*
> *Which only for the holy*
> *The Destinies array.*
> *O, happy mystic chorus,*
> *The blessed sunshine o'er us*
> *On us alone is smiling,*
> *In its soft sweet light:*
> *On us who strove for ever*
> *With holy, pure endeavour,*
> *Alike by friend and stranger*
> *To guide our steps aright.*[1]

Fragment 837 of Sophocles:

'Thrice happy are those mortals who see these rites before they depart for Hades; for to them alone is it granted to have true life on the other side. To all the rest there is evil.'[2]

the sober testimony of Cicero and Plutarch, the statement of Diodorus:

'The claim is also made that men who have taken part in the

[1] *The Frogs of Aristophanes*, tr. Benjamin B. Rogers (London, 1902), pp. 68–71.
[2] Tr. William Chase Greene, *Moira Fate, Good, and Evil in Greek Thought* (Cambridge (Mass.), 1948), p. 51.

mysteries become both more pious and more just and better in every respect than they were before.'[1]

and, finally, the great prayer of Apuleius to the goddess:

'O holy and blessed dame, the perpetual comfort of human kind, who by Thy bounty and grace nourishest all the world, and bearest a great affection to the adversities of the miserable as a loving mother, Thou takest no rest night or day, neither art Thou idle at any time in giving benefits and succouring all men as well on land as sea; Thou art she that puttest away all storms and dangers from men's life by stretching forth Thy right hand, whereby likewise Thou dost unweave even the inextricable and tangled web of fate, and appeasest the great tempests of fortune, and keepest back the harmful course of the stars. The Gods supernal do honour Thee; the Gods infernal have Thee in reverence; Thou dost make all the earth to turn, Thou givest light to the sun, Thou governest the world, Thou treadest down the power of hell. By Thy mean the stars give answer, the seasons return, the Gods rejoice, the elements serve; at Thy commandment the winds do blow, the clouds nourish the earth, the seeds prosper, and the fruits do grow. The birds of the air, the beasts of the hill, the serpents of the den, and the fishes of the sea do tremble at Thy majesty: but my spirit is not able to give Thee sufficient praise, my patrimony is unable to satisfy Thy sacrifices; my voice hath no power to utter that which I think of Thy majesty, no, not if I had a thousand mouths and so many tongues and were able to continue for ever. Howbeit as a good religious person, and according to my poor estate, I will do what I may: I will always keep Thy divine appearance in remembrance, and close the imagination of Thy most holy godhead within my breast.'[2]

to counter-balance their criticisms. As to the extent and virulence of the attacks on the mysteries by the Fathers, these may be taken as a kind of praise in reverse, for the Church recognized quite clearly that in the mysteries it had one of its most appealing and formidable rivals. 'For', as Paul said, 'I am persuaded, that neither death, nor life, nor angels, nor principalities, nor powers, nor things present, nor things to come, nor height, nor depth, nor any other creature, shall be able to separate us from the love of God, which is in Christ

[1] Diodorus Siculus, op. cit., III, p. 235.
[2] Apuleius, *The Golden Ass*, op. cit., pp. 583–5.

Jesus our Lord.' (Romans 8, 38–9.) Thus, from the old agricultural God, the 'Soter', he who '. . . slew the Enemy and brought back the Dead God, or was himself the dead God restored',[1] there emerged in the long course of time the pagan concept of the Saviour God whose special gift to man was *philanthropy*, for he loved compassion, which he gave to man as a refuge from his sorrows.

The mystery religions have been defined as a:

> '. . . divine drama which portrayed before the wondering eyes of the privileged observers the story of the struggles, sufferings, and victory of a patron deity, the travail of nature in which life ultimately triumphs over death, and joy is born of pain.'[2]

They repeat both in form and content, but with the variations introduced by new needs and under the impetus of the differing characters of different peoples, the myth and ritual pattern of the ancient Near East. Unfortunately, we are in the dark when it comes to settling down what actually took place in the mysteries; by and large, the vows of secrecy which the initiates had to take were faithfully kept, and often our information must be drawn from those writers who were sharply antagonistic to them and who were themselves outsiders.[3] But a kind of idealized version of the mystic rites can be reconstructed, and Professor Angus has arranged them into three divisions: (1) the preparation and probation of the candidate for admission into membership, or *catharsis*; (2) the initiation and communion of the candidate into membership, or *muesis*; and (3) the blessedness and salvation of the newly accepted member, or *epopteia*.[4] Not only did the cult practices form a divine drama of death and resurrection, then, but the individual initiate himself went through a similar progression; in other words, as in the rituals which we have considered, the thing done was the very means whereby the thing sought was accomplished; in drama, however, there is a separation of the two, the action being an end in itself which the spectator

[1] Gilbert Murray, *Stoic, Christian and Humanist* (London, 1940), p. 67.

[2] S. Angus, *The Mystery-Religions and Christianity* (London and New York, 1925), p. 59.

[3] The paucity of information about the mysteries has led one scholar to go so far as to deny, in one case at least, their very existence; see Ivan M. Linforth, *The Arts of Orpheus* (Berkeley, 1941). Cf. A. D. Nock, 'Orphism or Roman Philosophy?', *HTR*, XXXIII (1940), pp. 301–15 but see, too, W. K. C. Guthrie, *Orpheus and Greek Religion* (London, 1935), pp. 301–15; Franz Cumont, *Lux Perpetua* (Paris, 1949), pp. 235–74; and W. K. C. Guthrie, *The Greeks and Their Gods* (London, 1950), pp. 145–82, 307–32.

[4] S. Angus, *The Mystery-Religions*, op. cit., p. 76.

contemplates with another kind of pleasure, nor does he seek to achieve some specific ritual change in himself, though he can, and does, secure the pleasure of moral insight which links the drama to its source in ritual, but which at the same time, by virtue of its non-active and non-participating effects, distinguishes the drama from the ritual. In the first stage, the initiate went through a period of preparation, with vows of secrecy, confession, lustral purification, sacrifice, ascetic acts, penitential pilgrimages, self-mortification, and the wearing of proper garments, leading to *enthronismos*, or the enthronement of the candidate. The second stage was that of initiation and communion, of which very little is actually known, since this was the very heart of the mystery. But we do know that the sacrament of the *taurobolium*, or bath in bull's blood, and sometimes the *criobolium*, or sacrifice of a ram, took place at this stage. The centre of the mystery lay in *palingenesia* or regeneration in which the old was shed and the spirit made new; the *mystes* was thus twice-born, for he passed from death through his identity with the deity to a new life. In the Hymn of Regeneration of the *Liturgy of Mithra*, we read:

'Lord, having been regenerated, I depart in exaltation, and having been exalted I die. Born again for rebirth of that life-giving birth, and delivered unto death, I go the way, as thou hast established, as thou hast decreed, as thou hast created the sacrament.'[1]

As a result of the process of regeneration, the *mystes* became, through communion, identified with God. In the trance induced by ecstasy and enthusiasm, the initiate underwent apotheosis, being in all respects identical with God, for, as the Orphic tablets stated: 'Happy and blessed one, thou shalt be God instead of mortal.'[2] *The Bacchae* of Euripides is shot through with the language of intoxication derived from the mysteries; a chorus of maidens speaks:

*Oh, blessèd he in all wise,*
*Who hath drunk the Living Fountain,*
*Whose life no folly staineth,*
*And his soul is near to God;*
*Whose sins are lifted, pall-wise,*
*As he worships on the Mountain,*
*And where Cybele ordaineth,*
*Our Mother, he has trod:*

[1] Ibid., p. 100. [2] Jane Harrison, *Prolegomena*, op. cit., p. 586.

*His head with ivy laden*
*And his thyrsus tossing high,*
*For our God he lifts his cry;*
*'Up, O Bacchae, wife and maiden,*
*Come, O ye Bacchae, come;*
*Oh, bring the Joy-bestower,*
*God-seed of God the Sower,*
*Bring Bromios in his power*
*From Phrygia's mountain dome;*
*To street and town and tower,*
*Oh, bring ye Bromios home!'*

*Whom erst in anguish lying*
*For an unborn life's desire,*
*As a dead thing in the Thunder*
*His Mother cast to earth;*
*For her heart was dying, dying,*
*In the white heart of the fire;*
*Till Zeus, the Lord of Wonder,*
*Devised new lairs of birth;*

*Yea, his own flesh tore to hide him,*
*And with clasps of bitter gold*
*Did a secret son enfold,*
*And the Queen knew not beside him;*
*Till the perfect hour was there;*
*And a God with serpents crowned;*
*And for that are serpents wound*
*In the wands his maidens bear,*
*And the songs of serpents sound*
*In the mazes of their hair.*[1]

And Teiresias, describing the powers of Dionysus, who rests man's spirit, dim from grieving, says:

*A prophet is he likewise. Prophecy*
*Cleaves to all frenzy, but beyond all else*
*To frenzy of prayer. Then in us verily dwells*
*The God himself, and speaks the thing to be.*[2]

[1] *The Bacchae of Euripides*, tr. Gilbert Murray (London, n.d.), pp. 11–12.
[2] Ibid., p. 20.

Another means of communion with God was through the divine marriage, which particularly aroused the ire of the Fathers, though they themselves were not at all averse from using the imagery drawn from the concept of the divine marriage to depict the relationship of Christ to his worshippers. The divine marriage occupied a prominent place in the Eleusinian, Dionysian, Cybele, Attis, and Great Mother cults; and in the ritual of the cult of Sabazios, a snake was inserted into the robe of the novice and then drawn out from below to symbolize the union of Zeus in the form of a serpent with Persephone, the snake representing the God and the initiate the Goddess.[1] Moreover, communion with the God was effected through the ritual of the divine services in which the sacred procession and the *agape* were of outstanding importance.[2] Likewise of particular efficacy in bringing about the communion of the initiate with God was the sacramental meal, as we learn from Clement of Alexandria:

> *I have eaten out of the drum:*
> *I have drunk out of the cymbal:*
> *I have carried the* Kernos:
> *I have entered the bridal chamber.*[3]

Again, though the Church Fathers bitterly opposed the sacrament of eating, they adapted it to their own purposes. Finally, the rites of initiation ended with a vision of the epiphany of the deity:

> *But there, methinks, the God had wrought—I speak but as I guess—*
> *Some dream-shape in mine image;*[4]

The illumination which the mystic experience afforded has been vividly described by Plutarch:

'At first wanderings and wearisome hurryings to and fro, and unfinished journeys half-seen as through a darkness; then before the consummation itself all the terrors, shuddering and trembling, sweat and wonder; after which they are confronted by a wonderful light, or received into pure regions and meadows, with singing and dancing and sanctities of holy voices and sacred revelations, wherein, made perfect at last, free and absolved, the initiate worships with crowned head in the company of those pure and undefiled, looking down on

[1] W. O. E. Oesterley, 'The Cult of Sabazios: A Study in Religious Syncretism', in *The Labyrinth*, ed. S. H. Hooke (London, 1935), pp. 143–4.
[2] S. Angus, *The Mystery-Religions*, op. cit., pp. 121–7.
[3] Cited by Harold R. Willoughby, op. cit., p. 134.
[4] *The Bacchae*, op. cit., p. 39.

the impure, uninitiated multitude of the living as they trample one another under foot and are herded together in thick mire and dust.'[1]

Professor Rostovtzeff has called attention to the picture of the apse in the basilica of the Porta Maggiore; he writes:

'Rocks in the sun. On one, the beautiful erect figure of Apollo, extending his right hand towards a girl who is standing on the top of another rock ready to plunge into the sea, guided and gently urged by the God of love. In the sea, Tritons and Nereids (or Sirens) ready to help the girl and to receive her. The extreme left corner is occupied by a young man in deep sorrow, seated, looking at the scene of the plunge.'

What is the meaning of the picture? Basing his answer on the researches of his predecessors, Professor Rostovtzeff answers:

'The picture coincides in all the essential points with the fifteenth Heroid of Ovid, in which he describes the leap of Sappho from the Leucadian rock. Neither Ovid nor our picture represents the vulgar tradition of the suicide of the poetess, betrayed in her love to Phaon. Their conception is much loftier. Sappho does not intend to commit suicide. She is putting her fate into the hands of the great God of light and wisdom, Apollo. Her earthly love of Phaon is an obstacle to her sacred union with Apollo. By the mystic leap into the sea, by a ritual death, her immortal part is to be purified and made ready for her divine bridegroom—the God of light, Apollo. The beautiful painting was an eloquent symbol for the mystae who gathered in the underground basilica.'[2]

We may take this picture, then, as the representation and as the symbol, equally, of what the mysteries, seen in their best light, offered their communicants: salvation and immortality through their participation in the cycle of death and rebirth.[3]

It is not my purpose to take up here the problem of the origins of Greek tragedy except to recall Jane Harrison's brilliant account of the development of tragedy from the *dromenon* or enaction of the New Birth into the tribe, or group life, which is represented by the

[1] *De Anima*, as translated by George Thomson, *Aeschylus and Athens* (London, 1941), p. 124.

[2] Michael I. Rostovtzeff, *Mystic Italy* (London and New York, 1927), pp. 141–2.

[3] For a trenchant criticism of the influence of the mysteries on Christianity, see Hastings Rashdall, *The Idea of Atonement in Christian Theology* (London, 1918), pp. 479–92.

figure of the Daimon. In the course of her demonstration, she showed that the Cretan cult of the Kouretes and the Thracian religion of Dionysos were substantially one, the cardinal doctrine of both religions being that of the New Birth. The Dithyramb likewise, from which the drama ultimately descended, was a *dromenon* intended to induce a New Birth as well. From the *Omphagia*, or communal meal of the *dromenon*, developed the seasonal *dromenon*, particularly that of the spring, which was celebrated to induce the coming of new life, and from this in turn came the *agones* and the *agon* of the drama itself. 'This drama', she writes, 'might with equal appropriateness be represented as a Death followed by a Rebirth or as a contest followed by a victory.'[1] Then, turning to an examination of the origins of the hero, she found that he was a dead ancestor performing his ritual functions as the Eniautos-Daimon, or year daimon, and from his death and resurrection arose the idea of *palingenesia*; indeed, from the *dromena* of the Eniautos-Daimon came the ritual forms of the drama. The elements of the Eniautos myth are few and simple, Miss Harrison points out; they are: a contest, a *pathos* or a death or a defeat, and a triumphant Epiphany with an abrupt change from lamenting to rejoicing.[2] Building on this foundation, Professor Murray worked out the ritual form of the Greek tragedy as composed of:

'1. An *Agon* or Contest, the Year against its enemy, Light against Darkness, Summer against Winter.

2. A *Pathos* of the Year-Daimon, generally a ritual or sacrificial death.

3. A Messenger. . . .

4. A *Threnos* or Lamentation. Specially characteristic, however, is a clash of contrary emotions, the death of the old being also the triumph of the new: . . .

5. and 6. An *Anagnorisis*—discovery or recognition—of the slain and mutilated Daimon, followed by his Resurrection or Apotheosis or, in some sense, his Epiphany in glory. This I shall call by the general name *Theophany*. It naturally goes with a *Peripeteia* or extreme change of feeling from grief to joy.'[3]

[1] Jane Harrison, *Themis: A Study of the Social Origins of Greek Religion* (Cambridge, 1912), p. xii. Miss Harrison's thesis has been given a popular exposition in her *Ancient Art and Ritual* (Oxford, 1948).

[2] Ibid., pp. 331–2.

[3] Gilbert Murray, 'Excursus on the Ritual Forms Preserved in Greek Tragedy', ibid., pp. 342–3.

In a later work, Professor Murray summarized the dependence of tragedy on the *dromenon* in this way:

'At the great spring Dromenon the tribe and the growing earth were renovated together: the earth arises afresh from her dead seeds, the tribe from its dead ancestors; and the whole process, charged as it is with the emotion of pressing human desire, projects its anthropomorphic God or daemon. A vegetation-spirit we call him, very inadequately; he is a divine Kouros, a Year-Daemon, a spirit that in the first stage is living, then dies with each year, then thirdly rises again from the dead, raising the whole dead world with him—the Greeks called him in this phase "the Third One", or the "Saviour". The renovation ceremonies were accompanied by a casting off of the old year, the old garments, and everything that is polluted by the infection of death. And not only of death; but clearly, I think, in spite of the protests of some Hellenists, of guilt or sin also. For the life of the Year-Daemon, as it seems to be reflected in Tragedy, is generally a story of Pride and Punishment. Each Year arrives, waxes great, commits the sin of Hubris, and then is slain. The death is deserved; but the slaying is a sin; hence comes the next Year as Avenger, or as the Wronged-One re-risen. "All things pay retribution for their injustice one to another according to the ordinance of time." '[1]

Thus, the very soil out of which Greek tragedy grew was saturated with the theme of the dying-rising God, as re-shaped by the special character of the Hellenic mind and adapted to its own particular needs and uses.[2]

Try as they might, the Hebrew people could never dissociate

[1] Gilbert Murray, *Five Stages of Greek Religion* (London and New York, 1925), pp. 48–9.

[2] The Jane Harrison-Gilbert Murray thesis as to the origins of tragedy have come under very strict scrutiny and criticism; see, for example, A. W. Pickard-Cambridge, *Dithyramb Tragedy and Comedy* (Oxford, 1927), pp. 185–208; but, in the light of the evidence which has come from the parallel developments in the ancient Near East, their point of view has received fresh support. George Thomson, utilizing the Harrison-Murray point of departure and adding to it new materials drawn from anthropology, has traced the origin of tragedy from the totemic rites to the secret society whose principal rite, designed to promote the fertility of the soil, contained three elements: orgiastic exodus, tearing a victim to pieces, and a triumphant return. In time, the procession turned into a hymn, and the sacrament became a passion-play; from the first came the dithyramb and from the second, tragedy. *Aeschylus and Athens* (London, 1941), pp.195–6. For the theory of the origin of comedy out of the same nexus as tragedy, see Francis M. Cornford, *The Origins of Attic Comedy* (Cambridge, 1934).

themselves from the other peoples of the ancient Near East. We recall how Isaiah complained bitterly of the ravages wrought on the Hebrews by the Assyrian armies; Deutero-Isaiah denounced the Persians for their depredations; Jeremiah warned the people against Nebuchadnezzar; and Ezekiel foretold the destruction of the Temple by Babylon. But armed conquest also brought with it cultural contact; Jeremiah saw with shame the worship of the Queen of Heaven, of Moloch, and of astral deities, and Ezekiel in his visions saw the Temple profaned by the idolatrous worship of Shamash.[1] The Hebrews met the threat of this contact in three ways: first, they placed more and more emphasis on the forms and legalisms of worship, drawing themselves together into a tightly knit group bound together by their strict devotion to the letter of the law. With the introduction of the priestly code, as described in Nehemiah, the character of Hebrew religion underwent a change in the direction of the rigid devotion to the letter of the law; we read in Nehemiah:

'And the rest of the people, the priests, the Levites, the porters, the singers, the Nethinim, and all they that had separated themselves from the peoples of the lands unto the law of God, their wives, their sons, and their daughters, everyone that had knowledge and understanding; they clave to their brethren, their nobles, and entered into a curse and into an oath, to walk in God's law, which was given by Moses the servant of God, and to observe and do all the commandments of the LORD our Lord, and his judgments and his statutes; and that we would not give our daughters unto peoples of the land, nor take their daughters for our sons: and if the peoples of the land bring ware or any victuals on the sabbath day to sell, that we would not buy of them on the sabbath, or on a holy day: and that we would forgo the seventh year, and the exaction of every debt. (Nehemiah 10, 28–31.)

This attitude found its culmination in the codification of the Mishnah, promulgated by Rabbi Judah, 'The Prince', shortly before A.D. 219. The second way we shall soon see: the reassertion of the omnipotence of the one God by the major prophets. But there were still others who succumbed to the temptations of other religions, and what the Exile had begun, the conquest of Alexander accelerated immensely. Josephus quotes Strabo as saying of the Jews:

[1] See William F. Albright, *Archaeology and the Religion of Israel* (Baltimore, 1942), pp. 155–75.

'This people has already made its way into every city, and it is not easy to find any place in the habitable world which has not received this nation and in which it has not made its way.'[1]

And similarly did Haman speak to Ahasuerus:

'There is a certain people scattered abroad and dispersed among the peoples in all the provinces of thy kingdom; and their laws are diverse from *those of* every people; neither keep they the king's laws: therefore it is not for the king's profit to suffer them.' (Esther 3, 8.)

From the second book of the Maccabees, we learn what effect contact with Greek ways had on the Jewish men; after Jason succeeded to the high priesthood:

'. . . he forthwith brought over them of his own race to the Greek fashion . . . he brought in new customs forbidden by the law: for he eagerly established a Greek place of exercise under the citadel itself; and caused the noblest of the young men to wear the Greek cap. And thus there was an extreme of Greek fashions, and an advance of an alien religion, by reason of the exceeding profaneness of Jason, that ungodly man and no high priest; so that the priests had no more any zeal for the services of the altar: but despising the sanctuary, and neglecting the sacrifices, they hastened to enjoy that which was unlawfully provided in the palaestra, after the summons of the discus; making no account the honours of their fathers, and thinking the glories of the Greeks best of all.' (*The Apocrypha*, p. 390 of the 1926 edition of the revised version in *The World's Classics*.)

The young men even went so far as to join the *epheboi*, that is, those who pretended that they were uncircumcized. The reaction against the Hellenization of the Jews led to the various Maccabean revolts, but their ultimate failure caused the Jews to turn in on themselves once more. While the Pharisees and Sadducees held, as Josephus says, different opinions concerning human affairs, for:

'. . . the Pharisees had passed on to the people certain regulations handed down by former generations and not recorded in the Laws of Moses, for which reason they are rejected by the Sadducaean group, who hold that only those regulations should be considered valid which were written down (in Scripture), and that those which had been handed down by former generations need not be observed.'[2]

[1] Josephus, *Jewish Antiquities*, tr. Ralph Marcus (London, 1943), VII, p. 509.
[2] Josephus, ibid., III, p. 377.

nevertheless, both sects were agreed on their insistence on the law as the ultimate authority, and it is of some significance that it was the Pharisees, that 'body of Jews who profess to be more religious than the rest, and to explain the laws more precisely' (Josephus), who relied only on the written law and its many and detailed regulations, and who believed in 'the survival of the soul, the revival of the body, the great judgment, and the life of the world to come',[1] who, having always the masses on their side, won out over the more aristocratic Sadducees. But even here the Hellenistic influences were strong, and the Pharisees show in their exegetic and dialectic methods the impress of Hellenistic thought. Nor was Hellenism the only influence on Jewish thought; account must also be taken of the Iranian religion, proto-gnosticism, and the Logos concepts, all of which exercised strong influences on the eschatologists and particularly on the sect of the Essenes.[2] To go into further detail concerning the mysteries and on the Hellenizing of Jewish thought previous to the time of Christ would, I think, serve no useful purpose here. But I think that enough has been shown to indicate that in the Aegean area ideas similar to those of the myth and ritual pattern of the ancient Near East were widely and deeply held. Even if we should adopt a conservative position, we can safely say that two great streams of similar ideas, one rising in the Near East, and the other in the Aegean area, slowly converged on Palestine to form one single sea out of which Christianity emerged.

[1] George F. Moore, *Judaism in the First Centuries of the Christian Era* (Oxford and Cambridge (Mass.), 1927), I, p. 68.

[2] For detailed studies of Hellenic and non-Hellenic influences on later Hebrew thought, see W. O. E. Oesterley and T. H. Robinson, *Hebrew Religion* (London and New York, 1937), pp. 340–410; and William F. Albright, *From the Stone Age to Christianity* (Baltimore, 1940), pp. 265–92. For Philo's distinction between the three types of Jewish apostates, 'those who forsook Judaism out of the weakness of the flesh', 'the vulgar delusion of social ambition', and the 'unconscious shifting of intellectual interest', see Harry A. Wolfson, *Philo Foundations of Religious Philosophy in Judaism, Christianity, and Islam* (Cambridge (Mass.), 1947), I, pp. 73–85. As to Philo's position generally, E. R. Goodenough goes so far as to say '. . . that Judaism in the Greek diaspora did, for at least an important minority, become a . . . mystery'. *By Light, Light* (New Haven (Conn.), 1935), p. 5, but see Wolfson's discussion of the Hellenistic Jewish attitude toward Greek religion and philosophy and of Philo on polytheism, mythology, and the mysteries.

## CHAPTER V

# *The Paradox of the Fortunate Fall in Hebrew Thought*

WE turn now to a consideration of the myth and ritual pattern of the ancient Near East as it was taken over, developed, and transformed in and by Hebrew thought. We shall find that each of the elements in the pattern remains present in Hebrew thought, but we shall find also that they have been reworked in terms of the needs and character of the Hebrew people. At the outset, it would appear that Hebrew thought uncompromisingly rejects the pattern in a revulsion against its pagan origins and associations, but it is not long before we realize that the animus of the Hebrews is directed not against the pattern itself but against what they considered to be its brutalization and perversion by the pagans. In the process of taking over the pattern and cleansing it of what they supposed to be its foulness, the Hebrews tended to neglect some elements in the pattern while, at the same time, they gave others greater prominence, and in so doing revealed their particular character as a distinctive people. Thus, by contrasting how one people utilizes the myth and ritual pattern as compared with another, we have a more precise means of defining their unique nature, for, while the form remains essentially the same, the variations which are introduced in it are the result of differing qualities.

There are two accounts of the foundation of the Hebrew monarchy; the first reads as follows:

'Now the LORD had revealed unto Samuel a day before Saul came, saying, Tomorrow about this time I will send thee a man out of the land of Benjamin, and thou shalt anoint him to be prince over my people Israel, and he shall save my people out of the hand of the Philistines: for I have looked upon my people, because their cry is come unto me. And when Samuel saw Saul, the LORD said unto him, Behold the man of whom I spake to thee! this man shall have authority over my people.' (1 Samuel 9, 15–18.)

But the other account has it that the people themselves demanded a king over them '. . . that we also may be like all the nations; and that our king may judge us, and go out before us, and fight our battles', though Samuel has warned them that a king will degrade their sons and daughters, take their fields and vineyards, and '. . . ye shall cry out in that day because of your king which ye shall have chosen you; and the LORD will not answer you in that day.' (1 Samuel 8, 18–20.) Such a divergence may very well be attributed to the struggle over the control of the nation waged by the monotheistic minority and the polytheistic majority (James): 'And Elijah came near unto all the people, and said, 'How long halt ye between two opinions? If the LORD be God, follow him: but if Baal, then follow him.' (1 Kings 18, 21.) How tenacious the hold of Baalism was can be vividly seen by the measures taken to exterminate it: '. . . Jehu said to the guard and to the captains, Go in, and slay them; let none come forth. And they smote them with the edge of the sword; and the guard and the captains cast them out and went to the city of the house of Baal. And they brought forth the pillars that were in the house of Baal, and burned them. And they brake down the pillar of Baal, and brake down the house of Baal, and made it a draught house, unto this day. Thus Jehu destroyed Baal out of Israel.' (2 Kings 10, 25–9.) But the solution seemed after all to be in the nature of a compromise, for, in actual practice, the king was treated in many ways as was the king in the other civilizations of the ancient Near East. Thus, as Professor Cook points out, the king is the head and representative of the people he is in control of the temple and cult; he prays, makes sacrifices, and consults the God and oracles; he can bring guilt upon the people as well as serve as the people's scapegoat; his coronation ceremony symbolizes his divine recognition; he is Yahweh's anointed and sits upon Yahweh's throne, that is, Jerusalem.[1] 'The spirit of the LORD will come mightily upon thee', Samuel tells Saul, 'and thou shalt prophesy with them, and shalt be turned into another man.' (1

[1] Stanley A. Cook, 'Israel Before the Prophets', *Cambridge Ancient History* (Cambridge, 1920), III, pp. 453–6.

Samuel 10, 6.) In the course of the coronation ceremony, the king received the power of the Lord: 'Then he brought out the king's son, and put the crown upon him, and *gave him* the testimony; and they made him king, and anointed him; and they clapped their hands, and said, God save the king. . . . And Jehoida made a covenant between the LORD and the king and the people, that they should be the LORD's people; between the king also and the people'. (2 Kings 11, 12, 17.) The position of the king in the community, the nature and extent of his powers, and his relationship with God are exemplified in Psalm 72:

*Give the king thy judgements, O God,*
*And thy righteousness unto the king's son.*
*He shall judge thy people with righteousness,*
*And the poor with judgement.*
*The mountains shall bring peace to the people,*
*And the hills, in righteousness.*
*He shall judge the poor of the people,*
*He shall save the children of the needy,*
*And shall break in pieces the oppressor.*
*They shall fear thee while the sun endureth,*
*And so long as the moon, throughout generations.*
*He shall come down like rain upon the mown grass;*
*As showers that water the earth.*
*In his days shall the righteous flourish;*
*An abundance of peace, till the moon be no more.*
*He shall have dominion also from sea to sea,*
*And from the River to the ends of the earth.*
*They that dwell in the wilderness shall bow before him;*
*And his enemies shall lick the dust.*
*The kings of Tarshish and of the isles shall bring presents:*
*The kings of Sheba and Seba shall offer gifts.*
*Yea, all kings shall fall down before him:*
*All nations shall serve him.*
*For he shall deliver the needy when he crieth;*
*And the poor, that hath no helper.*
*He shall have pity on the poor and needy,*
*And the souls of the needy he shall save.*
*He shall redeem their soul from oppression and violence;*
*And precious shall be their blood in his sight;*
*And they shall live; and to him shall be given of the gold of Sheba:*

*And men shall pray for him continually;*
*They shall bless him all the day long.*
*There shall be abundance of corn in the earth upon the top of the mountains;*
*The fruit thereof shall shake like Lebanon.*
*And they of the city shall flourish like grass of the earth.*
*His name shall endure for ever;*
*His name shall be continued as long as the sun:*
*And men shall be blessed in him:*
*All nations shall call him happy.* (Psalm 72, 1–17.)

The rôle of the king as sublimated vegetation-deity is especially noteworthy in this Psalm, for he is the bringer of fertility and the success of the crops; in him is epitomized the fortunes of his people. Yet more evidence for the existence of the divine kingship in the thought of the Hebrews can be adduced, and Professor Engnell calls attention to the facts that the patriarchical figures, such as Adam, Noah, Abraham, Isaac, Jacob, Joseph, and Moses are referred to in royal terms; that the king is of divine origin, being the product of 'the performance of the fingers of God'; that he is installed and enthroned; that his function in the cult is that of high priest; that he confesses and passes through a passion and a death; and that he is the bringer of peace, justice, and wisdom.[1] Finally, the king played the chief rôle in the ceremonies connected with the New Year Festival, since he was the head priest of the nation.[2] All in all, then, we must conclude that the Hebrews in pre-exilic times knew of the concept of divine kingship and adapted it to their purpose by retaining its potency though stripping it of what they termed its grosser associations. In the course of time, after the exile had taken place, the powers which had once been vested in the king were now transferred to the chief priest, and, as pagan practices persisted, seemingly with the connivance of the kings and despite the exertions of the prophets, the institution of kingship fell into disrepute under the repeated hammer-blows of the prophets, and so we hear the voice of the prophet Amos lamenting:

'Shall not the day of the LORD be darkness, and not light? even

[1] Ivan Engnell, *Studies in Divine Kingship of the Ancient Near East* (Uppsala, 1943), pp. 174–6. Cf. W. O. E. Oesterley, 'Early Hebrew Festival Ritual', in *Myth and Ritual*, ed. S. H. Hooke (Oxford, 1933), pp. 125–8; and William A. Irwin in *The Intellectual Adventure of Ancient Man*, ed. H. Frankfort (Chicago, 1946), pp. 326–54.

[2] See, in addition to the study, 'A Chapter in the History of the High Priesthood', Professor Morgenstern's article, 'Amos Studies', *HUCA*, XII-XIII (1937–8), pp. 1–34.

very dark, and no brightness in it? I hate, I despise your feasts, and I will take no delight in your solemn assemblies. Yea, though ye offer me your burnt offerings and meal offerings, I will not accept them: neither will I regard the peace offerings of your fat beasts. Take thou away from me the noise of thy songs; for I will not hear the melody of thy viols. But let judgement roll down as waters, and righteousness as a mighty stream. Did ye bring me sacrifices and offerings in the wilderness forty years, O house of Israel? Yea, ye have borne Siccuth your king and Chiun your images, the star of your god, which ye made to yourselves. Therefore I will cause you to go into captivity beyond Damascus, saith the LORD, whose name is the God of hosts.' (Amos 5, 20–7.)

Therefore: 'Woe to them that are at ease in Zion', warned the prophet, for the kings '. . . know not, neither do they understand; They walk to and fro in darkness'. (Psalm 82, 5.)[1]

Next, we consider the combat theme in Hebrew myth. To be sure, the prophetic reformers despised the myth and ritual pattern of the ancient Near East and did everything in their power to eradicate it from the minds of the people, but it is virtually impossible to expunge an idea once it has established itself and has demonstrated its attraction and power. So the Hebrews in their attempts to erase the influence of the myth and ritual pattern could not destroy it, but they did something better; they took it over and infused it with new meaning; they spiritualized it by making it symbolic rather than actual; and in so doing they created a notable precedent for adaptation, which the later Christians were to employ in their own attempts to convert both the myth and ritual pattern and Hebrew thought to their special uses. Accordingly, we do find the theme of combat in Hebrew thought, but now refined and symbolized, and the vitality of

[1] The steps in the disintegration of the institution of Hebrew kingship have been traced by J. Powis Smith, 'Traces of Emperor-Worship in the Old Testament', *AJSL*, XXXIX (1929), pp. 32–9. Among other studies of the Hebrew idea of kingship, in addition to the articles already cited of Morgenstern and Patai, and of the pioneering work of Gressmann and Mowinckel, see James G. Frazer, *Adonis Attis Osiris* (London, 1919), pp. 18–25; E. Goodenough, 'Kingship in Early Israel', *JBL*, XLVIII (1929), pp. 169–205; E. G. Kraeling, 'The Real Religion of Ancient Israel', *JBL*, XLVII (1928), pp. 133–59; H. G. May, 'Some Aspects of Solar Worship at Jerusalem', *ZAW*, LV (1937), pp. 269–81; H. G. May, 'The Departure of the Glory of Yahweh', *JBL*, LVI (1937), pp. 309–21; C. R. North, 'The Religious Aspects of Hebrew Kingship', *ZAW*, L (1930), pp. 8–38; and Joh. Pedersen, *Israel, Its Life and Culture* (Oxford, 1947), III, pp. 33–106. The transformation of the king into Messiah is described by Raphael Patai, *Man and Temple in Ancient Jewish Myth and Ritual* (London, 1947), pp. 172–215.

the pattern continues therefore to exercise its sway on the minds of men. 'In the beginning God created the heaven and the earth. And the earth was waste and void; and darkness was upon the face of the deep: and the spirit of God moved upon the face of the waters.' (Genesis 1, 1–2.) The sublimity of creation as narrated in Genesis puts in the shadow the precedent combat which probably took place before the actual act of creation so that God's power might be the more fully realized, but the waste and void out of which God created the universe is *Tehom*, the deep, and is linked with the antagonist of Marduk, Tiamat. Job gives us a more detailed, though perhaps less awesome, picture of the creation:

*He stretcheth out the north over empty space,*
*And hangeth the earth upon nothing.*
*He bindeth up the waters in his thick clouds;*
*And the cloud is not rent under them.*
*He closeth in the face of his throne,*
*And spreadeth his cloud upon it.*
*He hath described a boundary upon the face of the waters,*
*Unto the confines of light and darkness.*
*The pillars of heaven tremble*
*And are astonished at his rebuke.*
*He stirreth up the sea with his power,*
*And by his understanding he smiteth through Rahab.*
(Job 26, 7–12.)

God defeats Rahab ('The helpers of Rahab do stoop under him'. Job 9, 13.) as he defeats the leviathan whose head he breaks (Psalm 74, 13) and who, when he comes forth to punish the inhabitants of the earth for their iniquity, in that day '. . . with his sore and great and strong sword shall punish leviathan the swift serpent, and leviathan the crooked serpent; and he shall slay the dragon that is in the sea.' (Isaiah 27, 1.) Again and again, God is depicted in his rôle as slayer of the beast and victor over the forces of the sea:

*Thou rulest the pride of the sea:*
*When the waves thereof arise, thou stillest them.*
*Thou hast broken Rahab in pieces, as one that is slain;*
*Thou hast scattered thine enemies with the arm of thy strength.*
(Psalm 89, 9–10.)

And again in Isaiah we read:

'Art thou not it that cut Rahab in pieces, that pierced the dragon? Art thou not it which dried up the sea, the waters of the great deep; that made the depths of the sea a way for the redeemed to pass over?' (Isaiah 5, 9–10.)

But the enemy becomes more and more a symbol of evil, rather than an actual combatant: 'For Egypt helpeth in vain, and to no purpose: therefore have I called her Rahab that sitteth still.' (Isaiah 30, 7.) And Ezekiel reports that, when the word of the Lord came to him, he was told to set his face against Pharaoh king of Egypt and to prophesy against him, saying: 'Thus saith the Lord GOD: Behold, I am against thee, Pharaoh king of Egypt, the great dragon that lieth in the midst of his rivers, which hath said, My river is mine own, and I have made it for myself.' (Ezekiel 29, 3.) For the Lord will fish him up out of the rivers and throw him into the wilderness. Thus, in Hebrew thought, the element of combat in the myth and ritual pattern of the ancient Near East has been retained but in a spiritualized. and symbolic form.[1] For now the theme of combat has been transformed into the struggle of good over evil, the victory of the chosen people over their enemies, the establishment of the way of righteousness over the path of evil:

'The LORD hath broken the staff of the wicked, the sceptres of the rulers; that smote the peoples in wrath with a continual stroke, that ruled the nations in anger, with a persecution that none restrained. . . How art thou fallen from heaven, O day star, son of the morning! how art thou cut down to the ground, which didst lay low the nations!' (Isaiah 14, 5–6, 12.)

The presence of the combat in Hebrew ritual is much less easy to detect than its occurrence in Hebrew myth, but the very fact of its prevalence in the myth suggests that it was not lacking in the ritual pattern either. Here we must base our suppositions on the evidence for the reconstruction of the installation ceremonies of the Hebrew kings. Thus, in Psalm 2, we read:

[1] Other references to the combat theme in Hebrew myth will be found in T. H. Robinson, 'Hebrew Myths', in *Myth and Ritual*, op. cit., pp. 175–9; Alexander Heidel, *The Babylonian Genesis* (Chicago, 1942), pp. 87–96; and Theodor H. Gaster, 'Ugaratic Mythology', *JNES*, VII (1948), p. 185, footnote 5. Professor Patai has selected examples from later sources in *Man and Temple*, op. cit., pp. 71–87.

*Why do the nations rage,*
*And the peoples imagine a vain thing?*
*The kings of the earth set themselves,*
*And the rulers take counsel together,*
*Against the Lord, and against his anointed,* saying,
*Let us break their bands asunder,*
*And cast their cords from us.*

*He that sitteth in the heavens shall laugh:*
*The Lord shall have them in derision.*
*Then shall he speak unto them in his wrath,*
*And vex them in his sore displeasure:*
*Yet have I set my king*
*Upon my holy hill of Zion.* (Psalm 2, 1–6.)

And in another Psalm, after the Lord has been praised for breaking Rahab in pieces and having scattered his enemies with the arm of his strength, he is addressed in this way:

*Strong is thy hand, and high is thy right hand.*
*Righteousness and judgement are the foundation of thy throne:*
*Mercy and truth go before thy face.*
*Blessed is the people that know the joyful sound:*
*They walk, O Lord, in the light of thy countenance.*
*In thy name do they rejoice all the day:*
*And in thy righteousness are they exalted.* (Psalm 89, 13–16).

These passages, and others which could be added, are seen as evidence of the existence of the theme of combat in Hebrew ritual, but, as we observed in connection with the combat in Hebrew myth, the Hebrews took over this element from the myth and ritual pattern of the ancient Near East not merely to repeat but rather to transform and spiritualize it. Therefore, for the Hebrews, the theme of combat was seen as more than the repetition of the actual act; it symbolized the victory of the Lord, his people, and his principles over the forces of the pagan Gods, their devotees, and their abominations. It is to the meaning of the outcome of the battle that the Hebrews look:

*Come, behold the works of the Lord,*
*What desolations he hath made in the earth.*
*He maketh wars to cease unto the end of the earth;*
*He breaketh the bow, and cutteth the spear in sunder;*

*He burneth the chariots in the fire.*
*Be still, and know that I am God:*
*I will be exalted among the nations,*
*I will be exalted in the earth.*
*The Lord of hosts is with us;*
*The God of Jacob is our refuge.* (Psalm 46, 8–11.)

For, when the cords of Sheol were round about the Psalmist and the snares of death came upon him, he called out to the Lord, who heard his voice; then the earth shook and the heavens bowed, and he sent out his arrows and scattered them; and in consequence of the victory of the Lord:

*He sent from on high, he took me;*
*He drew me out of many waters.*
*He delivered me from my strong enemy,*
*And from them that hated me, for they were too mighty for me.*
*They came upon me in the day of my calamity:*
*But the Lord was my stay.*
*He delivered me, because he delighted in me.*
*The Lord rewarded me according to my righteousness;*
*According to the cleanness of my hands hath he recompensed me.*
*For I have kept the ways of the Lord,*
*And have not wickedly departed from my God.*
*For all his judgements were before me,*
*And I put not away his statutes from me.* (Psalm 18, 16–22.)

It is, as I have said, to the significance of the end of the combat as the triumph of good over evil that the Hebrews looked for the meaning of the ritual combat, and, by so doing, they elevated it to the height of an ethical concept, beyond what it had been before it reached and was moulded in their hands.

Again, it is in Hebrew thought that the theme of suffering takes on depth, for, though in some places the idea of suffering is treated very much as we find it in the Tammuz liturgies, soon we see that an ethical dimension has been added, and the suffering is infused with a profundity of meaning which marks it apart from the previous expressions of the theme. We begin with the Song of Songs in which the lamentations for the departed lover are, after all, not far different from Ishtar's cries over the loss of Tammuz; we read, for example:

*I was asleep, but my heart waked:*
*It is the voice of my beloved that knocketh,* saying,
*Open to me, my sister, my love, my dove, my undefiled:*
*For my head is filled with dew,*
*My locks with the drops of the night.*
*I have put off my coat; how shall I put it on?*
*I have washed my feet; how shall I defile them?*
*My beloved put in his hand by the hole* of the door,
*And my heart was moved for him.*
*I rose to open to my beloved;*
*And my hands dripped with myrrh,*
*And my fingers with liquid myrrh,*
*Upon the handles of the bolt.*
*I opened to my beloved;*
*But my beloved had withdrawn himself,* and *was gone.*
*My soul had failed me when he spake:*
*I sought him, but I could not find him;*
*I called him, but he gave me no answer.*
*The watchmen that go about the city found me,*
*They smote me, they wounded me;*
*The keepers of the walls took my mantle from me.*
*I adjure you, O daughters of Jerusalem, if you find my beloved,*
*That ye tell him, that I am sick of love.*

(Song of Songs 5, 2–8.)

Yet, though Canticles has its roots in the fertility cult,[1] we quickly recognize that the theme is in process of deepening and spiritualization. Thus, in the Lamentations, a woman weeps for her departed lover, but now the woman is transformed into Israel and she suffers for her lost glory:

[1] See Theophile J. Meek, 'Canticles and the Tammuz Cult', *AJSL*, XXXIX (1922), pp. 1–14; and Theophile J. Meek, 'The Song of Songs and the Fertility Cult', in *The Song of Songs a Symposium*, ed. Wilfred H. Schoff (Philadelphia, 1924), pp. 48–79. For a criticism of this approach to Canticles, see Nathaniel Schmitt, 'Is Canticles an Adonis Liturgy?', *JAOS*, XLVI (1926), pp. 154–64; and H. H. Rowley, 'The Song of Songs: An Examination of Recent Theory', *JRAS*, 1938, pp. 251–76. Other books of the Old Testament have been treated in terms of the fertility cult; see, for example, W. F. Albright, 'Historical and Mythical Elements in the Story of Joseph', *JBL*, XXXVII (1918), pp. 111–43; H. G. May, 'The Fertility Cult in Hosea', *AJSL*, XLVIII (1932), pp. 73–98; J. G. Matthews, 'Tammuz Worship in the Book of Malachi', *JPOS*, XI (1931), pp. 42–50; and W. E. Staples, 'The Book of Ruth', *AJSL*, LIV (1937), pp. 145–57.

*How doth the city sit solitary, that was full of people!*
How *is she become as a widow!*
*She that was great among the nations*, and *princess among the provinces*,
How *is she become tributary!*
*She weepeth sore in the night, and her tears are on her cheeks;*
*Among all her lovers she hath none to comfort her:*
*All her friends have dealt treacherously with her,*
*They are become her enemies.*
*Judah is gone into captivity because of affliction, and because of great servitude;*
*She dwelleth among the heathen, she findeth no rest;*
*All her persecutors overtook her within the straits.*
(The Lamentations of Jeremiah 1, 1–3.)

And, though the Psalmist uses the imagery of lamentation, he has elevated it by expressing in its terms an idea more profound than had hitherto been conveyed by it:

*My God, My God, why hast thou forsaken me?*
Why art thou so far *from helping me*, and from *the words of my roaring?*
*O my God, I cry in the day-time, but thou answereth not;*
*And in the night season, and am not silent. . . .*
*But be not thou far off, O Lord:*
*O thou my succour, haste thee to help me.*
*Deliver my soul from the sword;*
*My darling from the power of the dog.*
*Save me from the lion's mouth;*
*Yea, from the horns of the wild-oxen thou hast answered me.*
(Psalm 22, 1–2, 19–21.)

More forceful is the unfolding of suffering and death into a spiritualized concept in Hosea:

'Come, and let us return unto the LORD: for he hath torn, and he will heal us; he hath smitten, and he will bind us up. After two days will he revive us: on the third day he will raise us up, and we shall live before him. And let us know, let us follow on to know the LORD; his going forth is sure as the morning; and he shall come unto us as the rain, as the latter rain that watereth the earth.' (Hosea 6, 1–3.)

Thus we are led to the confrontation of evil by suffering it in order to overcome it: did not the Preacher plant his vineyards and make his pools of water, and did they not turn into vanity and a striving after the wind, so that there was no profit under the sun? This, too, he says:

'. . . there is a righteous man that perisheth in his righteousness, and there is a wicked man that prolongeth *his life* in his evil-doing.' (Ecclesiastes 7, 15.)

But he learns from his suffering:

'For all this I laid to my heart, even to explore all this; that the righteous, and the wise, and their works are in the hand of God: whether it be love or hatred, man knoweth not; all is before them. All things come alike to all: there is one event to the righteous and to the wicked; to the good and to the clean and to the unclean; to him that sacrificeth and to him that sacrificeth not; as is the good, so is the sinner; *and* he that sweareth, as he that feareth an oath. This is an evil in all that is done under the sun, that there is one event unto all: yea also, the heart of the sons of men is full of evil, and madness is in their heart while they live, and after that *they go* to the dead.' (9, 1–3.)

Yet even more can be learned; the counsel of despair of the Preacher which Job knew only too well, and perhaps better, gives way to the acceptance through suffering of God's way:

*Then Job answered the Lord, and said,*
*I know that thou canst do all things,*
*And that no purpose of thine can be restrained.*
*Who is this that hideth counsel without knowledge?*
*Therefore have I uttered that which I understood not,*
*Things too wonderful for me, which I knew not.*
*Hear, I beseech thee, and I will speak;*
*I will demand of thee, and declare thou unto me.*
*I had heard of thee by the hearing of the ear;*
*But now mine eye seeth thee,*
*Wherefore I abhor* myself, *and repent*
*In dust and ashes.* (Job 42, 1–6.)

For the end of suffering is the understanding and acceptance of God's mercy and his way:

*O Lord, rebuke me not in thine anger,*
*Neither chasten me in thy hot displeasure.*
*Have mercy upon me, O Lord; for I am withered away:*

*O Lord, heal me; for my bones are vexed.*
*My soul also is sore vexed:*
*And thou, O Lord, how long?*
*Return, O Lord, deliver my soul;*
*Save me for thy loving kindness' sake.*
*For in death there is no remembrance of thee:*
*In Sheol who shall give thee thanks:*
*I am weary with my groaning;*
*Every night make I my bed to swim;*
*I water my couch with my tears.*
*Mine eye wasteth away because of grief;*
*It waxeth old because of mine adversaries.*
*Depart from me, all ye workers of iniquity;*
*For the Lord hath heard the voice of my weeping.*
*The Lord hath heard my supplication;*
*The Lord will receive my prayer.*
*All mine enemies shall be ashamed and sore vexed:*
*They shall turn back, they shall be ashamed suddenly.*

(Psalm 6.)

But it is in Deutero-Isaiah that the theme of suffering reaches its most poignant and revealing heights in Hebrew thought. The immensity of the step which the prophet took to advance the imagery of the Tammuz lamentations to an ethical view of the universe is displayed in one stark and striking sentence: 'The grass withereth, the flower fadeth: but the work of our God shall stand for ever.' (Isaiah 40, 8.) Isaiah faces the decay and vanity of the world as clearly as ever the Preacher did; he, too, sees that: 'One generation goeth, and another generation cometh; and the earth abideth for ever. The sun also ariseth, and the sun goeth down, and hasteth to his place where he ariseth.' (Ecclesiastes 1, 4–5.) But the word of our God shall stand for ever, for:

'Behold the Lord God will come as a mighty one, and his arm shall rule for him: behold, his reward is with him, and his recompence before him. He shall feed his flock like a shepherd, he shall gather the lambs in his arm, and carry them in his bosom, and shall gently lead those that give suck.' (Isaiah 40, 10–11.)

We have gone beyond the mere acceptance of the mystery of the way of God which was Job's portion; now it is God's mercy and righteousness, his compassion for his suffering servants which make that suffering endurable. God has given his promise:

'But thou, Israel, my servant, Jacob whom I have chosen, the seed of Abraham my friend; thou whom I have taken hold of from the ends of the earth, and called thee from the corners thereof, and said unto thee, Thou art my servant, I have chosen thee and not cast thee away; fear thou not, for I am with thee; be not dismayed, for I am thy God: I will strengthen thee; yea, I will help thee; yea, I will uphold thee with the right hand of my righteousness.' (Isaiah 41, 8–10.)

For him will God open rivers on the bare heights and fountains in the midst of the valleys, and in the wilderness will he plant the cedar, the acacia tree, and the myrtle. Here again we have the language of the fertility cult, but transfigured into an idea of transcendent meaning for man. Therefore, though:

'He was despised, and rejected of men; a man of sorrows, and acquainted with grief: and as one from whom men hid their face he was despised, and we esteemed him not. . . . He was oppressed, yet he humbled himself and opened not his mouth; as a lamb that is led to the slaughter, and as a sheep before her shearers is dumb; yea, he opened not his mouth. . . .

'Yet it pleased the LORD to bruise him; he hath put him to grief: when thou shalt make his soul an offering for sin, he shall see *his* seed, he shall prolong his days, and the pleasure of the LORD shall prosper in his hand.' (Isaiah 53, 3, 7, 10.)

For he knows that his suffering shall not be in vain:

'For a small moment have I forsaken thee; but with great mercies will I gather thee.' (Isaiah 54, 7.)

The very heart of man's fate is encompassed in that small moment; in that moment is man lost and saved; in that moment is the blindness lifted from his eyes, he learns, and is saved. Somewhat in this manner, then, is the theme of suffering given its meaning in Hebrew thought.[1] Jeremiah's bitter complaint:

[1] There is, of course, a large literature on the theme of the suffering servant, but I cite a few recent treatments which sum up the latest research and thought on the subject: William F. Albright, *From the Stone Age to Christianity* (Baltimore, 1940), pp. 250–5; J. Philip Hyatt, 'The Sources of the Suffering Servant Idea', *JNES*, III (1944), pp. 79–86; Edwin O. James, *Origins of Sacrifice* (London, 1933), pp. 206–12; W. O. E. Oesterley and Theodore H. Robinson, *Hebrew Religion* (London and New York, 1937), pp. 261–5, 303–9, 344–51.

'O LORD, thou hast deceived me, and I was deceived: thou art stronger than I, and hast prevailed: I am become a laughing stock all the day, every one mocketh me.' (Jeremiah 20, 7.)

is answered by Isaiah's realization of the meaning of suffering:

'... because he poured out his soul unto death, and was numbered with the transgressors: yet he bare the sin of many, and made intercession for the transgressors.' (Isaiah 53, 12.)

We have already met with the theme of the going down and coming up in Hosea (6, 1–3); and in Ezekiel the imagery is even more pronounced:

'They shall bring thee down to the pit; and thou shalt die the deaths of them that are slain, in the heart of the seas.' (Ezekiel 28, 8.)

Similarly, does Joseph descend into the pit. Nor is the humiliation of the king absent from the ritual of the Hebrews; thus, in Psalm 89 we read:

*But thou hast cast off and rejected,*
*Thou hast been wroth with thine anointed.*
*Thou hast abhorred the covenant of thy servant:*
*Thou hast profaned his crown* even *to the ground.*
*Thou hast broken down all his hedges;*
*Thou hast brought his strong holds to ruin.*
*All that pass by the way spoil him:*
*He is become a reproach to his neighbours.*
*Thou hast exalted the right hand of his adversaries;*
*Thou hast made all his enemies to rejoice.*
*Yea, thou turnest back the edge of his sword,*
*And hast not made him to stand in the battle.*
*Thou hast made his brightness to cease,*
*And cast his throne down to the ground.*
*The days of his youth thou hast shortened:*
*Thou hast covered him with shame.'* (Psalm 89, 38–45.)[1]

Jahweh himself dwelt on the mountains and Sinai was known as 'the mount of Yahweh', though other heights were held to be sacred too, such as Nebo, Peor, Pisgah, Carmel, Tabor, Gibeah, and the

[1] For other examples of the theme of humiliation in Hebrew ritual, see Raphael Patai, 'Hebrew Installation Rites', *HUCA*, XX (1947), pp. 179–81, 202–4. Cf. Raffale Pettazoni, *La Confessione dei Peccati* (Rome, 1936), III, pp. 140–311.

Mount of Olives. Ezekiel speaks of 'the holy mountain of God', and in Isaiah, the day star is mocked for saying:

'And thou saidst in thine heart, I will ascend into heaven, I will exalt my throne above the mount of congregation, in the uttermost parts of the north: I will ascend above the heights of the clouds; I will be like the Most High.'

But the punishment of this usurpation of the Lord's place is swift and sure:

'Yet thou shalt be brought down to hell, to the uttermost parts of the pit.' (Isaiah 14, 13–15.)

And twice in Isaiah the Lord warns that His enemies 'shall not hurt nor destroy in all my holy mountain'. (Isaiah 11, 9; 65, 25.) And we may remember from our analysis of the installation rites of the divine king that one of his most significant acts was to mount a hill, that is, to ascend to his throne, in a symbolic ritual designed to enable the king to partake in himself, and through him to the people, of the life-giving force which lay in the primeval hill, the first act in creation. The sacred mountain, then, from which life came, on which was received the Law when Moses went up to the top of the Mount for forty days and forty nights, on which the sacred temple was built, and which the king symbolically mounted at his coronation and on New Year's Day, possessed the sacred power of passing on to the people, through the king, the vitality with which it had been infused on the day of creation.

For the Hebrews, however, the resurrection of the God became the symbol of the eternal life of the nation in God:

'Wilt thou confide in him, that he will bring home thy seed, and gather *the corn of* thy threshing-floor?' (Job 39, 12.)

But the identification of the rising God with the revivified vegetation persists in Hebrew myth, though again the imagery, while familiar enough in its origins, is used to convey a deeper meaning:

*He turneth a wilderness into a pool of water,*
*And a dry land into watersprings.*
*And there he maketh the hungry to dwell,*
*That they may prepare a city of habitation;*
*And sow fields, and plant vineyards,*
*And get them fruits of increase.*

*He blesseth them also, so that they are multiplied greatly;*
*And he suffereth not their cattle to decrease.*
*Again they are minished and bowed down*
*Through oppression, trouble, and sorrow.*
*He poureth contempt upon princes,*
*And causeth them to wander in the waste, where there is no way.*
*Yet setteth he the needy on high from affliction,*
*And maketh* him *families like a flock.*
*The upright shall see it, and be glad;*
*And all iniquity shall stop her mouth.* (Psalm 107, 35–42.)

When the Psalmist cries, 'And now, Lord, what wait I for?' for, as he says:

*For my heart was grieved,*
*And I was pricked in my reins:*
*So brutish was I, and ignorant:*
*I was* as *a beast before thee.*

he knows:

*Thou hast holden my right hand.*
*Thou shalt guide me with thy counsel,*
*And afterward receive me to glory.*
(Psalm 73, 21–4.)

For, wherever he is, the right hand of the Lord holds him, in heaven, or in Sheol, in the wings of the morning, and in the uttermost parts of the sea. Isaiah has a terrifying vision of the apocalypse: the Lord has made the earth empty and waste; it mourns and fades away: 'The new wine mourneth, the vine languisheth, all the merryhearted do sigh.' For fear, and the pit, and the snare are upon the inhabitants of the earth. But the Lord shall punish the host of the great ones on high, and the kings of the earth upon the earth: 'As the heat in a dry place shalt thou bring down the noise of strangers; as the heat by the shadow of a cloud, the song of the terrible ones shall be brought low.' But there will come a day—'Shall not the day of the LORD be darkness, and not light, even very dark, and no brightness in it?' (Amos 5, 20.)—this cry from the depths of despair had already been answered: 'And it shall be said in that day, Lo, this is our God; we have waited for him, and he will save us: this is the LORD; we have waited for him, and we will be glad and rejoice in his salvation.' What is his salvation? It is thus described:

'LORD, in trouble have they visited thee, they poured out a prayer *when* thy chastening was upon them. Like as a woman with child, that draweth near the time of her delivery, is in pain and crieth out in her pangs; so have we been before thee, O LORD. We have been with child, we have been in pain, we have as it were brought forth wind; we have not wrought any deliverance in the earth; neither have the inhabitants of the world fallen. The dead shall live; my dead bodies shall arise. Awake and sing, ye that dwell in the dust: for thy dew is *as* the dew of herbs, and the earth shall cast forth the dead. . . .

'In that day the LORD with his sore and great and strong sword shall punish leviathan the swift serpent, and leviathan the crooked serpent; and he shall slay the dragon that is in the sea.

'In that day: A vineyard of wine, sing ye to it. I the LORD do keep it; I will water it every moment: lest any hurt it, I will keep it night and day. Fury is not in me: would that the briars and thorns were against me in battle! I would march upon them, I would burn them together. Or else let him take hold of my strength, that he may make peace with me; *yea*, let him make peace with me. In days to come shall Jacob take root; Israel shall blossom and bud; and they shall fill the face of the world with fruit.' (Isaiah 26, 16–19; 27, 1–6.)

Jeremiah's righteous branch is seen in the night visions of Daniel, for there came '. . . one like unto a son of man', who was given dominion, and glory, and a kingdom which shall not be destroyed (Daniel 7, 13–14). Then will come the days when '. . . the plowman shall overtake the reaper, and the treader of grapes him that soweth seed; and the mountains shall drop sweet wine, and all the hills shall melt'. (Amos 9, 13.) Again we hear the language of the fertility cult in Micah, but again transformed: 'Woe is me! for I am as when they have gathered the summer fruits, as the grape gleanings of the vintage; there is no cluster to eat; my soul desireth the first ripe fig.' (Micah 7, 1.) But the Lord of Hosts has promised his people: 'For *there shall be* the seed of peace; the vine shall give her fruit, and the ground shall give her increase, and the heavens shall give their due; and I will cause the remnant of this people to inherit all these things.' (Zechariah 8, 12.) The godly man is perished, continues Micah; instead, they hunt every man his brother with a net, the best of them is as a brier, and a man's enemies are the men of his own house. But, cries Micah:

'But as for me, I will look unto the LORD; I will wait for the God of my salvation: my God will hear me. Rejoice not against me, O mine enemy:'

and then we get one of the most magnificent expressions of the paradox of the fortunate fall in the Bible:

'when I fall, I shall arise; when I sit in darkness, the LORD shall be a light unto me.'

But the responsibility is his:

'I will bear the indignation of the LORD, because I have sinned against him; until he plead my cause, and execute judgement for me: he will bring me forth to light, *and* I shall behold his righteousness.' (Micah 7, 7–9.)

Jewish Apocalyptic literature, into which so many eastern streams of thought poured, finds itself occasionally overwhelmed by the hopelessness of man's fate:

'O thou Adam what hast thou done? For though it wast thou hast sinned, the fall was not thine alone but also ours who are thy descendants. For how does it profit us that eternal age is promised us whereas we have done the works that bring death? And that there is foretold us an imperishable hope whereas we are so miserably brought to futility.' (IV Ezra 7, 118–20.)

It is at this point that the paradox of the fortunate fall is stretched almost to the point of dissolution, where the fall itself overweighs the good which is to come of it. But another Apocalyptist overcame the hopelessness of Ezra and restored the balance:

*But with the righteous he will make peace,*
*And will protect the elect,*
*And mercy shall be upon them.*
*And they shall belong to God,*
*And they shall be prospered,*
*And they shall all be blessed.*
*And he will help them all,*
*And light shall appear to them,*
*And he will make peace with them.* (Enoch 1, 8.)

'And I heard,' cried Daniel:

'but I understood not: then said I, O my lord, what shall be the issue of these things? And he said, Go thy way, Daniel, for the words are shut up and sealed till the time of the end. Many shall purify themselves, and make themselves white, and be refined; but the wicked shall do wickedly; and none of the wicked shall understand: but they that be wise shall understand.' (Daniel 12, 8–10.)

Though the words are shut up and sealed till the time of the end, yet Daniel holds out to man his greatest hope and challenge: he himself has the power to make of himself what he will: many shall purify themselves but the wicked shall do wickedly.

Finally, a word must be said concerning the presence of the theme of resurrection in Hebrew ritual, as distinct from its treatment in Hebrew thought, which we have already considered. Of the two main patterns of ritualistic resurrection, that of the installation ceremony of the king and that of the Hebrew festivals, enough has been demonstrated about the first to show how it repeats in its programme the theme of death and resurrection in the symbolic acts of the king. Much more difficult, however, is the attempt to indicate the movement of the pattern in the festivals themselves. Mainly, the problem revolves around the interpretation of the early Israelite festivals, and of these we have certain knowledge only of the feast of Passover, based on Exodus 1–15, as revised in post-exilic times. For the rest of the festivals, we have to look for our evidence in the interpretation of the Psalms, and here we must assume that by far the largest number of them is pre-exilic, if we are to read them in the light of cultic practices. Professor Pederson holds that the Psalms celebrate actual actions of worship because of the fact that:

'. . . they treat of processions in which Yahweh "goes up" and sits on his throne. In connection with this he subdues the Gods, who, terrified, prostrate themselves before him, and takes over the rule of the world, i.e. the dominion over all peoples and their Gods. He "judges" the world by throwing down the powerless strange Gods from their false dignity, exalting the righteous among his people, and seeing that strange peoples subject themselves to them.'

Moreover, Yahweh substantiates his claims to dominion because he created the world, defeated the dragon, that is to say, overcame chaos, and instituted order in the world. So far, the practice of the Israelite cult agrees with that of the Canaanite ritual, but, as Professor Pedersen acutely points out:

'When Yahweh goes in a procession and is enthroned, this does not mean that he has for some time lost some of his power or even his life, but only that he corroborates his will to exercise this power for the benefit of his people. His fight with the dragon and the chaos-waters becomes an expression of his power over the world, as he has created it and constantly renews his promise to maintain it with its law and order. His fight against other Gods is not a fight to maintain a balance in this world; the Gods are the Gods of other peoples, and Yahweh's victorious fight against them means that he alone is the real God and has a claim to the rule over the world, a rule to be exercised over his people through his king in Zion.'[1]

Thus, the myth of the resurrection of the dead God has been transformed in Hebrew myth and ritual from the return of the circle to an ascent to a higher stage, and we have here in essence the greatest single contribution of Hebrew thought to the myth and ritual pattern of the ancient Near East. Hitherto, such a pattern was based on the assumption of recurrence in which a cycle of birth, life, death, and rebirth[2] is repeated over and over again at each New Year's Day to secure for the coming year the well-being of the community; in this cycle, death and rebirth are equal in opposite directions and, while no loss is made, no gain is recorded either, and at the end the forces of opposition are in a state of uneasy truce. But the Hebrews introduced a new and far-reaching idea; the cycle begins as before; birth, life, death, and rebirth, but at the end, instead of coming round to the position as before, when the cycle began, the Hebrews leaped out to a tremendous concept: the end of the cycle was not mere repetition but actual advance, and for them there took place a dialectical transformation in which out of the conflict of opposites came not a simple truce, but rather a new and different stage, partaking, to be sure, of the nature of the two elements from which it was born, that is to say, the myths and rituals of the ancient Near East, but now become something entirely different: the concept of a God who does not die, but by his just rule imposes order on chaos because he has created and laid out the world according to his plan which man can for himself understand and live by. Seen in this light, we can accept the idea that Hebrew cult did employ the practices of the other Near Eastern rituals, but always transformed and spiritualized. Thus, in Psalm 24, we read:

[1] J. Pedersen, 'Canaanite and Israelite Culture', *Acta Orientalia*, XVIII (1940), pp. 1–17; J. Pedersen, *Israel*, op. cit., III, pp. 441–3.

[2] Edwin O. James, *Comparative Religion* (London, 1938), p. 77.

*The earth is the Lord's, and the fulness thereof;*
*The world, and they that dwell therein*
*For he hath founded it upon the seas,*
*And established it upon the floods.*
*Who shall ascend into the hill of the Lord?*
*And who shall stand in his holy place?*
*He that hath clean hands, and a pure heart;*
*Who hath not lifted up his soul unto vanity,*
*And hath not sworn deceitfully.*
*He shall receive a blessing from the Lord,*
*And righteousness from the God of his salvation.*
*This is the generation of them that seek after him,*
*That seek thy face, O* God of *Jacob.* (Psalm 24, 1–6.)

The same idea appears in Psalm 93:

*The world also is stablished, that it cannot be moved.*
*Thy throne is established of old:*
*Thou art from everlasting.* (Psalm 93, 1–2.)

as well as in Psalms 94, 95, 96, 97, 98 and 99, but most clearly in Psalm 47:

*O clap your hands, all ye peoples;*
*Shout unto God with the voice of triumph.*
*For the Lord Most High is terrible;*
*He is a great King over all the earth.*
*He shall subdue the peoples under us,*
*And the nations under our feet.*
*He shall choose our inheritance for us,*
*The excellency of Jacob whom he loved.*
*God is gone up with a shout,*
*The Lord with the sound of a trumpet.*
*Sing praises to God, sing praises:*
*Sing praises unto our King, sing praises.*
*For God is the King of all the earth:*
*Sing ye praises with understanding.*
*God reigneth over the nations:*
*God sitteth upon his holy throne.*
*The princes of the people are gathered together*
To be *the people of the God of Abraham:*
*For the shields of the earth belong to God;*
*He is greatly exalted.*

Now, these are the very songs which celebrate the enthroning of Yahweh at the beginning of the new year and at the installation of the king, the two events being celebrated interchangeably and simultaneously.[1] For these reasons, therefore, Professor Johnson treats the Feast of Tabernacles as a New Year Festival.[2]

The same conclusion can be drawn concerning the Feast of Unleavened Bread, into which the Passover Feast was later merged, as well as concerning the Feast of Weeks; and it is particularly interesting to see how these elements were transmuted in the later Hannukah festival.[3] We can therefore accept that idea that in Hebrew ritual the programme of the myth and ritual pattern of the ancient Near East was utilized but so modified as to deepen and universalize its meaning.

When we turn to the creation story in Hebrew myth, we meet in the thought and language certain similarities to the creation myths we have already considered, but once more we find similarity of expression merely superficial: the language is simultaneously heightened and deepened by the thought it conveys. Actually, Genesis contains two creation myths, that of the Yahwist and that of the priestly writer. Genesis 2 introduces a much more subtle form of the creation; in Genesis 1, there are some possible parallels to the Babylonian myth of creation, such as God's spirit and the winds of Marduk, the dividing of the waters and the cutting up of Tiamat's body, and the similarity between Tiamat and the Hebrew word for the deep, *Tehom*. But Genesis 2, even though it uses the language of lustration, plunges immediately into the problem of the origin of evil in the world and from the very outset man is confronted with the most frightening and momentous of choices. In Sumerian myth, man is created in order to serve the Gods:

[1] A. J. Wensinck, 'The Semitic New Year and the Origin of Eschatology', *Acta Orientalia*, I (1923), p. 180.

[2] Aubrey R. Johnson, 'The Rôle of the King in the Jerusalem Cultus', in *The Labyrinth*, ed. S. H. Hooke (London, 1935), pp. 110–11.

[3] I have already cited some of the literature on the Hebrew festivals. Further details of Hebrew ritual practice will be found in S. H. Hooke, *The Origins of Early Semitic Ritual* (London, 1932), pp. 45–68. It is only fair to point out that the interpretation of the Hebrew festivals in the light of transformed cultic practice has been criticized; see for example, the criticism of the approach as a whole in Professor Snaith's *The Jewish New Year Festival* (London, 1947); for a criticism of Professor Johnson's conclusions, see Julian Morgenstern, 'Psalm 48', *HUCA*, XVI (1941), pp. 1–95, where Professor Morgenstern objects to the notion that the ancient Israelites possessed a ritual drama, but he himself has proved conclusively in his other articles the significant rôle of the king in the cultus.

*For the sake of the good things in their pure sheep-folds,*
Man was given breath.[1]

Moreover, his very origins are often the result of what can only be described as a complicated indifference. But God created man as an act, placed him in Eden, and then put upon him his prohibition not to eat of the tree of knowledge of good and evil; Adam falls, but in his fall, and God himself admits: 'Behold, the man is become as one of us, to know good and evil.' (Genesis 3, 22.) And in that one magnificent stroke, the duality of man's nature, the very source of his depths and heights, is at once revealed; he at one and the same time partakes of good and evil, knowledge and ignorance, death and immortality, and in these seeming contradictions lies his very being. Rightly, therefore, does the Psalmist link together the creation and man's own mixed state:

*O Lord, our Lord,*
*How excellent is thy name in all the earth!*
*Who hast set thy glory upon the heavens.*
*Out of the mouths of babes and sucklings hast thou established strength.*
*Because of thine adversaries, that thou mightest still the enemy and the avenger.*
*When I consider thy heavens, the work of thy fingers,*
*The moon and the stars, which thou hast ordained;*
*What is man, that thou art mindful of him?*
*And the son of man, that thou visitest him?*
*For thou hast made him but little lower than God,*
*And crownest him with glory and honour.*
*Thou madest him to have dominion over the works of thy hands;*
*Thou hast put all things under his feet:*
*All sheep and oxen,*
*Yea, and the beasts of the field;*
*The fowl of the air, and the fish of the sea,*
*Whatsoever passeth through the paths of the seas.*
*O Lord, our Lord,*
*How excellent is thy name in all the earth!* (Psalm 8.)

I need not add to the references to the creation in the Psalms, but I do wish to emphasize again the relationship expressed between the

[1] Samuel N. Kramer, *Sumerian Mythology* (Philadelphia, 1944), p. 73.

creation and man's responsibility; the Lord knows our frame, he remembers that we are dust and our days are as grass:

> *But the mercy of the Lord is from everlasting to everlasting*
> *upon them that fear him,*
> *And his righteousness unto children's children;*
> *To such as keep his covenant,*
> *And to those that remember his precepts to do them.*
>
> (Psalm 103, 17–18.)

Similarly does Job answer Bildad, the Shuhite: he that stretches out the north over empty space and hangs the earth upon nothing, he who has described a boundary upon the face of the waters, he who in his power made the creation:

> *God forbid that I should justify you:*
> *Till I die I will not put away mine integrity from me.*
> *My righteousness I hold fast, and will not let it go:*
> *My heart shall not reproach* me *so long as I live.* (Job 27, 5–6.)

For Job sees that in the very act of creation God made man to accept the responsibility for his acts, and as long as Job does not speak unrighteousness nor his tongue utter deceit, then does he dwell in God's ways.

Before the earth was created:

> *When he established the heavens, I was there:*
> *When he set a circle upon the face of the deep:*
> *When he made firm the skies above:*
> *When the fountains of the deep became strong:*
> *When he gave to the sea its bound,*
> *That the waters should not transgress his commandment:*
> *Then I was by him,* as *a master workman:*
> *And I daily was* his *delight,*
> *Rejoicing always before him;*
> *Rejoicing in his habitable earth:*
> *And my delight was with the sons of men.*

Therefore:

> . . . *whoso findeth me findeth life,*
> *And he shall obtain favour of the Lord.*
> *But he that sinneth against me wrongeth his own soul:*
> *All they that hate me love death.*
>
> (Proverbs 8, 13, 22–3, 27–31, 35–6.)

Thus the Hebrews converted the theme of creation from what was essentially a magical rite into an ethical concept of deep significance.[1] For we remember that though the Lord said: 'I will destroy man whom I have created from the face of the ground,' yet we know '. . . Noah found grace in the eyes of the Lord'. (Genesis 6, 7–8.) Thus, twice does God fail to make good his threats: once when he tells Adam that if he eats of the tree of knowledge of good and evil in that day will he surely die, yet Adam does not die on that day, and again when God decides to destroy man yet permits him to live in the person of Noah with whom he goes so far as to make a covenant, for the Lord said in his heart: 'I will not again curse the ground any more for man's sake . . . neither will I again smite any more every living thing, as I have done;' therefore, in his covenant 'neither flesh shall be cut off any more by the waters of the flood; neither shall there any more be a flood to destroy the earth.' (Genesis 8, 21; 9, 11.) Here is the final transformation of the waters of creation: they have become the agent of God's punishment which he in his love for man then repudiates, never again to use against man.

Finally, in Hebrew ritual, in addition to the evidence to be drawn from the Psalms already considered, evidence which has led Professors Oesterley and Robinson to say that '. . . the great New Year festival probably involved in Israel (as it certainly did elsewhere in the ancient world) a dramatic representation of the myth of Creation in one form or another',[2] we can point to the use of water in the consecration rites whereby its life-giving properties were transmitted to the king or high priest. Professor Gaster calls attention to the imagery of the Lord dominating the waters in Psalm 93:

> *The Lord reigneth; he is apparelled with majesty;*
> *The Lord is apparelled, he hath girded himself with strength:*
> *The world also is stablished, that it cannot be moved.*
> *Thy throne is established of old:*
> *Thou art from everlasting.*
> *The floods have lifted up,* O *Lord,*

[1] Professor Morgenstern regards Genesis 1, 1–2, 4, as composed of two versions, Creation A, in which the universe is created by God alone, and Creation B, in which the physical acts of God are emphasized; see his articles 'The Sources of the Creation-Story-Genesis 1: 1–2: 4', *AJSL*, XXXVI (1920), pp. 169–212; and 'Psalms 8 and 19a', *HUCA*, XIX (1945–6), pp. 491–523. For the latest study of the relationship between Genesis and its Babylonian sources, see Professor Heidel's edition of the *Enuma Elish*, already cited, pp. 71–118.

[2] W. O. E. Oesterley and T. H. Robinson, *Hebrew Religion*, op. cit., p. 199.

*The floods have lifted up their voice;*
*The floods lift up their waves.*
*Above the voices of many waters,*
*The mighty breakers of the sea,*
*The Lord on high is mighty.*
*Thy testimonies are very sure:*
*Holiness becometh thine house,*
*O Lord, for evermore.*

But, as usual, the imagery is transformed into something far more significant: the floods are made to acknowledge the power of God over them. And, though the use of lustration as a means of expiatory cleansing was not unknown to the other peoples of the ancient Near East, again the Hebrews spiritualized the concept of cleansing by waters:

'And I will sprinkle clean water upon you, and ye shall be clean: from all your filthiness, and from all your idols, will I cleanse you. A new heart also will I give you, and a new spirit put within you: and I will take away the stony heart out of your flesh, and I will give you an heart of flesh.' (Ezekiel 36, 25–6.)

Thus, the use of water as the symbol of life, either as anointment or as expiation, was widespread in the myth and ritual pattern.[1] Indeed, the whole cultus of initiation, which Mr. Hocart regarded as a popularized form of the installation rites of the king, is in itself but another form of the chain of birth, life, death, and rebirth, but by the time of the Hebrews it had become, as we have already seen, so spiritualized that it no longer bore the traces of its antecedents.[2]

The pressing needs of an agricultural people push forward to the head of the ritual the rôle of the sacred marriage as the act by which the revitalization of the crops is ensured, and both the imagery, particularly that of the rains, and the thought, reflect this somewhat spiritually limited demand. It is, therefore, not surprising that the God-drenched, if I may use so violent an adjective, Hebrew prophets rejected so narrow a use of the myth and ritual pattern as crude and uninspiring, yet, at the same time, they themselves recognized, pos-

[1] This double use in Hebrew ritual has been treated by Raphael Patai, 'Hebrew Installation Rites', op. cit., pp. 166–8; 'The "Control of Rain" in Ancient Palestine', *HUCA*, XIV (1939), pp. 251–86; and *Man and Temple*, op. cit., pp. 24–71.

[2] For an analysis of the initiatory rituals of the Hebrews, see the essay by Professor James in *Myth and Ritual*, op. cit., pp. 147–71.

sibly in spite of themselves, the spiritual symbolism inherent in the pattern, and with consummate poetic skill made it serve a purpose far higher than its original intent. By taking over the essential elements in the pattern, they linked themselves with the best thought in which the ancient Near Eastern mind up to that time had been capable, but at the same time they added to it a range of insight and meaning it had not hitherto possessed, thus affording the measure both of the intrinsic worth of the pattern as one capable of endless re-employment and re-interpretation and of their own particular genius.[1]

That there were vestiges of the ritual practice of sacred marriage in the early Hebrew religion seems clear from the prohibitions against it. Thus, we read in Deuteronomy:

'There shall be no harlot of the daughters of Israel, neither shall there be a Sodomite of the sons of Israel. Thou shalt not bring the hire of a whore, or the wages of a dog, into the house of the LORD thy God for any vow: for even both these are an abomination unto the LORD thy God.' (Deuteronomy 23, 17–18.)

And Hosea had some harsh things to say about the people for '. . . the spirit of whoredom hath caused them to err, and they have gone a whoring from under their God.' (Hosea 4, 12.) Similarly did Amos complain that '. . . a man and his father will go unto the same maid, to profane my holy name': (Amos 2, 7.) The actual practices of the fertility cult associated with the lunar goddess were fully described by Jeremiah:

'But we will certainly perform every word that is gone forth out of our mouth, to burn incense unto the queen of heaven, and to pour out drink offerings unto her, as we have done, we and our fathers, our kings and our princes, in the cities of Judah, and in the streets of Jerusalem: for then we had plenty of victuals, and were well, and saw no evil. But since we left off to burn incense to the queen of heaven, and to pour out drink offerings unto her, we have wanted all things, and have been consumed by the sword and by the famine. And when we burned incense to the queen of heaven, and poured

[1] For a survey of the influence of the Ras Shamra materials on Hebrew thought, see René Dussaud, *Les découvertes de Ras Shamra (Ugarit) et l'ancien testament*, (Paris, 1941); J. P. Hyatt, 'The Ras Shamra Discoveries and the Interpretation of the Old Testament', *JBR*, X (1942), pp. 67–75; R. de Langhe, *Les textes de Ras Shamra—Ugarit et leurs rapports avec le milieu biblique de l'ancien testament*, 2 vols. (Paris, 1945); and J. Patton, *The Canaanite Parallels to the Book of Psalms* (Baltimore, 1944).

out drink offerings unto her, did we make her cakes to worship her, and pour out drink offerings unto her, without her husbands?' (Jeremiah 44, 17–19.)

Nor must we forget the two sisters, Oholah and Oholibah, who doted on their lovers, all of them desirable young men, and multiplied their whoredoms, so vividly described by Ezekiel (23). But if the people did in their obstinacy perform their every word, yet the prophetic reformers strove mightily against them and, in spite of the attractions of the moon-fertility cults, managed to transform the sacred marriage from what was to them an abominable and profane cultic practice into an idea of deep spiritual significance, that is, the union of man with his God. Already Hosea symbolizes offending Israel as a harlot: 'Though thou, Israel, play the harlot, yet let not Judah offend.' (Hosea 4, 15.) For the Lord will show his mercy, and, in language drawn from the fertility cult but elevated in quality, Hosea concludes:

'I will heal their backsliding, I will love them freely: for mine anger is turned away from him. I will be as the dew, unto Israel: he shall blossom as the lily, and cast forth his roots as Lebanon. His branches shall spread, and his beauty shall be as the olive tree, and his smell as Lebanon. They that dwell under his shadow shall return; they shall revive *as* the corn, and blossom as the vine: the scent thereof shall be as the wine of Lebanon.' (Hosea 14, 4–7.)

Similarly is this transformation seen in Joel, where the pastures of the wilderness do spring, the tree beareth her fruit, the fig tree and the vine do yield their strength:

'And it shall come to pass in that day, that the mountains shall drop sweet wine, and the hills shall flow with milk, and all the brooks of Judah shall flow with waters; and a fountain shall come forth of the house of the Lord, and shall water the valley of Shittim. . . . But Judah shall abide for ever, and Jerusalem from generation to generation. And I will cleanse their blood that I have not cleansed: for the Lord dwelleth in Zion.' (Joel 3, 18–21.)

But the final step in the transformation of the sacred marriage into the union of God and man was taken in the Apocrypha. Thus we read in Ecclesiasticus:

'What is man, and whereto serveth he? What is his good, and

what is his evil? The number of man's days at the most are a hundred years. As a drop of water from the sea, and a pebble from the sand; so are a few years in the day of eternity. For this cause the Lord was long-suffering over them, and poured out his mercy upon them. He saw and perceived their end, that it is evil; therefore he multiplied his forgiveness. The mercy of a man is upon his neighbour; but the mercy of the Lord is upon all flesh; reproving, and chastening, and teaching, and bringing again, as a shepherd doth his flock. He hath mercy on them that accept chastening, and that diligently seek after his judgments.' (Ecclesiasticus 18, pp. 226–7 of the 1926 edition of the revised version in *The World's Classics*.)

And in the description of Simon, the son of Onias, the great priest, the wisdom of Jesus the son of Sirach transforms the practices of the temple ritual into a symbol of God's union with man by describing it in the language of the fertility cult, now heightened and refined:

'How glorious was he when the people gathered round him at his coming forth out of the sanctuary! As the morning star in the midst of a cloud, as the moon at the full; as the sun shining forth upon the temple of the Most High, and as the rainbow giving light in clouds of glory: as the flower of roses in the days of new fruits, as lilies at the water spring, as the shoot of the frankincense tree in the time of summer: as fire and incense in the censer, as a vessel all of beaten gold adorned with all manner of precious stones: as an olive tree budding forth fruits, and as a cypress growing high among the clouds. When he took up the robe of glory, and put on the perfection of exultation, in the ascent of the holy altar, he made glorious the precinct of the sanctuary. And when he received the portions out of the priests' hands, himself also standing by the hearth of the altar, his brethren as a garland round about him, he was as a young cedar in Libanus; and as stems of palm trees compassed they him about, and all the sons of Aaron in their glory, and the Lord's offering in their hands, before all the congregation of Israel.' (Ecclesiasticus 50, ibid., p. 279.)

All the epithets which had been used to exalt the God-king of the fertility cult are here applied to the priest Simon, who led the people in prayer before the Lord Most High. But the ultimate transformation of the sacred marriage is found in the Apocalypse of Ezra:

'For behold the days come, and it shall be when the signs come which I have foretold to thee, and the bride shall be revealed, appearing as a city, and there shall be revealed she that is now cut off: and whoever is delivered from these evils which have been predicted, he shall see my wonders. For my son the Messiah shall be revealed together with those who (are) with him, and shall rejoice those that remain thirty years. And it shall be after these years my son the Messiah shall die, and all those in whom is human breath. And the world shall return to its first silence seven days, as it was at the beginning, so that no man is left.

'And it shall be after seven days that the world shall be awakened, which now is not awake, and corruption shall perish. . . .

'And the Most High shall be revealed upon the throne of judgment:

and the end shall come,
and compassion pass away,
and pity be far off,
and long-suffering be gathered;
But my judgment alone shall remain,
And truth shall stand,
and faith flourish;
And the work shall come,
and the reward be made known;
and acts of righteousness shall awake
and acts of ungodliness shall not sleep.'

(2 Esdras VII, 26–31, 33–5, as translated by G. H. Box (London, 1917), pp. 51–2.)

For the old Jerusalem, too, came down out of heaven from God, made ready as a bride adorned for her husband: 'And do thou give us the seed and culture of a new heart whence (may) come fruits, so that everyone that is corruptible may be able to live who is clothed with the form of man.' (2 Esdras VIII, 6, ibid., p. 68.) Just as the Christians were to take over from Hebrew thought its spiritual heights, so did Hebrew thought take over from the fertility cult its most significant insights and transform them: 'For, behold, I create new heavens and a new earth; and the former things shall not be remembered, nor come into mind.' (Isaiah 65, 17.) Finally, as to the presence of the sacred marriage in Hebrew ritual, the evidence is only conjectural since it is possible that the booths of greenery associated with the Feast of Tabernacles may have been connected with the sacred marriage.[1] It has been suggested that the '. . . pavilion for a shadow in the day-time from the heat, and for a refuge and for a covert from storm and from rain' (Isaiah 4, 6) has reference to the booth or tent in which the sacred marriage took place; if so, the original use has been so completely transformed that it is now intended as a spiritual harbour. Similarly is the process of change to be observed in Hosea where the language of carnal love can be seen undergoing spiritualization even as we read:

'Plead with your mother, plead; for she is not my wife, neither am I her husband: and let her put away her whoredom from her face, and her adulteries from between her breasts; lest I strip her naked, and set her as in the day that she was born, and make her as a wilderness, and set her like a dry land, and slay her with thirst; yea, upon her children will I have no mercy; for they be children of whoredom. For their mother hath played the harlot: she that conceived them hath done shamefully: for she said I will go after my lovers, that give me bread and my waters, my wool and my flax, mine oil and my drink. Therefore, behold, I will hedge up thy way with thorns, and I will make a fence against her, that she shall not find her paths. And she shall follow after her lovers, but she shall not overtake them; and she shall seek them, but shall not find them: then shall she say, I will go and return to my first husband; for then was it better with me than now. For she did not know that I gave her the corn, and the wine, and the oil, and multiplied unto her silver and gold, which they used for Baal. Therefore will I take back my corn in the time thereof, and my wine in the season thereof, and will pluck away my wool and my flax which should have covered her nakedness. And now I will discover her lewdness in the sight of her lovers, and none shall deliver her out of mine hand. I will also cause all her mirth to cease, her feasts, her new moons, and her sabbaths, and all her solemn assemblies. And I will lay waste her vines and her fig trees, whereof she hath said, These are my hire that my lovers have given me: and I will make them a forest, and the beasts of the field shall eat them. And I will visit upon her the days of the Baalim, unto which she burned incense; when she decked herself with her ear-rings and her jewels, and went after lovers, and forgat me, saith the LORD. There-

[1] W. O. E. Oesterley, in *Myth and Ritual*, op. cit., pp. 139–40; T. H. Robinson, ibid., pp. 184–6; S. H. Hooke, *Origins*, op. cit., p. 54; Raphael Patai, 'Hebrew Installation Rites', op. cit., pp. 164–6; and Raphael Patai, *Man and Temple*, op. cit., pp. 87–94.

fore, behold, I will allure her, and bring her unto the wilderness, and speak comfortably unto her. And I will give her her vineyards from thence, and the valley of Achor for a door of hope: and she shall make answer there, as in the days of her youth, and as in the day when she came up out of the land of Egypt. And it shall be at that day, saith the LORD, that thou shalt call me Ishi; and shall call me no more Baali. For I will take away the names of the Baalim out of her mouth, and they shall no more be mentioned by their name. And in that day will I make a covenant for them with the beasts of the field, and with the fowls of heaven, and with the creeping things of the ground: and I will break the bow and the sword and the battle out of the land, and I will make them to lie down safely. And I will betroth thee unto me for ever; yea, I will betroth thee unto me in righteousness, and in judgment, and in loving kindness, and in mercies. I will even betroth thee unto me in faithfulness: and thou shalt know the LORD. And it shall come to pass in that day, I will answer saith the LORD, I will answer the heavens, and they shall answer the earth; and the earth shall answer the corn, and the wine, and the oil; and they shall answer Jezreel. And I will sow her unto me in the earth; and I will have mercy upon her that had not obtained mercy; and I will say to them that were not my people, Thou art my people; and they shall say, *Thou art* my God.' (Hosea 2, 2–23.)

The Lord is indeed a jealous God; he reviles the unfaithfulness of his people as he would an unfaithful wife, and he withdraws from them the fruit and increase of the earth; but he is a compassionate God and will take back his unfaithful wife, and restore to her the corn and the wine, and he will renew his marriage contract with her in a covenant which will bring peace and plenty to man in an era of righteousness, judgment, loving kindness, mercy, and faith. Thus, from the language of the fertility cult, Hosea has drawn the image of the faithless wife reconciled to her forgiving husband to create from it and in its place the idea of God's spiritual relation with his chosen people.

When we turn to Hebrew ritual, we find that the association of the procession with fertility figures prominently. Thus, Beth-Ghoglah, near Jericho, 'the house, or sanctuary, of the hobbler,' was associated with the worship of the holy waters and of the holy tree by means of a sacred dance or procession in the ritual there.[1] In the Book of

[1] W. O. E. Oesterley and T. H. Robinson, *Hebrew Religion*, op. cit., p. 37, and the reference there to W. Robertson Smith.

Judges, we learn of the men of Shechem who '. . . went out into the field, and gathered their vineyards, and trode the *grapes*, and held festival, and went into the house of their God, and did eat and drink, and cursed Abimelech.' (Judges 9, 27.) In addition to other processions associated with fertility directly, as, for example, Judges 11, 40 and Judges 21, 21, there are references to the procession in connection with the installation rites of the king. Thus, in the installation rites of Saul, he makes two processions: once, before the installation when he goes to the sepulchre of Rachel, to the oak of Tabor, and to the hill of God, where he meets '. . . a band of prophets coming down from the high place with a psaltery, and a timbrel, and a pipe, and a harp, before them;' and he is turned into another man (1 Samuel 10, 2–7), and again, after his installation when he goes down to Carmel, '. . . and is gone about, and passed on, and gone down to Gilgal'. (1 Samuel 15, 12.)[1] Again, David asks that Solomon be put on his own mule to be brought down to Gihon where Zadok the priest and Nathan the prophet will anoint him king over Israel: 'And all the people came up after him, and the people played with pipes, and rejoiced with great joy, so that the earth rent with the sound of them.' (1 Kings 1, 32–46.) But it is in the Psalms that the theme of procession receives its most eloquent and spiritually heightened expression. I have already quoted Psalm 47 in which the people are called on to clap their hands and shout unto God with the voice of triumph, for 'God is gone up with a shout', and '. . . sitteth upon his holy throne'. In Psalm 48 we read:

*Walk about Zion, and go round about her:*
*Tell the towers thereof.*
*Mark well her bulwarks,*
*Consider her palaces;*
*That ye may tell it to the generation following:*
*For this God is our God for ever and ever:*
*He will be our guide even unto death.*

(Psalm 48, 12–14.)

Here the procession is utilized to proclaim the people's eternal faith in their God. Psalm 68 brings together the theme of fertility and the procession:

[1] For the procession in the installation rites of Saul, see further, Raphael Patai 'Hebrew Installation Rites', op. cit., pp. 174–6.

*Thou, O God, didst send a plentiful rain,*
*Thou didst confirm thine inheritance, when it was weary . . .*
*Thou hast ascended on high, thou hast led thy captivity captive; . . .*
*They have seen thy goings, O God,*
*Even the goings of my God, my King, into the sanctuary.*
*The singers went before, the minstrels followed after,*
*In the midst of the damsels playing with the timbrels.*
*Bless ye God in the congregations,*
*Even the Lord,* ye that are *of the fountain of Israel.*

(Psalm 68, 9, 18, 24–6.)

One other example from the Psalms must suffice:

*Make a joyful noise unto the Lord, all ye lands,*
*Serve the Lord with gladness:*
*Come before his presence with singing.*
*Know ye that the Lord he is God:*
*It is he that hath made us, and we are his;*
*We are his people, and the sheep of his pasture.*
*Enter into his gates with thanksgiving,*
*And into his courts with praise:*
*Give thanks unto him, and bless his name.*
*For the Lord is good; his mercy* endureth *for ever;*
*And his faithfulness unto all generations.*

(Psalm 100.)

It is noteworthy that this Psalm is among those which commemorate the installation of Yahweh on his throne.[1] The final transformation of the procession and its relation with new life into the theme of God's everlasting love is found in Isaiah:

'For as the rain cometh down and the snow from heaven, and returneth not thither, but watereth the earth, and maketh it bring forth and bud, and giveth seed to the sower and bread to the eater; so shall my word be that goeth forth out of my mouth; it shall not return unto me void, but it shall accomplish that which I please, and it shall prosper in the thing whereto I sent it. For ye shall go out with joy, and be led forth with peace: the mountains and the hills shall break forth before you into singing, and all the trees of the

[1] Other examples of the procession in the Psalms will be found in W. O. E. Oesterley, in *Myth and Ritual*, op. cit., pp. 130–8; and in his book, *A Fresh Approach to The Psalms* (London and New York, 1937), pp. 32–5.

field shall clap their hands. Instead of the thorn shall come up the fig tree, and instead of the brier shall come up the myrtle tree; and it shall be to the LORD for a name, for an everlasting sign that shall not be cut off.' (Isaiah 55, 10–13.)

We can now consider the concept of judgment and justice in Hebrew thought, as it pertains to the determination of destiny. I begin with Psalm 85, which reads:

*Lord, thou hast been favourable unto thy land:*
*Thou hast brought back the captivity of Jacob.*
*Thou hast forgiven the iniquity of thy people,*
*Thou hast covered all their sin.*
*Thou hast taken away all thy wrath:*
*Thou hast turned thyself from the fierceness of thine anger.*
*Turn us, O God of our salvation,*
*And cause thine indignation toward us to cease.*
*Wilt thou be angry with us for ever?*
*Wilt thou draw out thine anger to all generations?*
*Wilt thou not quicken us again:*
*That thy people may rejoice in thee?*
*Shew us thy mercy, O Lord,*
*And grant us thy salvation.*
*I will hear what God the Lord will speak:*
*For he will speak peace unto his people, and to his saints:*
*But let them not turn again to folly.*
*Surely his salvation is nigh them that fear him;*
*That glory may dwell in our land.*
*Mercy and truth are met together;*
*Righteousness and peace have kissed each other.*
*Truth springeth out of the earth;*
*And righteousness hath looked down from heaven.*
*Yea, the Lord shall give that which is good;*
*And our land shall yield her increase.*
*Righteousness shall go before him;*
*And shall make his footsteps a way* to walk in.

In this single beautiful psalm is quietly summed up the best of Hebrew thought on the relations of man to his God. Its central idea is the concept of *Sedek*, defined by Professor Cook as: '. . . what is due or just, what should be; and men have certain convictions, not only of the proper behaviour among men, and of men towards the Gods, but even of the Gods toward men.'[1] The consciousness of his sin is ever present in man:

> *Behold, I was shapen in iniquity;*
> *And in sin did my mother conceive me.* (Psalm 51, 5.)

Yet, continues the Psalmist, his God will wash him clean:

> *Behold, thou desirest truth in the inward parts:*
> *And in the hidden part thou shalt make me to know wisdom.*
> *Purge me with hyssop, and I shall be clean:*
> *Wash me, and I shall be whiter than snow.*
> *Make me to hear joy and gladness;*
> *That the bones which thou hast broken may rejoice.*
> *Hide thy face from my sins,*
> *And blot out all mine iniquities.*
> *Create in me a clean heart, O God;*
> *And take not thy holy spirit from me.*
> *Restore unto me the joy of thy salvation:*
> *And uphold me with a free spirit.* (Psalm 51, 6–12.)

But God does not despise a broken and contrite heart: altogether on the contrary, he is the God of salvation, for as long as the soul panteth after God as the hart panteth after the water brooks (Psalm 42, 1), so will he be merciful:

> *For thou, Lord, art good, and ready to forgive,*
> *And plenteous in mercy unto all them that call upon thee.*
> (Psalm 86, 5.)

He alone can do this, because there is none like him among the Gods; he is God alone, full of compassion and gracious, slow to anger, and plenteous in mercy and truth. The Psalmist knows that the God of his salvation will show him his ways and will not remember his sins and transgressions; then will:

> *His soul . . . dwell at ease;*
> *And his seed shall inherit the land.* (Psalm 25, 13.)

How deeply moving is the appeal of man to be with his maker we el when we read Psalm 130:

[1] S. A. Cook, in *CAH*, op. cit., II, p. 398.

*Out of the depths have I cried unto thee, O Lord.*
*Lord, hear my voice:*
*Let thine ears be attentive*
*To the voice of my supplications.*
*If thou, Lord, shouldst mark iniquities,*
*O Lord, who shall stand?*
*But there is forgiveness with thee,*
*That thou mayest be feared.*
*I wait for the Lord, my soul doth wait,*
*And in his word do I hope.*
*My soul* looketh *for the Lord,*
*More than watchmen* look *for the morning;*
Yea, more than *watchmen for the morning.*
*O Israel, hope in the Lord;*
*For with the Lord there is mercy,*
*And with him is plenteous redemption.*
*And he shall redeem Israel*
*From all his iniquities.*

Man is assured that he can attain to the understanding of the way of God:

*Blessed is the man that walketh not in the counsel of the wicked,*
*Nor standeth in the way of sinners,*
*Nor sitteth in the seat of the scornful.*
*But his delight is in the law of the Lord;*
*And in his law doth he meditate day and night.*
*And he shall be like a tree planted by the streams of water,*
*That bringeth forth its fruit in its season,*
*Whose leaf also doeth not wither,*
*And whatsoever he doeth shall prosper.* (Psalm 1, 1–3.)

The Psalmist's vision far transcends man and his works, and he looks through and behind nature and through all the visible fabric of creation to see his God immanent in the universe:

*Praise ye the Lord,*
*Praise the Lord, O my soul.*
*While I live will I praise the Lord:*
*I will sing praises unto my God while I have any being.*
*Put not your trust in princes,*
*Nor in the son of man, in whom there is no help.*

*His breath goeth forth, he returneth to his earth;*
*In that very day his thoughts perish.*
*Happy is he that hath the God of Jacob for his help,*
*Whose hope is in the Lord his God:*
*Which made heaven and earth,*
*The sea, and all that in them is;*
*Which keepeth truth for ever:*
*Which executeth judgment for the oppressed;*
*Which giveth good to the hungry:*
*The Lord looseth the prisoners;*
*The Lord openeth* the eyes of *the blind;*
*The Lord raiseth up them that are bowed down;*
*The Lord loveth the righteous;*
*The Lord preserveth the strangers;*
*He upholdeth the fatherless and widow;*
*But the way of the wicked he turneth upside down.*
*The Lord shall reign for ever,*
*Thy God, O Zion, unto all generations.*
*Praise ye the Lord.* (Psalm 146.)

In this Psalm, the Psalmist has gone almost to the utmost reaches of human faith; in his faith and passion, he has rejected the dying God, he has rejected the divine king, he has rejected the very processes of nature and of history to attain to his absolute belief in a transcendent God. Yet the most striking thought of all is the idea of the indissoluble link between man and God who interpenetrate each other and become as one:

*O Lord, thou hast searched me, and known* me.
*Thou knowest my downsitting and mine uprising,*
*Thou understandest my thought afar off.*
*Thou searchest out my path and my lying down,*
*And art acquainted with all my ways.*
*For there is not a word in my tongue,*
*But, lo, O Lord, thou knowest it altogether.*
*Thou hast beset me behind and before,*
*And laid thine hand upon me.*
Such *knowledge is too wonderful for me;*
*It is high, I cannot attain to it.*
*Whither shall I go from thy spirit?*
*Or whither shall I flee from thy presence?*

*If I ascend up to heaven, thou art there:*
*If I make my bed in Sheol, behold, thou art there.*
*If I take the wings of the morning,*
*And dwell in the uttermost parts of the sea;*
*Even there shall thy hand hold me.*
*If I say, Surely the darkness shall overwhelm me,*
*And the light about me shall be night;*
*Even the darkness hideth not from thee,*
*And the night shineth as the day:*
*The darkness and the light are both alike* to thee.
*For thou hast possessed my reins:*
*Thou hast covered me in my mother's womb.*
*I will give thanks unto thee; for I am fearfully and wonderfully made:*
*Wonderful are thy works;*
*And that my soul knoweth right well.*
*My frame was not hidden from thee,*
*When I was made in secret,*
And *curiously wrought in the lowest part of the earth.*
*Thine eyes did see mine unperfect substance,*
*And in thy books were all* my members *written,*
*Which day by day were fashioned,*
*When as yet there were none of them.*
*How precious also are my thoughts unto me, O God!*
*How great is the sum of them!*
*If I should count them, they are more in number than the sand:*
*When I am awake, I am still with thee. . . .*
*Search me, O God, and know my heart:*
*Try me, and know my thoughts:*
*And see if there be any way of wickedness in me,*
*And lead me in the way everlasting.*

(Psalm 139, 1–18, 23–4.)

It is at this point that the myth and ritual pattern of the ancient Near East once more comes close to being shattered, for in this tremendous vision of a God in and through all things, who permeates all his own creation, to whom nothing is secret or unknown, there is suggested the thought that a God need not die for man, nor a man for man, that man might live, but that the one and only God of mercy and salvation so orders his creation that he and man can live in perfect and whole harmony. Here we are past the point of passion, past torturing doubts, past questioning and fear and sacrifice; we are in the very heart of being, in God. In man's surrender, after travail and suffering, in his utter yielding to this force which can be represented only partially and faintly in a symbolism which must partake of concrete reality in order to attain to spiritual transcendence, in the very abdication of the will of man to the will of God, lies his ultimate salvation. 'And the Lord spake unto you out of the midst of the fire: ye heard the voice of words, but ye saw no form: only *ye heard* a voice.' (Deuteronomy 4, 12.) Similarly is the commandment of the Lord to be understood, not so much as a legal document prescribing specific actions, but as an expression of the spirit:

'For this commandment which I command thee this day, it is not too hard for thee, neither is it far off. It is not in heaven, that thou shouldest say, Who shall go up for us to heaven, and bring it unto us, and make us to hear it, that we may do it? Neither is it beyond the sea, that thou shouldest say, Who shall go over the sea for us, and make us to hear it, that we may do it? But the word is very nigh unto thee, in thy mouth, and in thy heart, that thou mayest do it.' (Deuteronomy 30, 11–14.)

For the choice is between life and good, and death and evil, the blessing and the curse. So we have come to the very heart and core of belief and faith: on the one hand, God (or the process of history) sweeps man inevitably to his salvation; on the other, man must of his own free will choose to immerse and lose himself in God (or the process of history) in order that he may be saved. There the contradiction stands, seemingly not to be overcome in its logical rigour, yet in all great religions and beliefs it has, in fact, been overcome by a leap in which man in his actions leaves behind the logical contradiction which he realizes is, after all, merely one of words and not of deeds. In the final analysis, then, it is what man does which conquers on another, higher, level the impasse into which words have gotten him: he achieves salvation by his own identification with the will of God (or the process of history). The interpenetration of God's will with that of man is seen by Isaiah:

'And there shall come forth a shoot out of the stock of Jesse, and a branch out of his roots shall bear fruit: and the spirit of the Lord shall rest upon him, the spirit of wisdom and understanding, the spirit of counsel and might, the spirit of knowledge and of the fear of the

LORD; and his delight shall be in the fear of the LORD: and he shall not judge after the sight of his eyes, neither reprove after the hearing of his ears: but with righteousness shall he judge the poor, and reprove with equity for the meek of the earth: and he shall smite the earth with the rod of his mouth, and with the breath of his lips shall he slay the wicked. And righteousness shall be the girdle of his loins, and faithfulness the girdle of his reins. And the wolf shall dwell with the lamb, and the leopard shall lie down with the kid; and the calf and the young lion and the fatling together: and a little child shall lead them. And the cow and the bear shall feed; their young ones shall lie down together: and the lion shall eat straw like the ox. And the sucking child shall play on the hole of the asp, and the weaned child shall put his hand on the basilisk's den. They shall not hurt nor destroy in all my holy mountain: for the earth shall be full of the knowledge of the LORD, as the waters cover the sea.' (Isaiah 11, 1–9; cf. 32, 1–8; 44, 1–5, 60; 65, 8–25.)

Again, the prayer of Jonah reveals how God and man by their actions in concert resolve the dilemma involved in the relationship between God's universal plan on the one hand and man's individual will on the other:

> *I called by reason of mine affliction unto the Lord,*
> *And he answered me;*
> *Out of the belly of hell cried I,*
> And *thou heardest my voice.*
> *For thou didst cast me into the depth, in the heart of the seas,*
> *And the flood was round about me;*
> *All thy waves and thy billows passed over me;*
> *And I said, I am cast out from before thine eyes;*
> *Yet I will look again toward thy holy temple.*
> *The waters compassed me about, even to the soul;*
> *The deep was round about me;*
> *The weeds were wrapped about my head.*
> *I went down to the bottoms of the mountains;*
> *The earth with her bars* closed *upon me for ever:*
> *Yet hast thou brought up my life from the pit, O Lord my God.*
> *When my soul fainted within me, I remembered the Lord:*
> *And my prayer came in unto thee, into thine holy temple.*
> *They that regard lying vanities*

*Forsake their own mercy.*
*But I will sacrifice unto thee with the voice of thanksgiving;*
*I will pay that which I have vowed.*
*Salvation is of the Lord.* (Jonah 2, 2–19.)

Salvation is indeed of the Lord, but Jonah must look to the holy temple and must remember the Lord of his own free will; then salvation is of the Lord. Here, in this brief prayer of Jonah, are the very libretto and imagery, if we may use the terms, of the myth and ritual pattern of the ancient Near East: the God deflated in combat and submerged in the waves of death, humiliated and plunged into the pit of hell, yet when he reaches the nether bottoms, then is he resurrected, but now how transformed, how risen in spiritual significance, is the pattern, and this is the very epitome of the Hebrew contribution to the myth and ritual pattern of the ancient Near East. It is in this light that we must understand the use of the theme of the settling of the destinies in Hebrew thought, for the idea of a transcendent God who judges the world in righteousness goes beyond judgment of the dying God himself:

*God, standeth in the congregation of God;*
*He judgeth among the Gods.*
*How long will ye judge unjustly,*
*And respect the persons of the wicked?*
*Judge the poor and fatherless:*
*Do justice to the afflicted and destitute.*
*Rescue the poor and needy:*
*Deliver them out of the hand of the wicked.*
*They know not, neither do they understand;*
*They walk to and fro in darkness:*
*All the foundations of the earth are moved.*
*I said, Ye are Gods,*
*And all of you sons of the Most High.*
*Nevertheless ye shall die like men,*
*And fall like one of the princes.*
*Arise, O God, judge the earth:*
*For thou shalt inherit all the nations.* (Psalm 82.)

The uncompromising rejection of the dying God in this terse Psalm comes almost as a shock, but in the end mercy: 'For his mercy *endureth* for ever' does win out over zealous narrowness of spirit: 'The word of the LORD came unto me again, saying, What mean ye, that ye use this proverb concerning the land of Israel, saying, The fathers have eaten sour grapes, and the children's teeth are set on edge? As I live, saith the Lord GOD, ye shall not have *occasion* any more to use this proverb in Israel.' (Ezekiel 18, 1–2.) Much more generous and warm in affection is the transformation of the elements in the myth and ritual pattern, procession, combat, creation, resurrection, and the settling of destinies, in the stirring Psalm 33:

*Rejoice in the Lord, O ye righteous:*
*Praise is comely for the upright.*
*Give thanks unto the Lord with harp:*
*Sing praises unto him with the psaltery of ten strings.*
*Sing unto him a new song;*
*Play skilfully with a loud noise.*
*For the work of the Lord is right;*
*And all his work is* done *in faithfulness.*
*He loveth righteousness and judgment:*
*The earth is full of the lovingkindness of the Lord.*
*By the word of the Lord were the heavens made;*
*And all the host of them by the breath of his mouth.*
*He gathereth the waters of the sea together as an heap:*
*He layeth up the deeps in storehouses.*
*Let all the earth fear the Lord:*
*Let all the inhabitants of the world stand in awe of him.*
*For he spake, and it was done;*
*He commanded, and it stood fast.*
*The Lord bringeth the counsel of the nations to nought:*
*He maketh the thoughts of the peoples to be of none effect.*
*The counsel of the Lord standeth fast for ever,*
*The thoughts of his heart to all generations.*
*Blessed is the nation whose God is the Lord;*
*The people whom he hath chosen for his inheritance.*
*The Lord looketh from heaven;*
*He beholdeth all the sons of men;*
*From the place of his habitation he looketh forth*
*Upon all the inhabitants of the earth;*
*He that fashioneth the hearts of them all,*
*That considereth all their works.*
*There is no king saved by the multitude of an host:*

*A mighty man is not delivered by great strength:*
*A horse is a vain thing for safety:*
*Neither shall he deliver any by his great power.*
*Behold, the eye of the Lord is upon them that fear him,*
*Upon them that hope in his mercy;*
*To deliver their soul from death,*
*And to keep them alive in famine.*
*Our soul hath waited for the Lord:*
*He is our help and our shield.*
*For our heart shall rejoice in him,*
*Because we have trusted in his holy name.*
*Let thy mercy, O Lord, be upon us,*
*According as we have hoped in thee.*

The fear with which the peoples of the ancient Near East awaited the resurrection of the dying God and the outcome of the settling of destinies is resolved now in the goodness of God:

*Yea, though I walk through the valley of the shadow of death,*
*I will fear no evil; for thou art with me:* (Psalm 23, 4.)

Since the time of the Exile, the Day of Atonement has become by far the most solemn of the Hebrew festivals, and to it have been drawn as well the portentous associations of the Day of Yahweh, the New Year's Day, and the Day of Judgment. Of all the Hebrew festivals, the Day of Atonement is the one which most retains its powerful hold on the Jews. The ten days from the first of Tishri, which is the first of the two days in celebration of Rosh Hashanah, the New Year Festival, to the tenth of Tishri, which is the Day of Atonement, are, to use Professor Langdon's telling phrase '. . . the ten terrible days of the world's judgment in Jewish tradition'.[1] For then it is that man stands naked before his creator, and, in the bitter and rending consciousness of all his guilt and sin, acknowledges the evil he has done, begs contritely for forgiveness, and promises that for the coming year he will lead a better life. *The Mishnah* reads as follows:

'There are four "New Year" days: on the 1st of Nisan is the New Year for kings and feasts; on the 1st of Elul is the New Year for the Tithe of Cattle (R. Eleazar and R. Simeon say: The 1st of Tishri); on

[1] Stephen Langdon, *Babylonian Menologies and the Semitic Calendars* (London, 1935), p. 100.

the 1st of Tishri is the New Year for [the reckoning of] the years [of foreign kings], of the Years of Release and Jubilee Years, for the planting [of trees] and for vegetables: and the 1st of Shebat is the New Year for [fruit-] trees (so the School of Shammai; and the School of Hillel say: on the 15th thereof).

'At four times in the year is the world judged: at Passover, through grain; at Pentecost, through the fruits of the tree; on New Year's Day all that come into the world pass before him like legions of soldiers, for it is written, *He that fashioneth the hearts of them all, that considereth all their works;* and at the Feast [of Tabernacles] they are judged through water.'[1]

Commenting on this passage, the *Gemara* reads:

'R. Kruspedai said in the name of R. Johanan: Three books are opened [in heaven] on New Year, one for the thoroughly wicked, one for the thoroughly righteous, and one for the intermediate. The thoroughly righteous are forthwith inscribed definitively in the book of life; the thoroughly wicked are forthwith inscribed definitively in the book of death; the doom of the intermediate is suspended from New Year till the Day of Atonement; if they deserve well, they are inscribed in the book of life; if they do not deserve well, they are inscribed in the book of the dead.'[2]

The authorities for the image of the book are cited by R. Abin as Psalm 69, verse 29, and Exodus 32, 32. The rabbis stressed the mercy of God on the Day of Judgment; thus we read:

'R. Abba b. Kahana said: On New Year God judges his creatures, and finds merit in them, for he desires to acquit, and not to condemn them, as it says, "As I live, I desire not the death of the wicked" (Ezekiel 33, 11.) God desires to justify his creatures, as it says, "It pleased the Lord to justify him". (Isaiah 42, 21, a playful mistranslation.) Resh Lakish said: God says, "In the hour when I conquer I suffer loss, but in the hour when I am conquered, I gain. I conquered at the generation of the flood, but I lost, for I destroyed all those masses. So it was with the generation of the Tower of Babel, and with the men of Sodom. But when the Golden Calf was made, Moses

[1] *The Mishnah*, tr. Herbert Danby (Oxford, 1933), p. 188.

[2] I. Epstein, ed. *The Babylonian Talmud Rosh Hashanah*, tr. Maurice Simon (London, 1938), p. 63.

conquered me, and I gained all those masses. So I acquit all my creatures, so that I may not suffer loss.'[1]

In this way, then, did the New Year, the Day of Atonement, and Judgment Day merge into one overwhelming period of confession, expiation, repentance, and salvation. Perhaps the most impressive moment in all the ritual is the evening before the Day of Atonement, when the congregation quietly gathers in the synagogue to listen to the cantor chant the pleading Kol Nidre:

'All vows, bonds, devotions, promises, obligations, penalties, and oaths: wherewith we have vowed, sworn, devoted, and bound ourselves: from this Day of Atonement unto the next Day of Atonement, may it come unto us for good: lo, all these, we repent us in them. They shall be absolved, released, annulled, made void, and of none effect: they shall not be binding nor shall they have any power. Our vows shall not be vows: our bonds shall not be bonds: and our oaths shall not be oaths.'[2]

Though the words do not quite reach the depth of feeling which the occasion demands, the traditional melody to which they are sung more than makes up in its moving quality for the deficiencies of the text. Then are all thoughts of gain and of the corruptions of the flesh and spirit put aside, and each person in the congregation stands alone before his God, in agony and in trembling, yet in faith and in the hope that he will be saved. Almost equally moving are the scenes of the casting out of evils as each worshipper recites the sins he has committed in the past year to the accompaniment of strong blows on the chest:

*For the sin wherein we have sinned before thee under compulsion or of freewill,*
*And for the sin wherein we have sinned before thee by hardening of the heart;*
*For the sin wherein we have sinned before thee unwittingly,*
*And for the sin where we have sinned before thee with utterance of the lips;*[3]

and so on through a long list of sins, ending with the prayer: 'And for all these, O God of forgiveness, forgive us, pardon us, grant us atonement'; the intercession of the priests at the sacred altar making

[1] In *A Rabbinic Anthology*, ed. C. G. Montefiore and H. Loewe (London, 1938), p. 236.
[2] Herbert M. Alder, ed. *Service of the Synagogue Day of Atonement. Part I, Evening Service* (London, n.d.), II, p. 15.
[3] Ibid., II, p. 26.

the mystic signs it is forbidden for the uninitiated to look on, and the blowing of the shofar, or ram's horn, now calling out with the voice of judgment, and now announcing triumphantly the coming in of the new year, after the long day of fasting, mortification, and penance has been done. The shofar is blown on Rosh Hashanah as well and a medieval rabbi has given ten reasons why it should then be blown, reasons which show unmistakably the inextricable connection of the themes of divine kingship, creation, humiliation, and judgment; the ten reasons of Rabbi Saadiyah run:

'1. Because this day is the beginning of creation, on which God created the world, and began to reign over it. And just as is the custom of kings, in that they sound the cornets and horns to make known and to cause to be heard in every place the commencement of their reign, so also we proclaim the Creator King over us this day. And thus said David in Psalm xcviii, 6: "With cornets and the sound of a Shofar shout about ye before the King Jehovah."

'2. As the day of Rosh Hashannah is the first of the ten days of penitence, so we sound on it the Shofar to proclaim to us as one who admonishes and says, Every one who is willing to return (and repent) let him return, and if he does not, he cannot say that he was not called, for he was fully informed. For so do kings publish their decrees at the beginning of their reigns, so that every passer-by may be informed, and none may plead that they did not hear.

'3. To remind us of the standing on Mount Sinai, as it is said in Ex. xix, 16: "And the sound of the Shofar exceeding loud." And that we ought to bind ourselves, as our fathers did, when they said, "We will do and hearken".

'4. To remind us of the words of the prophets who are likened unto (watchmen) blowing on the Shofar, as it is said (Ezek. xxxiii, 4): "Whoso heareth the sound of the Shofar and taketh not warning, and the sword cometh and taketh him away, his blood be upon his own head; but he that taketh warning shall save his life."

'5. To remind us of the destruction of the Temple, and the sound of the enemies' battle-cry, as it is said in Jer. iv, 19: "Because thou hast heard, O my soul, the sound of the Shofar and the alarm of war." Wherefore we, hearing the sound of the Shofar, ought to beseech the Almighty to rebuild the Temple.

'6. To remind us of the binding of Isaac, who submitted himself to the will of Heaven. So ought we to submit ourselves for the

Sanctification of His Name, and offer our memorial before Him for good.

'7. So that when we hear the sound of the Shofar we should fear, and be terrified, and humble ourselves before the Creator, for it is the nature of the Shofar to spread dread and terror, as it is said in Amos iii, 6: "Shall the Shofar be blown in the city, and the people not be afraid?"

'8. To remind us of the great and awful day of judgment, as it is said in Zeph. i, 16: "The great day of the Lord is near and hasteneth, a day of shofar and alarm."

'9. To remind us of the gathering of the outcasts of Israel, and to pray for it, as it is said in Isa. xxvii, 13: "And it shall come to pass on that day that the great shofar shall be sounded, and those that were perishing in the land of Assyria . . ."

'10. To remind us of the Resurrection of the Dead, and to believe firmly in it, as it is said in Isa. xviii, 3: "All ye that inhabit the earth, and ye dwellers on the earth, when the standard is lifted on the mountains, ye shall behold, and when the shofar is blown, ye shall hear." '[1]

Thus, in the blowing of the shofar is symbolized all the fearsome awe in the presence of judgment. This idea is found in Psalm 81:

*Sing aloud unto God our strength:*
*Make a joyful noise unto the God of Jacob.*
*Take up the psalm, and bring hither the timbrel,*
*The pleasant harp with the psaltery.*
*Blow up the trumpet in the new moon,*
*At the full moon, on our solemn feast day.*
*For it is a statute for Israel,*
*And ordinance of the God of Jacob.* (Psalm 81, 1–4.)

The translation does not quite catch the meaning of the Hebrew, for the word 'ordinance' fails to do justice to the Hebrew *mispat*, which means 'judgment', so that the solemn feast day is the Day of Judgment.

The Day of Atonement, or Yom Kippur (from the Sumerian *kuppuru*, 'to remove'?) is given its significance as the Day of Judgment in Leviticus, Chapter 16, where the Lord instructs Moses to

[1] Translated from the Hebrew in *Festival Prayers according to the German and Polish Rites, New Year Service,* by Professor Snaith, op. cit., pp. 160–2.

tell Aaron to dress himself in the holy linen coat and to bring a young bullock for the atonement of himself and his house. Then:

'he shall take the two goats, and set them before the LORD at the door of the tent of meeting. And Aaron shall cast lots upon the two goats; one lot for the LORD, and the other lot for Azazel. And Aaron shall represent the goat upon which the lot fell for the LORD, and offer him for a sin offering. But the goat, on which the lot fell for Azazel, shall be set alive before the LORD, to make atonement for him, to send him away for Azazel into the wilderness.' (Leviticus 16, 7–10.)

Whatever the meaning of Azazel, whether demon, or pagan god, or evil man, nevertheless the goat is used as the veritable scapegoat to convey away the sins of the people, just as in later times they were cast into the waters. Aaron is then to sprinkle the blood of the bullock and of the other goat upon and before the mercy-seat on the east for these reasons:

'. . . and he shall make atonement for the holy place, because of the uncleanness of the children of Israel, and because of their transgressions, even all their sins: and so shall he do for the tent of meeting, that dwelleth with them in the midst of their uncleannesses. And there shall be no man in the tent of meeting when he goeth in to make atonement in the holy place, until he come out, and have made atonement for himself, and for his household, and for all the assembly of Israel.' (Leviticus 16, 16–17.)

Similarly, the blood of the bullock and of the goat is to be sprinkled on the altar of the Lord. Then he shall present the live goat, that of Azazel, and '. . . lay both his hands upon the head of the live goat, and confess over him all the iniquities of the children of Israel, and all their transgressions, even all their sins; and he shall put them upon the head of the goat, and shall send him away by the hand of a man that is in readiness into the wilderness: and the goat shall bear upon him all their iniquities unto a solitary land: and he shall let go into the wilderness.' (Leviticus 16, 21–2.) Therefore, expiation having been made and the people cleansed of their sins and ready for the new year, the Lord commands Moses:

'And it shall be a statute for ever unto you: in the seventh month, on the tenth day of the month, ye shall afflict your souls, and shall do no manner of work, the homeborn or the stranger that sojourneth among you: for on this day shall atonement be made for you, to cleanse you, from all your sins shall ye be clean before the Lord. It is a sabbath of solemn rest unto you, and ye shall afflict your souls; it is a statute for ever.' (Leviticus 16, 29–31.)

That the New Year Day together with the Day of Atonement constituted indeed a time of affliction and of judgment was an idea which entered deeply and ineradicably into the Jewish mind, and it appears in the prayers for the New Year service which again and again speak of the fearful day of judgment to come when all creatures are dismayed with the fearful expectation and in the meditation *Un'saneh Tokef* ascribed to Rabbi Amnon of Mayence, but given its present form by R. Meshullam ben Kalonymos, recited in the course of the additional service of the First Day of Rosh Hashannah, these ideas are given the most striking expression as the members of the congregation, wailing and covering their heads with their prayer shawls, recite:

'We will celebrate the mighty holiness of this day, for it is one of awe and terror. Thereon is thy dominion exalted and thy throne is established in mercy, and thou sittest thereon in truth. Verily it is thou alone who art judge and arbiter, who knowest and art witness; thou writest down and settest the seal, thou recordest and tellest; yea, thou rememberest the things forgotten. Thou unfoldest the records, and the deeds therein inscribed proclaim themselves; for lo! the seal of every man's hand is set thereto. The great trumpet is sounded; the still small voice is heard; the angels are dismayed; fear and trembling seize hold of them as they proclaim, Behold the Day of Judgment! The host of heaven is to be arraigned in judgment. For in thine eyes they are not pure; and all who enter the world dost thou cause to pass before thee as a flock of sheep. As a shepherd seeketh out his flock and causeth them to pass beneath his crook, so dost thou cause to pass, and number, tell and visit every living soul, appointing the measure of every creature's life and decreeing their destiny.

'On the first day of the year it is inscribed, and on the Day of Atonement the decree is sealed, how many shall pass away and how many shall be born, who shall live and who shall die, who at the measure of man's days and who before it; who shall perish by fire and who by water, who by the sword, who by wild beasts, who by hunger and who by thirst; who by earthquake and who by plague, who by strangling and who by stoning; who shall have rest and who shall go wandering, who shall be tranquil and who shall be harassed, who shall be at ease and who shall be afflicted; who shall become poor and who shall wax rich; who shall be brought low and who shall be upraised.

'But Penitence, Prayer and Charity avert the severe decree.

'For according to thy Name so is thy praise. Thou art slow to anger and ever ready to be reconciled; for thou desirest not the death of the sinner, but that he turn from his way and live. And even until the day of his death thou waitest for him: and he return thou dost straightway receive him.

'In truth thou art their Creator, who knowest their nature, that they are flesh and blood. As for man, he is from the dust and unto the dust will he return; he getteth his bread with the peril of his life; he is like a fragile potsherd, as the grass that withereth, as the flower that fadeth, as a fleeting shadow, as a passing cloud, as the wind that bloweth, as the floating dust, and as a dream that flieth away.

'But thou art the King, the living and everlasting God.'[1]

To the Day of Atonement and the New Year Day were inevitably attached messianic and eschatological ideas, as we see, for example, in Zephaniah:

'The great day of the LORD is near, it is near and hasteth greatly, *even* the voice of the day of the LORD; the mighty man crieth there bitterly. That day is a day of wrath, a day of trouble and distress, a day of wasteness and desolation, a day of darkness and gloominess, a day of clouds and thick darkness, a day of the trumpet and alarm, against the fenced cities, and against the high battlements. And I will bring distress upon men, that they shall walk like blind men, because they have sinned against the LORD: and their blood shall be poured out as dust, and their flesh as dung. Neither their silver nor their

[1] *Service of the Synagogue New Year*, ed. Herbert M. Adler (London, n.d.), pp. 146–7. Descriptions of the New Year and Day of Atonement Services will be found in W. O. E. Oesterley and G. H. Box, *The Religion and Worship of the Synagogue* (London and New York, 1907), pp. 382–403; George F. Moore, *Judaism in the First Centuries of the Christian Era: The Age of the Tannaim* (Cambridge (Mass.), 1927), II, pp. 55–69; and Hayyim Schauss, *The Jewish Festivals*, tr. Samuel Jaffe (Cincinnati, 1938), pp. 112–69.

gold shall be able to deliver them in the day of the LORD's wrath; but the whole land shall make an end, yea, a terrible end, of all them that dwell in the land.' (Zephaniah 1, 14–18.)

Yet in this terrible end there is hope for Israel:

'In that day shalt thou not be ashamed for all thy doings, wherein thou hast transgressed against me: for then I will take away out of the midst of thee thy proudly exulting ones, and thou shalt no more be haughty in my holy mountain. But I will leave in the midst of thee an afflicted and poor people, and they shall trust in the name of the LORD.' (Zephaniah 3, 11–12.)

The messianic hope had already been expressed by Isaiah:

'For unto us a child is born, unto us a son is given; and the government shall be upon his shoulder: and his name shall be called Wonderful, Counsellor, Mighty God, Everlasting Father, Prince of Peace. Of the increase of his government and of peace there shall be no end, upon the throne of David, and upon his kingdom, to establish it, and to uphold it with judgment and with righteousness from henceforth even for ever. The zeal of the LORD of hosts shall perform this.' (Isaiah 9, 6–7.)

Finally, the union of the themes of judgment, eschatology, and messianism is effected by Daniel:

'I beheld till thrones were placed, and one that was ancient of days did sit: his raiment was white as snow, and the hair of his head; his throne was fiery flames, *and* the wheels thereof burning fire. A fiery stream issued and came forth from before him: thousand thousands ministered unto him, and ten thousand times ten thousand stood befor him: the judgment was set, and the books were opened. I beheld at that time because of the voice of the great words which the horn spake; I beheld even till the beast was slain, and his body destroyed, and he was given to be burned with fire. And as for the rest of the beasts, their dominion was taken away: yet their lives were prolonged for a season and a time. I saw in the night visions, and, behold, there came with the clouds of heaven one like unto a son of man, and he came even to the ancient of days, and they brought him near before him. And there was given him dominion, and glory, and a kingdom, that all the peoples, nations, and languages should serve him: his dominion is an everlasting dominion, which shall not pass away, and his kingdom that which shall not be destroyed.' (Daniel 7, 9–14.)

Two aspects of the day of judgment are of particular interest; the first throws considerable light on the moral implications of the later medieval fall of princes theme and of the point of view of the average Elizabethan writer of tragedy:

'Hear therefore, ye kings, and understand; learn, ye judges of the ends of the earth: give ear, ye that have dominion over much people, and make your boast in multitudes of nations. Because your dominion was given you from the Lord, and your sovereignty from the Most High; who shall search out your works, and shall make inquisition of your counsels: because being officers of his kingdom ye did not judge aright, neither kept ye law, nor walked after the counsel of God. Awfully and swiftly shall he come upon you; because a stern judgment befalleth them that be in high place: for the man of low estate may be pardoned in mercy, but mighty men shall be searched out mightily.' (*The Wisdom of Solomon* in *The Apocrypha*, op. cit., p. 171.)

The other aspect is that judgment is within the soul of the individual so that none can escape it; and in a Miltonic passage, *The Wisdom of Solomon* graphically describes the confusion which besets those evil men who think they can escape the judgment:

'For while they thought that they were unseen in their secret sins, they were sundered, one from another by a dark curtain of forgetfulness, stricken with terrible awe, and sore troubled by spectral forms. For neither did the dark recesses that held them guard them from fears, but sounds rushing down ran around them, and phantoms appeared, cheerless with unsmiling faces. And no force of fire prevailed to give them light, neither were the brightest flames of the stars strong enough to illumine the gloomy night: but only there appeared to them the glimmering of a fire self-kindled, full of fear; and in terror they deemed the things which they saw to be worse than that sight, on which they could not gaze.' (Ibid., p. 193.)

In this way, then, did later Hebrew thought speculate on the Day of Judgment, in language and imagery dark, obscured, and full of strange figures.[1] But at its spiritual height, Hebrew expression of the theme was lucid, direct, and infused with the breath of divine justice; thus, in the prayer of Hannah, we read:

> *My heart exulteth in the Lord,*
> *Mine horn is exalted in the Lord:*
> *My mouth is enlarged over mine enemies;*
> *Because I rejoice in thy salvation.*
> *There is none holy as the Lord;*
> *For there is none beside thee:*
> *Neither is there any rock like our God.*
> *Talk no more so exceeding proudly;*
> *Let not arrogancy come out of your mouth:*
> *For the Lord is a God of knowledge,*
> *And by him actions are weighed.*
> *The bows of the mighty men are broken,*
> *And they that stumbled are girded with strength.*
> *They that were full have hired out themselves with bread;*
> *And they that were hungry have ceased:*
> *Yea, the barren hath borne seven;*
> *And she that hath many children languisheth.*
> *The Lord killeth, and maketh alive:*
> *He bringeth down to the grave, and bringeth up.*
> *The Lord maketh poor, and maketh rich:*
> *He bringeth low, he also lifteth up.*
> *He raiseth up the poor out of the dust,*

[1] I cannot pursue the development of eschatological and messianic ideas in the later apocryphal and apocalyptic literature; the fullest account is that by R. H. Charles, *A Crictical History of the Doctrine of a Future Life in Israel, in Judaism, and in Christianity* (London, 1899), pp. 167–361. For a recent survey of the Apocrypha, see W. O. E. Oesterley, *An Introduction to the Books of the Apocrypha* (London, 1935). For the treatment of these ideas in the writings of the rabbis, see A. Buchler, *Studies in Sin and Atonement in the Rabbinic Literature of the First Century* (Oxford, 1928), and the more general treatments, covering the thought of Judaism, by W. O. E. Oesterley and G. H. Box, *The Religion and Worship of the Synagogue*, op. cit., pp. 196–254; and George F. Moore, op. cit., I, pp. 445–552; II, pp. 279–395. A striking manifestation of these ideas in art are the wall paintings of the Dura Synagogue, concerning which see E. L. Sukenik, *Ancient Synagogues in Palestine and Greece*, The Schweich Lectures of the British Academy, 1930 (London, 1934), pp. 82–5; C. H. Kraeling, 'The Wall Decorations', in *The Excavations at Dura-Europos*, 1932–3, ed. M. I. Rostovtzeff et al. (New Haven (Conn.), 1936), pp. 337–83; M. Rostovtzeff, *Dura-Europos and Its Art* (Oxford, 1938), pp. 110–34; Isaiah Soone, 'The Paintings of the Dura Synagogue', *HUCA*, XX (1947), pp. 324–49; and Rachel Wischnitzer, *The Messianic Theme in the Paintings of the Dura Synagogue* (Cambridge, 1949).

*He lifteth up the needy from the dunghill,*
*To make them sit with princes,*
*And inherit the throne of glory:*
*For the pillars of the earth are the Lord's,*
*And he hath set the world upon them.*
*He will keep the feet of his holy ones,*
*But the wicked shall be put to silence in darkness;*
*For by strength shall no man prevail.*
*They that strive with the Lodr shall be broken to pieces;*
*Against them shall be thunder in heaven:*
*The Lord shall judge the ends of the earth;*
*And he shall give strength unto his king,*
*And exalt the horn of his anointed.* (1 Samuel 2, 1–10.)

The Lord in the full strictness of his judgment is here uncompromisingly depicted; yet to this picture must be added his mercy and compassion for men, and this we find in the first of the Servant Songs of Isaiah:

'Behold my servant, whom I uphold; my chosen, in whom my soul delighteth: I have put my spirit upon him; he shall bring forth judgment to the Gentiles. He shall not cry, nor lift up, nor cause his voice to be heard in the street. A bruised reed shall he not break, and the smoking flax shall he not quench: he shall bring forth judgment in truth. He shall not fail nor be discouraged, till he have set judgment in the earth; and the isles shall wait for his law. Thus saith God the LORD, he that created the heavens, and stretched them forth; he that spread abroad the earth and that which cometh out of it; he that giveth breath unto the people upon it, and spirit to them that walk therein: I the LORD have called thee in righteousness, and will hold thine hand, and will keep thee, and give thee for a covenant of the people, for a light of the Gentiles; to open the blind eyes, to bring out the prisoners from the dungeon, and them that sit in darkness out of the prison house. I am the LORD; that is my name: and my glory will I not give to another, neither my praise unto graven images. Behold the former things are come to pass, and new things do I declare: before they spring forth I tell you of them.' (Isaiah 42, 1–9.)[1]

[1] I am aware that, while there is agreement that 42, 1–4 constitutes the first of the Servant Songs, it is not certain that 42, 5–9 should be taken as its continuation; nevertheless, I think the verses together form a unified whole. See, for this and other problems relating to Deutero-Isaiah, Christopher R. North, *The Suffering Servant in Deutero-Isaiah* (Oxford, 1948).

I think that with this passage we have reached the high point in the development of Hebrew thought in which the relations of God with his creatures have been elevated to the very heights of spirituality in compassion and in mercy. And at the same time, we have reached the high point in the development of the myth and ritual pattern of the ancient Near East which, as we have watched it, has undergone a slow yet steady process of refinement and spiritualization in which the grosser elements have been purged out of it and the others given a new and rich symbolic and ethical meaning. What had begun as a magical rite designed to effect a specific material end, has now become generalized into a pattern of human thought and behaviour intended to enable man to cope not only with the physical immediate but with the spiritual eternal.

While our attention has been centred on the dying-rising God theme in myth and ritual, it is essential that we realize that it constitutes but one illustration, so to speak, of the greater cycle of birth, life, death, and rebirth. The many and various rites connected with birth, with initiation, with marriage, and with death in the case of the individual, as well as the rites concerned with the planting, the harvesting, the new year celebrations, and with the installation ceremonies of the king in the case of the community, all these rites repeat each in its own way the deep-rooted and abiding cycle of birth-rebirth. Not only do these rituals symbolize the passage from death to life, from one way of life to another, but they are the actual means of achieving the change-over; they mark the transition by which, through the processes of separation, regeneration, and the return on a higher level, both the individual and the community are assured their victory over the forces of chaos which are thereby kept under control. Their purpose is by enaction to bring about a just order of existence in which God, nature, and man are placed in complete and final rapport with each other; they are both the defence against disorder and the guarantor of order. In the myth and ritual pattern, man has devised a mighty weapon by which he keeps at bay, and sometimes even seems to conquer, the hostile forces which endlessly threaten to overpower him. But before the Hebrews reshaped the myth and ritual pattern of the ancient Near East, the best that man could hope for was an uneasy truce between himself and chaos, because up to then the cycle merely returned to its beginnings: the God fought, was defeated, was resurrected, was momentarily triumphant, and thus ensured the well-being of the community for the coming year, but it was inevitable that in the course of the year he would again be defeated and would again have to go through his annual agony. Thus, nothing new could be expected nor was anticipated, and year after year man could hope for no more than a temporary gain which he was sure would soon be turned into an inevitable loss. To achieve genuine faith, therefore, was an act of courage difficult and infrequent to attain, and it is no wonder that we detect in the myth and ritual pattern of the ancient Near East before the Hebrews too strong a reliance on the mere machinery of ritual, ultimately leading not to faith but to superstition, as well as the melancholy notes of despair and pessimism. But Hebrew thought in the very process of adapting the pattern, transformed it, for by virtue of the Hebrews' unique and tenacious insistence on the mercy and judgment of their transcendent God, they introduced a new and vital element in the pattern, that of the dialectical leap from out of the endless circle on to a different and higher stage of understanding. For, once man places his will in the trust of a God of universal compassion and justice, he breaks out of the cycle; he attains to a new life for ever in which he no longer need fear his oppressors, whether of man or of nature, for he is with his God eternally. On this point Moses Maimonides was uncompromising; man, he says, has been given free will, and if he wishes to turn toward the good way and be righteous, the power is in his own hands; if he wishes to turn toward the evil way and be wicked, the power is likewise in his own hands. But the crucial moment is that in which man himself, by himself, must undertake on his own to make the leap; to him remains the decision and his is the responsibility: by making the leap, he makes himself. The Hebrews then, as did the other peoples of the ancient Near East, utilized the cycle of birth, life, death, and rebirth to conquer chaos and disorder, but they made their great contribution to the pattern by giving man the possibility of defeating chaos and disorder once and for all by a single, supreme act of human will which could wipe them out at one stroke. And in so doing, they preserved the potency of the pattern and retained its ancient appeal and, at the same time, they ensured its continued use by supplying the one element it had hitherto lacked to give it its permanent rôle as the means whereby man is enabled to live in an indifferent universe; they showed that man can, by himself, transcend that universe.

CHAPTER VI

# *The Paradox of the Fortunate Fall in Christian Thought*

By the time of the appearance of Christianity, we have found that there existed, and had existed for almost three millenia, a pattern of thought and action which had gripped and continued to grip the minds and emotions of men from the Persian Gulf far to the western gates of the Mediterranean. In the course of these millenia, and under the impact of the deep-seated needs of many peoples, this pattern underwent many significant changes, and particularly in the direction of symbolization and spiritualization. I do not mean to suggest that this process of adaptation was of the character of inevitable progress from superstition to religion, but, on the whole, the movement may be seen as proceeding in that direction. This statement, however, implies no more than that, as various peoples took up the myth and ritual pattern and adapted it to their needs in terms of their special characters, they built on the efforts of their predecessors and in the course of time refined out the dross, leaving the pattern clear and capable of sustaining and symbolizing the most elevated ideas, and particularly is this true of the Hebrews; more than this I do not mean to suggest, nor do I wish to be thought of saying that the process of refinement was inherent in the process of history as an inevitable development which slowly but surely prepared the way for the emergence of Christianity. Such an attitude does a grave injustice to the character of the peoples who left their imprint on the pattern; it makes them out to be the pliable and lifeless clay being worked by an omniscient creator, without force and vitality of their own; it sees Christianity as the final stage in the evolution of man's spiritual hopes and abruptly stops the process of history at that point, everything from that time on being regarded as retrogressive, even futile. But the myth and ritual pattern seems capable of yet further transformations, for neither man nor history stops; new conditions produce new needs for which new solutions, based on old experience and fresh insight, are brought forward; man keeps on remaking himself. To think of God as dwelling in the interstices of history through which he silently performs his will is to deny to man that which distinguishes him from the rest of creation—his ability to transform himself when he wills to do so.

As to the machinery by which the transmission of culture patterns takes place, Professor Hooke has suggested three ways: by adaptation, by disintegration, and by degradation,[1] the implication being that the idealized form of the myth and ritual pattern in the course of time disintegrates and degenerates. But, since there is no evidence that there ever was a primitive *ur-mythus*, a pristine, perfect archetype from which all real forms are a kind of platonic falling-off, such a view seems to me to fail to take into account the regenerative force of successive peoples infusing new form and fresh spirit into the conventional pattern which they take up from their predecessors and revitalize. A more evolutionistic position is taken by Professor Gaster, who holds that the myth and ritual pattern developed in five stages, as follows: in the first, when man, noticing the 'regular periodicity of the seasons', reasons therefrom that 'Life is a series of leases', and concludes that if he engages in periodic communal activities, he will be able mimetically to control the operations of nature. The second stage occurs when the king assumes in his own person the fortunes of the community and by his own death and rebirth ensures the well-being of the community. The third stage is marked '. . . by the projection of the entire programme, or ritual, into the realm of Theology', when man perceives that the series of leases is in fact a continuum so that the succession of kings merges into the concept of a 'continuous and seemingly eternal personality'. Professor Gaster continues:

'The present and immediate is immerged in the continuous and eternal, its representative (the king) becomes but the contemporary body of that larger personality which transcends the here and now (i.e. the God), and in which all moments are embraced. The periodic

[1] S. H. Hooke, in *Myth and Ritual*, ed. S. H. Hooke (Oxford, 1933), pp. 5–7.

programme, or ritual, then becomes a repetition of that which was at the beginning of all leases and of that which will be at the inauguration of the Last Lease. It is projected both backwards and forwards—backwards into Cosmogony and forwards into Eschatology.'[1]

In the fourth stage, the story of the myth is moralized and the God or king is transformed into a Divine King:

'. . . who, by battling against Sin and Evil and conquering them, establishes the new era (i.e. the new 'lease') of goodness, blessing, and prosperity, in which the bliss of the larger life may be enjoyed. In the terms of this development, Salvation is not, as formerly, the mere acquisition of new vigour; it is rescue from the requital which awaits wrongdoing.'[2]

Thus, the way is prepared for the Hero to conquer death and to give man life everlasting, as in the Christian myth.[3] The final stage in Professor Gaster's scheme is that in which the dichotomy of life and death begins to break down, for now life is seen as continuously eternal, and death only a transition 'from the moment of the present to the continuity of the eternal'. But Frazer had already expressed the same point of view when he said of the myth of Demeter and Persephone:

'. . . in the long course of religious evolution high moral and spiritual conceptions were grafted on this simple original stock and blossomed out into fairer flowers than the bloom of the barley and the wheat. Above all, the thought of the seed buried in the earth in order to spring up to new and higher life readily suggested a comparison with human destiny, and strengthened the hope that for man too the grave may be but the beginning of a better and happier existence in some brighter world unknown.'[4]

[1] Theodor H. Gaster, ' "Baal is Risen . . ." An Ancient Hebrew Passion Play from Ras Shamra-Ugarit', *Iraq*, VI (1939), p. 123.

[2] Ibid., p. 124.

[3] Professor Gaster's statement of the Christian myth as a drama of redemption is supported by Professor Gustaf Aulen's assertion that this idea of atonement is the 'classic' form and is 'dramatic' in its organization: 'Its central theme is the idea of the Atonement as a Divine conflict and victory; Christ—Christus Victor—fights against and triumphs over the evil powers of the world, the "tyrants" under which mankind is in bondage and suffering, and in Him God reconciles the world to Himself.' Gustaf Aulen, *Christus Victor*, tr. A. G. Herbert (London, 1940), p. 20.

[4] James G. Frazer, *Spirits of the Corn and of the Wild* (London, 1912), I, 90.

This evolutionary attitude seems to me more satisfactory than that expressed by Professor Hooke, because it makes room for change, and change for the better, for improvement, if we will. But it still leaves out of account the part which man himself plays in the making and transforming of the pattern. As it stands in Frazer, the evolutionary point of view is a little too mechanistic, and in Professor Gaster, a little too schematic to allow much, if any, free play for the fructifying power of the human mind; it is as though the scheme, once set into motion, proceeds inexorably to its fulfilment, regardless of whether men participate in its progress or not, and in fact, from this outlook, man is seen simply as the medium through which another and higher power executes its commands. Thus, both the Christian view and the evolutionary view of the way in which myth is unfolded are, in the last analysis, teleological in nature, and are therefore forced to deny man his proper place in the creation of myth, and, by implication, in the making of history. To read man out of history, as these schemes seem indeed to do, is to open the door to admit the intrusion of such forces as are beyond man and which compel him, through various devices, to do their bidding. One need not, however, be forced into accepting a naïve faith in simple progress if one opposes the notions of the divine will immanent in the historic process or of some self-sprung mechanism relentlessly unwinding its course. I am afraid that, denied these comforts, ours must be a more terrifying view. God, mechanism, and progress are the scapegoats of history; they serve to take the blame where history goes wrong and to receive the praise when it appears to go right. But by denying their relationship to history, we cut off at one stroke all the crutches on which man can rely and leave him to himself alone, a position at once more terrible and more encouraging than the others afford. For, if man no longer has these props on which to fall back, he is left with himself, and history is seen as the record of his own deeds for which he has to admit his own responsibility. If he has done ill, it follows that he can do well; the choice is his, and his alone to make. Therefore, in the making of myth, what barbarisms have been committed are his alone, but also what refinements have been made are his alone too. Nor can it be said that the process of transformation has any stopping-place, or culmination, or fulfilment. It is not the fitful yet destined working out of God's will from the depth of barbarism to the heights of Christianity; it is rather a process which begins with man and continues with him, and its meaning can be exhausted only when he dies, and his works with him.[1]

If it should be asked, why should the myth and ritual pattern exercise so strong a hold on the minds of such a great diversity of men for so many centuries and in so many forms, I think the answer lies in man's persistent, even stubborn, refusal to accept the evidence of what his reason and observation tell him is true, namely, that we live in a universe utterly indifferent to the will and desires of men, a universe in which the aspirations and ideals of men have no real meaning, and in which man is of no more or less consequence than the falling of a leaf. Bertrand Russell has poignantly expressed the depth of despair which is the result of the full acceptance of the candid view of the universe as it is, in *A Free Man's Worship*. But the myth and ritual pattern which we have been considering is man's obstinate answer to this bitter philosophy; in the face of all the evidence of the senses, it persists in claiming the victory of man over death, of good over evil, the victory in which, as Irenaeus says, captivity is led captive. There is no logic to this, the paradox remains a paradox, but man's unconquerable will asserts in the face of all the evidence to the contrary the reality of his hopes and ideals, and in and by that assertion, he transcends the reality of negation to achieve, instead, the reality of the ideal. Thus, in the myth and ritual pattern, there is not in the least any logical justification for the triumph of the God-king; even in its earliest forms, where the pattern, by repeating the alternations of the seasons, would seem to derive its efficacy from that repetition, there is always present the feeling that mere repetition is not sufficient, for the reason that the repetition of the pattern does not always secure the end it seeks. But what does make it work is not the impassive regularity of nature, but the active participation of man hoping, desiring, and winning the victory despite the obstacles before him. The paradox of the fortunate fall cannot therefore

[1] Among students of the antecedents of Christianity, the concept of a 'Praeparatio Evangelii' is firmly held; cf. Albright, Bailey, Graham and May, James, and Toynbee. Implicit in the idea is the thought that the divine purpose slowly prepared the world through a process of successive conditioning in higher and higher ethical concepts for the coming and acceptance of Christ. Niebuhr has repudiated this notion, but for reasons other than my own, for he holds that, while the '. . . goodness of Christ must be embodied in the stuff of history,' nevertheless '. . . it can never be so embodied that it does not also stand in contradiction to history in judgement and become the completion of history only by divine mercy rather than by human achievement'. *Faith and History* (New York, 1949), p. 213; cf. ibid., pp. 109–13.

be justified logically; it must be justified in another, and perhaps more significant, area of experience.

When we turn to the New Testament, we find that the elements which constitute the myth and ritual pattern have been telescoped together. Though the themes of the sacred king, combat, creation, the sacred marriage, and the procession do appear in the New Testament, they appear but faintly, and it is not until later that they are taken up again with renewed vigour. But in the New Testament the whole pattern has been coalesced and subsumed into the concept of rebirth, with the themes of suffering, death, and the settling of destinies dependent on it. For in the person of the Christ, the pattern is, as it were, brought down into one man who typifies man. In their use of the myth and ritual pattern, the peoples of the Near East made two major errors. On the one hand, the non-Hebrew peoples placed their faith in so many gods that none could claim the full affection of all his devotees; the result was a scattering of sympathy and a loss of focus; there was no single channel into which all the streams of devotion and love could be poured. On the other hand, the Hebrews in their most ecstatic moments so far spiritualized the concept of God that he lost that bond of affection which a perhaps less exalted yet more moving human figure could command. What the one lost in spreading its devotion too far, the other lost equally as much by its intensification. But in the figure of the Christ, Christian thought avoided the double error: as the one, single exemplar of human suffering, the Christ focused on himself alone all the adoration and love of which men were capable and, at the same time, because he was not only man but God, he personalized the concept of a transcendent God, and the combined force of the two appeals, reinforcing each other at the same point, created for man his most enduring image: in the Christ, man was both man and God; he was human and divine, for, as he could suffer in his own flesh the agonies of the Christ, so could he in Christ become God. In the creation of the Christ, then, the process of spiritualization and of symbolization through which the myth and ritual pattern passed reached its highest point.[1]

[1] Grant Allen long ago, in a rather blunt but accurate statement, said the same thing: 'In one word, Christianity triumphed, because it united in itself all the vital elements of all the religions then current in the world, with little that was local, national, or distasteful; and it added to them all a high ethical note and a social doctrine of human brotherhood. . . .' *The Evolution of the Idea of God* (London, 1901), p. 389. The same point of view is expressed in John M. Robertson, *Pagan Christs* (London, 1928). Cf. William F. Albright, *From the Stone Age to Christianity* (Baltimore, 1940), pp. 300–8, for a review of recent scholarship confirming this approach.

Another layer of meaning may, therefore, be added to Christ's repeated assertion of fulfilment:

'Think not that I came to destroy the law or the prophets: I came not to destroy, but to fulfil. For verily I say unto you, Till heaven and earth pass away, one jot or one tittle shall in no wise pass away from the law, till all things be accomplished.' (Matthew 5, 17–18.)

And again: 'But all this is come to pass, that the scriptures of the prophets might be fulfilled.' (Matthew 26, 56.) From Mark we learn that after John was delivered up, Jesus came into Galilee: '. . . preaching the gospel of God, and saying, The time is fulfilled, and the kingdom of God is at hand.' (Mark 1, 14–15.) And when Jesus came to Nazareth, he went into the synagogue to read and he read out of Isaiah that he had been sent to release the captives and to set at liberty those who are bruised; then he preached to the congregation, saying: 'To-day hath this scripture been fulfilled in your ears.' (Luke 4, 21.) John tells us that when the hour came and Jesus spoke plainly to his disciples, he prayed before them:

'While I was with them, I kept them in thy name which thou hast given me: and I guarded them, and not one of them perished, but the son of perdition; that the scripture might be fulfilled. But now I come to thee; and these things I speak in the world, that they may have my joy fulfilled in themselves.' (John 17, 12–13.)

Thus, fulfilment is of two kinds: Jesus came to fulfil the words of the prophets, to carry out in practice what they taught, and thereby to fulfil the end for which man was created, his salvation and redemption. In the first epistle of John, this double use is clearly brought out:

'Beloved, no new commandment write I unto you, but an old commandment which ye had from the beginning: the old commandment is the word which ye heard. Again, a new commandment write I unto you, which thing is true in him and in you; because the darkness is passing away, and the true light already shineth. He that saith he is in the light, and hateth his brother, is in the darkness even until now. He that loveth his brother abideth in the light, and there is none occasion of stumbling in him.' (1 John 2, 7–10.)

Jesus, then, came to fulfil the promise inherent in Hebrew thought, taht is, the highest expression of the myth and ritual pattern which had until then been made, and, in so doing, elevated it to a new height of spiritual awareness. How this fulfilment was brought about and how, in so doing, it was transformed, we shall see, beginning first with those elements in the pattern which Christian thought passed over and then going on to those elements which it sharpened, strengthened, and raised to a new level of ethical significance.

The idea of the kingship of Jesus does not in the New Testament play a very prominent part. To be sure, Jesus is referred to as the son of David (Matthew 9, 27; 15, 22; Mark 10, 48; Luke 18, 39); John reports that after Jesus recognized Nathanael, Nathanael said to him: 'Rabbi, thou art the Son of God; thou art the King of Israel.' (John 1, 49.) We have already seen what significance was attached to the kingship of the Davidic king, and in this sense Jesus did take on to himself the mantle of the divine king, but the other meanings of the divine kingship he in fact repudiated. In Matthew, Mark, and Luke, when Jesus is brought before Pilate who asks him: 'Art thou the King of the Jews?' Jesus merely replies: 'Thou sayest.' But in John, when the question is put to him, Jesus clearly indicates that his kingship is of a far different sort than we have so far considered: 'My kingdom is not of this world.' And when Pilate presses the question on him: 'Art thou a king then?' Jesus answers: 'Thou sayest that I am a king. To this end have I been born, and to this am I come into the world, that I should bear witness unto the truth.' (John 18, 36–7.) The kingship of Jesus is indeed divine but in an altogether other sense than we have hitherto met: 'But seek ye first his kingdom, and his righteousness; and all these things shall be added unto you.' (Matthew 6, 33.) It is not until later, however, that the concept of King Christ the Redeemer is re-introduced in the more familiar fashion in Christian thought. The reason for the failure of primitive Christianity to adopt the concept of the divine kingship is not too hard to find. Its strong anti-institutional bias: 'It is easier for a camel to go through a needle's eye, than for a rich man to enter into the kingdom of God' (Matthew 19, 24); its communist practice: 'Ye cannot serve God and mammon. Therefore I say unto you, Be not anxious for your life, what ye shall eat, or what ye shall drink; nor yet for your body, what ye shall put on' (Matthew 6, 24–5); and its whole stress on the things not of this world: 'for great is your reward in heaven' (Matthew 5, 12), all combined to make the idea of the divine kingship repugnant to it. But after Christianity had made its inevitable compromise with this world and received official sanction, the institution of kingship was defended on the grounds that it had been divinely instituted both as a corrective for the sins of man and as the instrument of divine justice. In such an intellectual atmosphere, the terms of praise which were applied to the earthly king could once more be extended without difficulty to the spiritual king.

In the very life of Jesus, the theme of combat plays a dramatically effective part as we see him engaged in a rising crescendo of conflict; first he is restrained by his friends, then he struggles with the Pharisees, and is next pitted against the leaders of the Jews and then against Pilate, and finally he goes to his defeat and triumph over death. It was therefore but a step to transfer the theme of conflict into a larger and more symbolic meaning; writing to the Ephesians, Paul says:

'Put on the whole armour of God, that ye may be able to stand against the wiles of the devil. For our wrestling is not against flesh and blood, but against the principalities, against the powers, against the world-rulers of this darkness, against the spiritual *hosts* of wickedness in the *heavenly* places. Wherefore take up the whole armour of God, that ye may be able to withstand in the evil day, and, having done all, to stand. Stand therefore, having girded your loins with truth, and having put on the breastplate of righteousness, and having shod your feet with the preparation of the gospel of peace; withal taking up the shield of faith, wherewith ye shall be able to quench all the fiery darts of the evil *one*. And take the helmet of salvation, and the sword of the Spirit, which is the word of God.' (Ephesians 6, 12–17.)

Therefore, does Paul tell Timothy: 'Fight the good fight of the faith, lay hold on the life eternal' (1 Timothy 6, 12), for he himself has '. . . fought the good fight, I have finished the course, I have kept the faith'. (2 Timothy 4, 7.) Sometimes the theme of combat is symbolized in the figure of a race: 'Know ye not that they which run in a race run all, but one receives the prize? Even so run, that ye may attain' (1 Corinthians 9, 24), and again: '. . . let us run with patience the race that is set before us.' (Hebrews 12, 1.) But it is in Revelation that the theme of combat is given its most eloquent expression:

'And there was war in heaven: Michael and his angels *going* forth to war with the dragon; and the dragon warred and his angels; and they prevailed not, neither was their place found any more in heaven. And the great dragon was cast down, the old serpent, he that is called the Devil and Satan, the deceiver of the whole world; he was cast down to the earth, and his angels were cast down with him.' (Revelation 12, 7–9.)

We hear clearly the echoes of the old combat with the dragon, but now the symbolic meaning has far outstripped the literal meaning. Again, the hymns take up the theme of combat and elaborate it in great detail: Jesus is often depicted in his rôle of victorious warrior over evil and death. Leaving aside for a moment the theme of the procession which is better considered in connection with Christian ritual, we may note that the theme of creation plays but a small part in the New Testament and that the *motif* of the sacred marriage is not of much greater import. Indeed, it is only in Revelation that the symbolism derived from the sacred marriage is significantly utilized: 'I will show thee the bride, the wife of the Lamb.' (Revelation 21, 9.) Once more, it is in the later literature that the *motif* of the sacred marriage is dealt with richly, especially after the emergence of Mariolatry.

Far different, however, is the use made in the New Testament of the themes of suffering, death, rebirth, and the settling of destinies. The myth and ritual pattern is compressed and stripped down to its essentials, which are thereby revealed all the more clearly and sharply so that the life of Christ stands for the lives of all men, the most moving symbol of our fate. The theme of suffering is introduced to us in the most touching way, through Jesus's own insight into what is to befall him: 'From that time began Jesus to shew unto his disciples, how that he must go unto Jerusalem, and suffer many things of the elders, and chief priests and scribes, and be killed, and the third day be raised up' (Matthew 16, 21), and again: 'And he began to teach them, that the Son of man must suffer many things, and be rejected by the elders, and the chief priests, and the scribes, and be killed, and after three days rise again.' (Mark 8, 31.) Even more moving is Jesus's own awareness of why he must suffer: '. . . the Son of man came not to be ministered unto, but to minister, and to give his life a ransom for many' (Matthew 20, 28), and 'For I am come down from heaven, not to do mine own will, but the will of him that sent me. And this is the will of him that sent me, that of all that which he hath given me I should lose nothing, but should raise it up at the last day. For this is the will of my Father, that every one that beholdeth the Son and believeth on him, should have eternal life; and I will raise him up at the last day.' (John 6, 39–40.) For Jesus came to save not a particular group or class or nation of men, but all men: 'All that came before me are thieves and robbers . . . I am the door: by me if any man enter in, he shall be saved, and shall go in and go out, and shall find pasture. . . . I am the good shepherd: the good shepherd layeth down his life for the sheep.' And Jesus then takes all men within his arms:

'And other sheep I have, which are not of this fold; them also must I bring, and they shall hear my voice; and they shall become one flock, one shepherd. Therefore doth the Father love me, because I lay down my life, that I may take it again. No one taketh it away from me, but I lay it down of myself. I have power to lay it down, and I have power to take it again.' (John 10, 8–18.)

Therefore Paul could well say: 'For in one Spirit were we all baptized into one body, whether Jews or Greeks, whether bond or free; and were all made to drink of one Spirit' (1 Corinthians 12, 13), and this idea was expanded in the magnificent passage in Galatians:

'So that the law hath been our tutor *to bring us* unto Christ, that we might be justified by faith. But now that faith is come, we are no longer under a tutor. For ye are all sons of Gods, through faith in Christ Jesus. For as many of you as were baptized into Christ did put on Christ. There can be neither Jew nor Greek, there can be neither bond nor free, there can be no male and female: for ye are all one *man* in Christ Jesus. And if ye are Christ's, then are ye Abraham's seed, heirs according to promise.' (Galatians 3, 24–9.)

The long evolution of the problem of who shall be saved thus comes to its great climax; at first, salvation is but for the few, indeed, initially only for the king and then later on for those close to him; gradually, those who belong to the same city or nation or class are brought within the fold; and finally, the universal salvation of all who would be saved, a concept to be discerned at the topmost heights of Hebrew thought, is by Jesus and Paul proclaimed to all in words that all can understand. In the Epistle to the Romans, Paul strongly binds the links between the suffering of Jesus and the universal salvation of mankind:

'Now we know that what things soever the law saith, it speaketh to them that are under the law; that every mouth may be stopped, and all the world may be brought under the judgment of God: because by the works of the law shall no flesh be justified in his sight; for through the law *cometh* the knowledge of sin. But now apart from the law a righteousness of God hath been manifested, being witnessed by the law and the prophets; even the righteousness of God through faith in Jesus Christ unto all them that believe; for there is no distinction; for all have sinned, and fall short of the glory of God; being justified freely by his grace through redemption that is in Christ Jesus: whom God set forth *to be* a propitiation, through faith, by his blood, to show his righteousness, because of the passing over of the sins done aforetime, in the forbearance of God; for the shewing, *I say*, of his righteousness at this present season: that he might himself be just, and the justifier of him that hath faith in Jesus.' (Romans 3, 19–26.)

Paul goes on to say:

'For if, while we were enemies, we were reconciled to God through the death of his Son, much more, being reconciled, shall we be saved by his life; and not only so, but we also rejoice in God through our Lord Jesus Christ, through whom we have received reconciliation.' (Romans 5, 10–11.)

Therefore, if in Christ suffer we all, likewise in him are we saved; no longer is the outcome of the passion of the God to be feared, for at one stroke Christian thought overcame the element of uncertainty that the suffering might be in vain; that, despite all the efforts of man, the chaos of the universe might win out over him; chaos is conquered when suffering achieves its purpose; and the sacrifice of one man, the gift by the grace of one man, abound unto the many:

'We were buried therefore with him through baptism into death: that like as Christ was raised from the dead through the glory of the Father, so we also might walk in newness of life. For if we have become united with him by the likeness of his death, we shall be also by the likeness of his resurrection; knowing this, that our old man was crucified with him, that the body of sin might be done away, so that we should no longer be in bondage to sin; for he that hath died is justified from sin. But if we died with Christ, we believe that we shall also live with him; knowing that Christ being raised from the dead dieth no more; death hath no more dominion over him.' (Romans 6, 4–9.)

That the suffering and resurrection of Jesus were the two foundation stones upon which Christian thought rested, we learn from Paul, the first being '. . . unto the Jews a stumbling block, and unto Gentiles foolishness; but unto them that are called, both Jews and Greeks, Christ the power of God, and the wisdom of God.' (1 Corinthians 1, 23–4); and of the second he said: '. . . if Christ hath not been raised, then is our preaching vain, your faith also is vain.' (1 Corinthians 15, 15.) Therefore, the idea of rebirth is emphasized over and over again in the New Testament. 'He that findeth his life shall lose it; and he that loseth his life for my sake shall find it.' (Matthew 10, 39.) And again: 'For whosoever would save his life shall lose it: and whosoever shall lose his life for my sake shall find it.' (Matthew 16, 25.) Similar expressions are found in Mark (8, 35), and in Luke we learn of the same concept in another way: 'Verily, I say unto you, Whosoever shall not receive the kingdom of God as a little child, he shall in no wise enter therein' (Luke 18, 17); for only one who is washed as clean of the old as the child is can enter into the new. In John, the idea of rebirth is repeated many times: 'Verily, verily, I say unto thee, Except a man be born anew, he cannot see the kingdom of God' (3, 3) and: 'Marvel not that I said unto thee, Ye must be born anew' (3, 8). Jesus said: 'He that followeth me shall not walk in the darkness, but shall have the light of life.' (8, 12). For, as Jesus said to Martha: 'I am the resurrection and the life: he that believeth on me, though he die, yet shall he live: and whosoever liveth and believeth on me shall never die.' (11, 25–6.)

It is not surprising, therefore, that the strong and subtle mind of Paul should have seized on the concept of rebirth as the very central doctrine of Christianity: '. . . that like as Christ was raised from the dead through the glory of the Father, so we also might walk in newness of life' (Romans 6, 4); and again: 'But now we have been discharged from the law, having died to that wherein we were holden; so that we serve in newness of the spirit, and not in the oldness of the letter.' (Romans 7, 6.) 'For', as he said, 'the mind of the flesh is death; but the mind of the spirit is life and peace: . . . But if the Spirit of him that raised up Jesus from the dead dwelleth in you, he that raised up Christ Jesus from the dead shall quicken also your mortal bodies through his Spirit that dwelleth in you.' (Romans 8, 6–7, 11.) Rebirth is universal to all: 'For none of us liveth to himself, and none dieth to himself. For whether we live, we live unto the Lord; or whether we die, we die unto the Lord: whether we live therefore, or die, we are the Lord's. For to this end Christ died, and lived *again*, that he might be Lord of both the dead and the living.' (Romans 14, 7–9.) Paul calls on the Corinthians to: 'Purge out the old leaven, that he may be a new lump, even as ye are unleavened' (1 Corinthians 5, 7); and he assures them that: '. . . as in Adam all die, so also in Christ shall all be made alive' (15, 22); for though the resurrection of the dead '. . . is sown in corruption; it is raised in incorruption: it is sown in dishonour; it is raised in glory: it is sown in weakness; it is raised in power: it is sown a natural body; it is raised a spiritual body.' (15, 42–4.) In the Second Epistle to the Corinthians, Paul reaffirms his faith in the resurrection: 'Wherefore if any man is in Christ, *he is* a new creature: the old things are passed away; behold they are become new.' (II Corinthians 5, 17.) To the Ephesians, he says and admonishes them: '. . . that ye put away, as concerning your former manner of life, the old man, which waxeth corrupt after the lusts of deceit; and that ye be renewed in the spirit of your mind, and put on the new man, which after God hath been created in righteousness and holiness of truth' (Ephesians 4, 22–4), for, he continues: ' . . . ye were once darkness, and now are light in the Lord.' (5, 8.) All things are revealed in and by the light: 'Wherefore he saith, Awake, thou that sleepest, and arise from the dead, and Christ shall shine upon thee.' (5, 14; cf. Colossians 1, 12–14; Philippians 3, 8–11; Hebrews 2, 9–16.) From darkness to light, from the old to the new, from death to life, this is the essence of the paradox of the fortunate fall, now compressed and refined into its ultimate significance.

With the resurrection comes judgment:

> 'Verily I say unto you, that ye which have followed me, in the regeneration when the Son of man shall sit on the throne of his glory, ye also shall sit upon twelve thrones, judging the twelve tribes of Israel. And every one that hath left houses, or brethren, or sisters, or father, or mother, or children, or lands, for my name's sake, shall receive a hundredfold, and shall inherit eternal life. But many shall be last *that are* first; and first *that are* last.' (Matthew 19, 28–30.)

When Jesus sat on the Mount of Olives, the disciples asked him, what shall be the sign of his coming, and of the end of the world. He tells them that there will be false reports of him, and wars, and famines and earthquakes; then when the sun shall be darkened and the powers of heaven shaken, the Son of man will sit upon the throne of his glory and the angels will gather together his elect from the four winds:

'But when the Son of man shall come in his glory, and all the angels with him, then shall he sit on the throne of his glory: and before him shall be gathered all the nations: and he shall separate them one from another, as the shepherd separateth the sheep from the goats: and he shall set the sheep on his right hand, but the goats on the left. Then shall the King say unto them on his right hand, Come, ye blessed of my Father, inherit the kingdom prepared for you from the foundation of the world: for I was an hungered, and ye gave me meat: I was thirsty, and ye gave me drink: I was a stranger, and ye took me in; naked, and ye clothed me: I was sick, and ye visited me: I was in prison, and ye came unto me.' (Matthew 25, 31–6.)

But to those on the left hand he shall say: 'Depart from me, ye cursed, into the eternal fire which is prepared for the devil and his angels.' (25, 41.) For the Father '. . . hath given all judgment unto the Son; that all may honour the Son, even as they honour the Father. . . . Verily, verily, I say unto you, The hour cometh, and now is, when the dead shall hear the voice of the Son of God; and they that hear shall live . . . for the hour cometh, in which all that are in the tombs shall hear his voice, and shall come forth; they that have done good, unto the resurrection of life; and they that have done ill, unto the resurrection of judgment.' (John 5, 23–9.) Nevertheless, '. . . if any man hear my sayings, and keep them not, I judge him not; for I came not to judge the world, but to save the world. He that rejecteth me, and receiveth not my sayings, hath one that judgeth him: the word that I spake, the same shall judge him in the last day.' (John 12, 47–8.)

The day of judgment is vivid in Paul's eye:

'Then *cometh* the end, when he shall deliver up the kingdom to God, even the Father; when he shall have abolished all rule and all authority and power. For he must reign, he hath put all his enemies under his feet. The last enemy that shall be abolished is death.' (1 Corinthians 15, 24–5.)

Therefore, Paul continues:

'We shall not all sleep, but we shall all be changed, in a moment, in the twinkling of an eye, at the last trump: for the trumpet shall sound, and the dead shall be raised incorruptible, and we shall be changed. For this corruptible must put on incorruption, and this mortal must put on immortality. But when this corruptible shall have put on incorruption, and this mortal shall have put on immortality, then shall come to pass the saying that is written, Death is swallowed up in victory.' (15, 51–4.)

We must all be prepared for judgment, Paul tells the Corinthians: 'For we must all be made manifest before the judgment-seat of Christ; that each may receive the things *done* in the body, according to what he hath done, whether *it be* good or bad.' (2 Corinthians 5, 10.) But it is in Revelation that the concept of the settling of destinies reaches its highest point in the New Testament. Hearkening to the call from heaven, John sees the throne set in heaven and surrounded by twenty-four thrones, with the seven lamps of fire burning before the throne and the four six-winged creatures praising the Lord. And in the right hand of him that sat on the throne was a book, closed with seven seals, which only the Lamb of the Lord, the Lion that is of the tribe of Judah, the Root of David, could open, for he alone purchased with his blood the men of every tribe, tongue, and nation, for he was slain that he might receive the power. Then the book is opened, the four horsemen rode out, the earth shook, and all men hid, for the day of wrath had come. Then came the three Woes; signs appeared in heaven; the dragon was defeated; the seven bowls of the wrath of God were poured into the earth; and then, after the final victory of the King of Kings, and Lord of Lords, the marriage of the Lamb is come, the dead are judged out of the book of life, and a new heaven and a new earth are come. Then shall God be with men, and he shall wipe away their tears: '. . . and death shall be no more; neither shall there be mourning, nor crying, nor pain, any more. . . . I will give unto him that is athirst of the fountain of the water of life freely.' (Revelation 21, 4, 6–7.) And with this last echo from the fertility *motif*, now completely transformed, the judgment has come.

Such, then, was the shape given the myth and ritual pattern by early Christian thought. In the main, the Hebrew tradition has been faithfully followed, for the vestiges of the old nature ritual have been either spiritualized or pruned away altogether, but in another sense the Christian version represents a kind of regression in the development of the pattern, for it is a return to the emphasis on the divine king as the symbol of man's struggle. We remember that in Hebrew thought the image of the divine king was ultimately obscured by the superior weight of the theme of the settling of destinies, by the preoccupation with the concept of justice. The effect of this preoccupation with abstract principle was a turning away from the essentially human vicissitudes of the divine king and a consequent loss of personal identification with his death and resurrection. Hebrew thought had pitched the combat on so exalted a spiritual level that only in rare moments of transport could the great range of the drama of salvation be seen in its vast unfolding. Such a vision could not be granted to many men for the reason that not many men could have the courage and strength to see with their own eyes the tremendous forces unleashed in the cosmic combat; the reward was great, but the price to be paid was great too, and most men preferred to seek safety in the intricacies of ritual rather than to expose themselves alone and unaided to the naked eye of God. Christian thought returned to the divine king as mediator between man and his maker; it retained the ethical insistence of the Hebrews, but at the same time restored the office of the divine king who in his own person was willing to bear the brunt of suffering for all men. The cosmic combat was softened and humanized; between man and his God there was interposed an intermediary who died that others might live; and if the pattern was in this way somewhat reduced in stature, it gained in intimacy and humanity. Christian thought was thus able to effect a balance between the excesses of the cultic practices of the nature ritual of the ancient Near East on the one hand and between the excesses of spirituality of the Hebrews on the other; to the efficacy of the pattern of the one, it added the ethical emphasis of the other, and recombined both in a new version of the pattern now placed on the human plane. It is probably owing to its skill in maintaining this delicate balance between nature and spirit, between the lowest and highest in man, giving each its just due, that enabled Christianity to emerge victorious out of the welter of competing religions.

The proliferation of the Christian versions of the myth and ritual pattern in the Middle Ages took many shapes and forms, but when we come to assess the influence of the pattern on Christian and medieval thought and practice, we must be on our guard to avoid a number of errors into which it would be temptingly easy to fall.

The first is that we may find the presence of the pattern everywhere, and hence nowhere. But the most that can be claimed for the influence of the pattern is that, in an atmosphere where the drama of redemption as symbolized in the death and resurrection of Christ was made the very heart of universal faith, it is not surprising that the pattern was given expression in an almost endless variety of ways and forms. This is not, however, the same as saying that the myth and ritual pattern was the sole, or even the largest, single inspiration of medieval expression; on the contrary, it means only that the medieval climate of opinion was in a large degree sympathetic to the pattern because of the pervading effect of its Christian shape. Second, there is the temptation to give too much weight to the appearance of the pattern in non-artistic forms, particularly in folk-custom and in folk-lore. Again, the most that can be said of these manifestations is that they created an atmosphere of acceptance and credence; they provided a predisposition for response; but in themselves they did not attain to the stature of art, nor did the folk-play in itself ever reach the status of tragedy. This consideration leads to the third warning, which is that we must not confuse the atmosphere and stuff out of which art may ultimately be made with the art product itself. Indeed, so far as tragedy is concerned, the commonly accepted Christian version of the pattern could not, given its bias and shape, lead directly to tragedy. Professor Willard Farnham has pointed out that '. . . by the very nature of its origin in the representation of incidents connected with the sacrificial death and the resurrection of Jesus, the drama of Christian Europe had tragic potentiality'. Yet, he goes on to say, '. . . the development of that potentiality was not a progress toward the profoundest realization of tragedy in the Passion of the God-man Jesus and through that toward the profoundest realization of tragedy in the suffering and death of man'.[1] The reasons for this failure are instructive; Professor Farnham gives them as follows:

'In the first place, one must consider the faith in the perfection of Jesus which was a cardinal principle of Christianity. He was not merely a god in human form, but very God in human form, and thus possessed all divine finality. Behind him and exterior to him Christianity could not conceive a higher operation of fate such as Aeschylus could conceive for Prometheus and even for Zeus, whose destiny

[1] Willard Farnham, *The Medieval Heritage of Elizabethan Tragedy* (Berkeley, 1936), p. 173.

included the threat of an overthrow similar to the overthrow of his father Cronus. . . . It was entirely possible for them to possess the flaws that lead to tragedy. But in order to represent Jesus in any such failure to embody true perfection, Christianity would have had to pass through a radical change in substance toward which, at the time, it was in no way disposed. . . . Hence the crucifixion could at the most be made to arouse a tragic pity for perfect goodness suffering ironically at the hands of lost creatures whom it had come to save; it could not be made to arouse the tragic terror that comes with the view of a hero helping to seal his own doom through imperfections recognizably like our own. A further consideration . . . must be the fact that the miraculous resurrection of Jesus and his divine victory over suffering and death, conceived as the true climax of his drama, went far toward nullifying the tragedy of pity in his crucifixion. His mortal agony could thus yield but little meaning in terms of this world such as great tragedy has always set itself to discover.'[1]

In short, medieval Christendom, fearing heresy, failed to give freedom of movement to the element of doubt in the pattern; the small amount of despair when it is uncertain which way the scales are going to tip was so hedged round with safeguards, the certainty of the victory of Christ was so well secured, that tragedy could not break through the wall of faith.

We begin with a group of related themes which, while not bearing directly on the concept of *felix culpa*, nevertheless, provided some degree of acceptance for it; these are the *de casibus*, the fall of princes, and the wheel of fortune themes. Though it would perhaps be going too far to think of them as vulgarized and debased versions of the paradox of the fortunate fall, yet they do approximate it and mimic the idea in debased form. But they differ from it in one essential point: they boggle at the element of doubt, for they either intrude the vagaries of chance in the destinies of man or else have recourse to intervention from the outside. Thus, in the tales of the fall of princes, the moral of the story is often forced upon a recalcitrant narrative, while, in the wheel of fortune theme, man is made either the victim of a 'fickle, whimsical, and careless mistress', or the tool

[1] Willard Farnham, ibid., pp. 174–6. The same reasons militate against the tragic potentialities of the miracle play; there is never any question that the suffering of the saint will ever be in vain; psychologically speaking, though his persecutors may be physically superior to him, they are, all the same, at the disadvantage, since we know that whatever they may do, they cannot possibly gain the victory.

of an omnipotent father who keeps him in a perpetual childhood of no responsibility. But neither Chaucer's Monk's definition of tragedy as the tale:

*Of him that stood in greet prosperitee*
*And is y-fallen out of heigh degree*
*Into miserie, and endeth wrecchedly, . . .*

(B. 3165–7.)

nor Virgil's explanation of Fortune to Dante:

*He whose high wisdom's over all transcendent*
*Stretched forth the Heavens, and guiding spirits supplied,*
*So that each part to each part shines resplendent,*

*Spreading the light equal on every side;*
*Likewise for earthly splendours He saw fit*
*To ordain a general minister and guide,*

*By whom vain wealth, as time grew ripe for it,*
*From race to race, from blood to blood, should pass,*
*Far beyond hindrance of all human wit.*

*Wherefore some nations minish, some amass*
*Great power, obedient to her subtle codes,*
*Which are hidden, like the snake beneath the grass.*

*For her your science finds no measuring-rods;*
*She in her realm provides, maintains, makes laws,*
*And judges, as do in theirs the other gods.*

*Her permutations never know truce nor pause;*
*Necessity lends her speed, so swift in fame*
*Men come and go, and cause succeeds to cause.*

*Lo! this is she that hath so curst a name*
*Even from those who should give praise to her—*
*Luck, whom men senselessly revile and blame.*

*But she is blissful and she does not hear;*
*She, with the other primal creatures, gay*
*Tastes her own blessedness, and turns her sphere.*[1]

neither of these medieval versions of tragedy, in which in one case man is utterly exposed to the blind machinations of chance, and in

[1] Dante, Hell, Canto VII, 73–96, tr. Dorothy Sayers, *The Comedy of Dante Alighieri* (Penguin Books, 1949), p. 112.

the other left without a will of his own, neither of these strikes that balance between determinism and freedom, between scepticism and faith, on which tragedy so delicately rests. Indeed, the conventional Christian view left the door open to the sentimentalism of poetic justice, to a system of the mathematical distribution of rewards for virtue and punishments for vices: man is now made over into a snivelling book-keeper cautiously huddling over his accounts. The ceaseless and senseless whirling of the wheel never pauses long enough for the small moment in which to make the perilous passage from ignorance through suffering to light, which is the mark of the paradox of the fortunate fall.[1]

The range of expression of the myth and ritual pattern in Christian and medieval thought and practice runs all the way from the scarcely concealed survivals of pagan cultic practices in the customs of the people through its formalized exposition in Christian and secular art and literature, and up to its official version in the doctrines and rites of the Church itself. In the area of folk-custom and folk-lore, the religion of the folk; the folk-festivals as well as the more sophisticated court festivals and triumphs; the sports and games, ranging from fencing and wrestling to jousts and the chase; the entertainers of the people, such as the minstrel, the jongleur, the swordsman, the fool, and the clown; the dances, including the burlesque dances; the children's games, dances, and rhymes; the folk hero; and magical rites; all these activities of the people seem in some measure to have been derived from ritual beliefs and practices.[2] Again, I do not sug-

[1] For the wheel of fortune, see H. R. Patch, *The Goddess Fortune in Medieval Literature* (Cambridge (Mass.), 1927); V. Ciofarri, *Fortune and Fate from Democritus to St. Thomas Aquinas* (New York, 1935); William Farnham, op. cit., *passim*; and William Chase Greene, *Moira Fate, Good, and Evil in Greek Thought* (Cambridge (Mass.), 1948). The interrelated treatment of the wheel of fortune in literature and art is treated by Samuel Chew, 'Time and Fortune', *ELH*, VI (1939), pp. 83–113. A survey of studies of the theme is made by David M. Robinson, 'The Wheel of Fortune', *CP*, XLI (1946), pp. 207–16.

[2] I append a few references which tend to substantiate this generalization. For the religion of the people, Edmund K. Chambers, *The Medieval Stage* (Oxford, 1903), I, pp. 89–115. For the village festivals, E. K. Chambers, ibid., I, pp. 116–15. For the observances at the beginning of winter, E. K. Chambers, ibid., I, pp. 228–48. For the New Year customs, E. K. Chambers, ibid., I, pp. 249–73. For the Feast of Fools, E. K. Chambers, ibid., I, pp. 274–335; Karl Young, *The Drama of the Medieval Church* (Oxford, 1933), I, pp. 104–6; Edwin O. James, *Christian Myth and Ritual* (London, 1933), pp. 293–8. For the Boy Bishop, E. K. Chambers, ibid., I, pp. 336–71; Karl Young, ibid., I, pp. 106–10; E. O. James, ibid., pp. 293–8. For the Fool, E. K. Chambers, ibid., I, pp. 372–89; and Enid Welsford, *The Fool* (London, 1935), pp. 55–75. For games and sports, E. K. Chambers, ibid., I, pp. 146–81; E. O. James, ibid., pp. 277–92; and Lewis Spence,

gest here any direct line of connection with the paradox of the fortunate fall; rather, we have here the atmosphere and the soil in which the concept of *felix culpa* could take root and grow, but no more.

When we turn to literature, we find that the ritual origin of romance has been examined by Professor Jessie L. Weston in that book which Mr. Eliot used to such good purpose, *From Ritual to Romance*. The Grail story, she argues, was the product of an ancient ritual '. . . having for its ultimate object the initiation into the secret of the sources of Life, physical and spiritual'. Vestiges of these cultic practices still persisted in folk ceremonies and came over into religion through the medium of the mysteries and thence into Christianity which '. . . boldly identified the Deity of Vegetation, regarded as Life Principle, with the God of the Christian Faith'. Particularly did the Naassene document link pre-Christian, and Christian, mystery tradition together. Now, the very first versions of the Grail story, as represented in the Bleheris form, '. . . relates the visit of a wandering knight to one of these hidden temples, a reference to the places of worship associated with the old nature ritual; his successful passing of the test into the lower grade of Life initiation, his failure to attain to the highest degree.' The Grail Quest then, was, a record of the practices of the nature ritual, which in its first form was a composite between Christianity and the nature ritual, '. . . as witnessed by the ceremony over the bier of the Dead Knight, the procession with Cross and incense, and the solemn Vespers for the Dead'. But then the tale came into the hands of those who knew nothing of its ritualistic origins so that the original sex symbols, the Lance and the Cup, came to be identified with the Weapon of the Crucifixion and the Cup of the Last Supper. The tale was now definitely Christianized when it was amalgamated with the Fescamp *Saint-Sang* tradition and with Glastonbury; this is the form of the *Perlesvaus* text. Then Robert De Borron '. . . radically remodelled the whole on the basis of the triple Mystery tradition, translated into terms of high Christian Mysticism. In time, other themes were attracted to the tale, as, for

*Myth and Ritual in Dance, Game and Rhyme* (London, 1947), pp. 11–94. For dancing, E. K. Chambers, ibid., I, pp. 182–204; Jessie L. Weston, *From Ritual to Romance* (Cambridge, 1920), pp. 77–85; and Lewis Spence, ibid., pp. 95–160. For popular rhyme, Lewis Spence, ibid., pp. 161–89. For the Folk Hero, Lord Raglan, *The Hero* (New York, 1937); Jessie L. Weston, ibid., pp. 11–22; and Hugh Ross Williamson, *The Arrow and the Sword* (London, 1947), pp. 91–136. For magical rites, Margaret A. Murray, *The Witch-Cult in Western Europe* (Oxford, 1921), and Eva M. Butler, *The Myth of the Magus* (Cambridge, 1948).

example, the tale of the Widow's Son, and finally, '. . . the rising tide of dogmatic Medievalism, with its crassly materialistic view of the Eucharist; its insistence on the saving grace of asceticism and celibacy; and its scarcely veiled contempt for women, overwhelmed the original conception.'[1] Such is the story of the origin of medieval romance. Once more, we can claim no more influence for this development than that of a contribution, at the most, to the making of a mood.

Of the many forms of folk drama, the 'most conspicuous', as Professor Karl Young calls it, is the Mummer's Play. Concerning the dramatic activities of the folk drama, Professor Young writes:

'The ultimate origin of these, we know, was certain pagan ceremonies of a quasi-religious nature, the purpose of which was to secure the fertility of the earth, of animals, and of human beings through the use of sympathetic magic. It was assumed that man could bring about the natural phenomena on which his life depended by imitating them. Thus the primitive worshipper fancied that by dressing himself in leaves and flowers, and by hanging such objects on trees, he could encourage the earth to re-clothe herself with verdure; or that by putting to death some representative of the principle of life and subsequently reviving him, he could bring about a repetition of this act on a comprehensive scale by the mighty forces which govern the physical world. The outward manifestations of these beliefs have been, from very early times to the present, a variety of festivals, games, processions and dances which centred in acts imitating or symbolizing the departure and return of life, and particularly the death of vegetation in winter and the revival of it in the spring. All of these ritualistic observances contained dramatic elements. . . . Some of them, however, developed out of folk festival, through symbolic dances, into independent spoken drama.'[2]

The Mummer's Play was originally a spring observance but, as a result of Christian influence, was attached to the Christmas season. I quote a normalized text, as reconstructed by Professor E. K. Chambers:

(Enter the PRESENTER.)

PRESENTER. *I open the door, I enter in;*
*I hope your favour we shall win.*

[1] Jessie L. Weston, *From Ritual to Romance*, op. cit., pp. 191–5.
[2] Karl Young, op. cit., I, pp. 10–11.

*Stir up the fire and strike a light,*
*And see my merry-boys act to-night.*
*Whether we stand or whether we fall,*
*We'll do our best to please you all.*

(Enter the actors, and stand in a clump.)

PRESENTER. *Room, room, brave gallants all,*
*Pray give us room to rhyme;*
*We're come to show activity,*
*This merry Christmas time;*
*Activity of youth,*
*Activity of age,*
*The like was never seen*
*Upon a common stage.*
*And if you don't believe what I say,*
*Step in St. George—and clear the way.*

(Enter ST. GEORGE.)

ST. GEORGE. *In come I, Saint George*
*The man of courage bold;*
*With my broad axe and sword*
*I won a crown of gold.*
*I fought the fiery dragon,*
*And drove him to slaughter,*
*And by these means I won*
*The King of Egypt's daughter.*
*Show me the man that bids me stand;*
*I'll cut him down with my courageous hand.*

PRESENTER. *Step in, Bold Slasher.*

(Enter BOLD SLASHER.)

SLASHER. *In come I, the Turkish Knight,*
*Come from the Turkish land to fight.*
*I come to fight St. George,*
*The man of courage bold;*
*And if his blood be hot,*
*I soon will make it cold.*

ST. GEORGE. *Stand off, stand off, Bold Slasher,*
*And let no more be said,*
*For if I draw my sword,*

*I'm sure to break thy head.*
*Thou speakest very bold,*
*To such a man as I;*
*I'll cut thee into eyelet holes,*
*And make thy buttons fly.*

SLASHER. *My head is made of iron,*
*My body is made of steel,*
*My arms and legs of beaten brass;*
*No man can make me feel.*

ST. GEORGE. *Then draw thy sword and fight.*
*Or draw thy purse and pay;*
*For satisfaction I must have,*
*Before I go away.*

SLASHER. *No satisfaction shalt thou have,*
*But I will bring thee to thy grave.*

ST. GEORGE. *Battle to battle with thee I call,*
*To see who on this ground shall fall.*

SLASHER. *Battle with battle with thee I pray,*
*To see who on this ground shall lay.*

ST. GEORGE. *Then guard thy body and mind thy head,*
*Or else my sword shall strike thee dead.*

SLASHER. *One shall die and the other shall live;*
*This is the challenge that I do give.*

(They fight. SLASHER falls.)

PRESENTER. *O cruel Christian, what hast thou done?*
*Thou hast wounded and slain my only son.*

ST. GEORGE. *He challenged me to fight,*
*And why should I deny't?*

PRESENTER. *O, is there a doctor to be found*
*To cure this deep and deadly wound.*
*Doctor, doctor, where art thou?*
*My son is wounded to the knee.*
*Doctor, doctor, play thy part,*
*My son is wounded to the heart.*
*I would put down a thousand pound,*
*If there were a doctor to be found.*

(Enter the DOCTOR.)

DOCTOR. *Yes, there is a doctor to be found,*
*To cure this deep and deadly wound.*

| | |
|---|---|
| | *I am a doctor pure and good,* |
| | *And with my hand can stanch his blood.* |
| PRESENTER. | *Where hast thou been, and where hast come from?* |
| DOCTOR | *Italy, Sicily, Germany, France and Spain,* |
| | *Three times round the world and back again.* |
| PRESENTER. | *What canst do and what canst cure?* |
| DOCTOR. | *All sorts of diseases,* |
| | *Just what my physic pleases;* |
| | *The itch, the stitch, the palsy and the gout,* |
| | *Pains within and pains without;* |
| | *If the devil is in, I can fetch him out.* |
| | *I have a little bottle by my side;* |
| | *The fame of it spreads far and wide.* |
| | *The stuff therein is elecampane;* |
| | *It will bring the dead to life again.* |
| | *A drop on his head, a drop on his heart.* |
| | *Rise up, bold slasher, and take thy part.* |

(SLASHER rises. Enter BIG HEAD.)

| | |
|---|---|
| BIG HEAD. | *In come I, as ain't been yet,* |
| | *With my big head and little wit,* |
| | *My head so big, my wit so small,* |
| | *I will dance a jig to please you all.* |

(Dance and Song *ad libitum*. Enter BEELZEBUB.)

| | |
|---|---|
| BEELZEBUB. | *In come I, old Beelzebub.* |
| | *On my shoulder I carry a club,* |
| | *In my hand a dripping-pan.* |
| | *Don't you think I'm a jolly old man?* |

(Enter JOHNNY JACK.)

| | |
|---|---|
| JOHNNY JACK. | *In come I, little Johnny Jack,* |
| | *With my wife and family at my back,* |
| | *My family's large and I am small,* |
| | *A little, if you please, will help us all.* |

(Enter DEVIL DOUT.)

| | |
|---|---|
| DEVIL DOUT. | *In come I, little Devil Dout;* |
| | *If you don't give me money, I'll sweep you out.* |
| | *Money I want and money I crave;* |
| | *If you don't give me money, I'll sweep you to the grave.* |

Quete.[1]

The play falls into three parts: the presentation; the drama, which consists of the vaunts, the combat, the lament, and the cure; and the *quete*. The classical elements of the ritual pattern are here exemplified in simplified form: the hero, the combat, the death, and the resurrection; sometimes, it is St. George who wins; sometimes, he is slain; but the important germ of the ritual is there, that of death and resurrection, which owes its origin, as Professor Chambers suggests, to some original European *ludus*, one more instance of the myth and ritual pattern which we have been considering.

The themes of death and resurrection, which form the apex of the myth and ritual pattern, are again the core of the drama of the medieval Church. Though the drama of the Church did not originate where one would naturally expect it to, in the liturgy itself, it did develop from the '. . . deliberate, and perhaps unsanctioned, literary additions to the authorized liturgical texts', the *tropes*.[2] From the simplest form of the *trope*, the *Quem quaeritis*, which reads:

Of the Lord's Resurrection.

Question of the angels:

*Whom seek we in the sepulchre, O followers of Christ?*

Answer of the Marys:

*Jesus of Nazareth, which was crucified, O celestial ones.*

The angels:

*He is not here, he is risen, just as foretold.*
*Go, announce that he is risen from the sepulchre.*[3]

to the most literary, the *Visitatio Sepulchri*, in the play-book from the monastery of St.-Benoit-sur-Loire, at Fleury, the theme of the death and resurrection of Christ is made the very heart of the action. The Sepulchrum begins with a lament by the three Marys, the first saying:

*Alas! the good shepherd is killed.*
*Whom no guilt stained.*
*O lamentable occurrence!*

[1] Edmund K. Chambers, *The English Folk-Play* (Oxford, 1933), pp. 6–9.

[2] The evidence for the failure of the liturgy to develop into drama is given by Karl Young, op. cit., I, pp. 79–111.

[3] Joseph Q. Adams, *Chief Pre-Shakespearean Dramas* (London, n.d.), p. 3.

The Marys ask why this righteous man deserved to be crucified, for

*Alas, what are we wretched ones to do,*
*Bereft of our sweet Master?*

They then do the only thing they can do: they go to anoint the most sacred body with preservatives of spices and a mixture of spikenard. But, since they need help to roll away the stone from the door of the sepulchre, an angel comes to the tomb, and he tells them:

*He is not here; he is risen, as he foretold his disciples.*

Now Mary Magdalene once more bewails the loss of Christ, and asks who bore away the body from the tomb; she is answered by Peter. She weeps once more:

*My heart is burning with desire*
*To see my Lord;*
*I seek, and I do not find*
*Where they have laid him.*

The two angels come to the door of the sepulchre and say:

*Be not affrighted:*
*Change now your sad countenance!*
*Proclaim Jesus living!*

And the three women cry out:

*The king of the angels has arisen today!*
*The throng of the righteous is led out of hell!*
*The door of the kingdom of heaven is opened!*[1]

A similar dramatic line is followed in certain of the secular plays. For example, the story of the temptation of man, as played by the Grocers of Norwich, ends on this triumphal note:

ADAM. *Oh! prayse to thee, Most Holye, that hast with me abode,*
*In mysery premonyshynge by this thy Holy Spright.*
*Howe fele I such great comforte, my syns they be unlode*
*And layde on Chrystes back, which is my joye and lyght.*
*This dolor and this mysery I fele to me no wight;*
*No! Deth is overcum by forepredestinacion.*
*And we attayned wyth Chryst in heavenly consolacion.*

[1] Ibid., pp. 15–20.

Therefore Adam calls on Eve to praise the Lord 'Who hath given himselfe over us to raygne and to governe us'.[1] The moral of the theme is made quite explicit by the Expositer in the Chester play, *The Sacrifice of Isaac:*

> *Lordinges, the significacioun*
> *Of this deed of devocion,*
> *And you will, you witten mone,*
> *May torne you to moche good.*
> *This deed you see done here in this place,*
> *In example of Jesu done it was,*
> *That for to wynne mankindes grace*
> *Was sacrifised on the roode.*
> *By Abraham I maie understande*
> *The father of heaven, that can fand*
> *With his sonnes bloode to breake the band,*
> *That the devill had broughte us to.*
> *By Isaake understande I maie*
> *Jesu, that was obedient aye,*
> *His fathers will to worke alwaie,*
> *And death for to confounde.*[2]

One more illustration of the presence of the pattern in medieval drama must suffice: after Everyman goes to his punishment, Knowledge speaks:

> *Now hath he suffred that we all shall endure;*
> *The good dedes shall make all sure.*
> *Now hath he made endynge,*
> *Me thynketh that I here aungelles synge,*
> *And make grete joy and melody,*
> *Where every mannes soule receyved shall bee.*[3]

Thus, at the very moment of his defeat, is Everyman triumphant. Christ, Adam, Everyman—each suffers, yet each is triumphant; and in the wings stands Hamlet.

The attitude of the Church toward the myth and ritual pattern was ambivalent. On the one hand, it strove to wipe out wherever it

[1] Ibid., p. 93.
[2] Alfred W. Pollard, *English Miracle Plays, Moralities and Interludes* (Oxford, 1927), pp. 29–30.
[3] Ibid., p. 95.

could find them the vestiges of the pagan cultic practices in the thought and customs of the people. On the other hand, however, the Church, where it encountered stubborn opposition, preferred to adapt these customs to its own ends; a notable example is the shifting of the important festival days of the Church to conform with the precedent pagan celebrations. We have already seen that in almost every case where the myth and ritual pattern has been taken over by one people from another, it seems at first to be forcefully rejected only in the end to reappear transformed and in its new form accepted. The acceptance of the pattern in Christian thought is no exception to this rule. The opposition of the Church was not to the pattern itself, whose potency it wished to retain, and indeed to monopolize for itself, but rather to those manifestations of it over which it could exercise no proper control. What the Church attempted to do, therefore, was to channelize the impulse toward the pattern in its own direction; it created an orthodox version of the pattern, which it claimed was the most effective exemplification of it; other versions it rejected as unworthy and ineffective. In short, the Church presented itself as the only vessel fit to preserve the vigour and power of the myth and ritual pattern. For all the scorn which the Fathers poured on the pagan Gods and pagan religions, at the same time they also argued that Christianity was a kind of sublimation of the wisdom and of the Gods of the pagans; passages in Justin Martyr, Irenaeus, Tertullian, Minucius Felix, Origen, Lactantius, and Augustine, among others, repeat the point that Christianity was after all in the same line of development of pagan religion, but represented its highest point of evolution. In his *Apology*, Tertullian writes:

'So all the subject-matter, all the material, all the origins, chronologies, sources, of every ancient pen you know—yes, and most of your races, your cities, famous in history, hoary of memory—nay, the very shapes of your letters, those witnesses and guardians of the past—and (for I seem to be understating things), I say, add your very gods, temples, oracles, rituals and all—the book of a single prophet notwithstanding, beats them all, with centuries to spare—that book in which is summed up the treasure of the whole Jewish religion, and in consequence of ours as well.'[1]

Much longer is the list given by Lactantius, who calls to witness the foretelling of the one God by the prophets, the poets and philo-

[1] Tertullian, *Apology*, tr. T. R. Glover (London, 1931), pp. 97–9.

sophers, the divine testimonies, the Sibyls and their predictions, the predictions of Apollo and the gods; but, he asks:

'. . . what can we suppose to have been the reason why it was not found, though sought with the greatest earnestness and labour by so many intellects, and during so many ages?'

He answers:

'Whence I am accustomed to wonder that, when Pythagoras, and after him Plato, inflamed with the love of searching out the truth, had penetrated as far as the Egyptians, the Magi, and Persians, that they might become acquainted with their religious rites and institutions (for they suspected that wisdom was concerned with religion), they did not approach the Jews only, in whose possession alone it then was, and to whom they might have gone more easily. But I think that they were turned away from them by divine providence, that they might not know the truth, because it was not yet permitted for the religion of the true God and righteousness to become known to men of other nations. For God had determined, as the last time drew near, to send from heaven a great leader, who should reveal to foreign nations that which was taken away from a perfidious and ungrateful people.'[1]

The brave Octavius, of the good old Plautine stock, answering the pagan Caecilius's dignified defence of the mysteries in which '. . . we see each people having its own individual rites and worshipping its local gods, the Eleusinians Ceres, the Phrygians the Great Mother, the Epidaurians Aesculapius, the Chaldeans Bel, the Syrians Astarte, the Taurians Diana, the Gauls Mercury, the Romans one and all', the Christian Octavius replies:

'And lastly, consider the sacred rites of the mysteries: you will find tragic deaths, dooms, funerals, mourning and lamentations of woebegone gods. Isis with her Cynocephalus and shaven priests, mourning, bewailing and searching for her lost son; her miserable votaries beating their breasts and mimicking the sorrows of the unhappy mother; then, when the stripling is found, Isis rejoices, her priests jump for joy, the Cynocephalus glories in his discovery; and, year by year, they cease not to lose what they find or to find what they lose. . . .

[1] Lactantius, *The Divine Institutes*, tr. William Fletcher (Edinburgh, 1871), I, pp. 213–14.

'Ceres, with lighted torches, serpent-girt, with anxious troubled footsteps follows the trail of her decoyed and ravished Libera—such are the Eleusinian mysteries. And what are the rites of Jupiter? His nurse is a she-goat; the infant is withdrawn from his greedy sire, for fear he should be eaten; the tinkling cymbals of the Corybants are clashed for fear the father should hear his infant wails. Of Cybele and Dindyma it is a shame to speak: unable to satisfy the affections of her luckless paramour—for mothering of many gods had made her plain and old—she reduced the god to impotence, and in deference to this fable her Galli priests inflict the same disablement upon their bodies. Such practices are not sacred rites, but tortures.'[1]

Filled with Hebrew Puritanism, the Christian Fathers rejected the pagan rites, only to revitalize them in terms of a spiritualized and humanized version of the myth and ritual pattern.[2]

It is therefore not surprising to find the basic themes of the myth and ritual pattern taken up and developed by the Fathers in terms of Christian doctrine and practice. Without attempting to cite all the relevant evidence, I call attention to the treatment of the themes of the pattern as follows: (1) The divine kingship: Justin Martyr, I, 212 ff., 267 ff.; Irenaeus, I, 448 ff., 548 ff.; Tertullian, III, 445 ff.; Cyprian, V, 526 ff.; Augustine, II, 430 ff. (2) The combat: Cyprian, V, 421 ff.; Augustine, II, 465 ff. (3) Suffering: Justin Martyr, I, 200 ff.; Irenaeus, I, 445 ff., 527 ff.; Tertullian, III, 158 ff., 335 ff.; Hippolytus, V, 158 ff.; Cyprian, III, 335 ff.; Methodius, VI, 400 ff.; Lactantius, VII, 116 ff.; Augustine, II, 355 ff., 500 ff. (4) Rebirth: Justin Martyr, I, 169 ff.; Irenaeus, I, 469 ff., 493 ff., 561 ff.; Tertullian, III, 231 ff., 421 ff., 447 ff., 552 ff.; Origen, IV, 293 ff.; Cyprian, V, 454 ff., 474 ff.; Lactantius, VII, 110 ff., 218 ff.; Augustine, II, 255 ff., 425 ff., 493 ff. (5) Divine marriage: Cyprian, V, 423 ff., 523 ff. (6) The settling of destinies: Irenaeus, I, 522 ff.; Tertullian, III, 300 ff., 589 ff.; Origen, IV, 293 ff.; Lactantius, VII, 211 ff.; and Augustine, II, 421 ff.[3] The

[1] Minucius Felix, *Octavius*, tr. Gerald H. Rendall (London, 1931), pp. 381–5.

[2] The first four books of Eusebius's *Ecclesiastical History* contain the most detailed account of the development of Christian religion as the highest stage of the religions of the past, tr. Kirsopp Lake (London, 1926), I, pp. 7–45. The patristic defence of Christianity as the continuation of ancient religion, but on a much higher level, is linked with a strong strain of anti-primitivistic thought in the Fathers; see the discussion and passages collected by George Boas, *Essays in Primitivism and Related Ideas in Antiquity* (Baltimore, 1948), pp. 175–205.

[3] The references to the Fathers, with the exception of Augustine, are to *The Ante-Nicene Fathers*, ed. Alexander Roberts and James Donaldson (New York, 1925); for Augustine, *A Select Library of Nicene and Post-Nicene Fathers*, ed. Philip Schaff (Buffalo, 1887).

authority of the Fathers was thus placed squarely behind the Christian version of the myth and ritual pattern.

We have already seen that the myth and ritual pattern is not a static thing, but a process, a movement, an action in which the divine king goes from one stage to another, from combat to defeat to victory. But, before the combat is resolved, there is that small moment of doubt, a suspension between the opposing forces when it would seem as though the outcome might go in either direction, in the direction of the triumph of evil, darkness, and death, or in the direction of the triumph of good, light, and life. Yet that small moment is never prolonged, nor is the ultimate triumph of good, light, and life ever too long delayed; indeed, implicit in the struggle is the assurance that the divine king will in fact emerge victorious. The opposing forces are given equal weight but not equal value; it is only in and through the struggle with evil, darkness, and death that good, light, and life can be given their proper place in a universe put together out of these essential but conflicting elements. Thus, at the very source of western thought, the principle of salvation through action, of the good emerging triumphant only after the struggle with evil, is sounded to give it its dominant key. The scheme is dualistic, but it is a dualism with a difference: evil, darkness, and death are not denied, but they are conquered by good, light, and life.[1] But there are some dualisms in which the outcome of the combat is left indefinitely suspended, in which both opponents are given equal weight and value, so that in fact the combat can never be ended. The struggle is made to stop at the small moment in a *stasis* of indecision: darkness and light, good and evil, life and death are frozen permanently in endless opposition to each other. Yet, as Mr. Steven Runciman has pointed out, the origin of Christian dualism must be sought '... in the same place and time as that in which orthodox Christianity was born'; both were inspired by the same religious feeling.[2] From the point of view of the use of the myth and ritual pattern, both the Christian dualists and the orthodox Christians, for all their differences, suspended the outcome of the divine combat, but the orthodox Christians, following the main impulse of western thought, went

[1] This problem has been restated in different terms by Arthur O. Lovejoy on the chapter on the origin of other-worldliness and this-worldliness in Plato in *The Great Chain of Being* (Cambridge (Mass.), 1948), pp. 24–66.

[2] Steven Runciman, *The Medieval Manichee* (Cambridge, 1947), p. 174. Professor Greene has given the reason in a brief sentence; we must admit at once, he says, '... that some sort of dualism is the condition of any ethical system', *Moira*, op. cit., p. 283.

on to resolve that conflict in the favour of the victory of the divine king, of good, light, and life, whereas the Christian dualists stopped abruptly short at that critical point and refused the combat any outcome at all. The struggle between medieval orthodoxy and medieval heresy of the dualist kind then, was one fought over the control of the potency of the myth and ritual pattern, the Church claiming that it alone was in the direct tradition of the effective employment of the pattern, as it argued in similar fashion against the claims of the pagan gods, and the heretical movements asserting in reply that their beliefs and practices were in fact closer to the original sources and intentions of the pattern than the Church could come. The Church had, therefore, from the very beginning to face the rivalry of existing forms of the pattern. The Gnostics solved the problem of the existence of evil in the world by separating the creator from his creation by interposing an almost endless series of aeons between them. In consequence, the disciples of Valentinus maintained, according to Irenaeus, that '. . . the good are those who become capable of receiving the spiritual seed; the evil by nature are those who are never able to receive that seed.'[1] Even more thorough-going in his dualism is Marcion, for he opposed, as Tertullian says, the cruel Jehovah with the Kind Stranger. Again, Zoroastrianism placed light and darkness in conflict with each other: Ormuzd, 'the source of light for the world', is engaged in endless struggle with Ahriman, 'the demon of destruction', but, while the victory of Ormuzd is forecast, in effect it can never happen; nevertheless, man is left free to choose his own salvation, whether for good or for evil.[2] According to the *Prose Refutations of Mani, Marcion and Bardaisan*, Mani's doctrines were the product of the ideas of Bardaisan and Marcion; Professor Burkitt quotes Moses bar Kepha as saying that Bardaisan held that the world was composed of Fire, Wind, Water, Darkness, and Light, with the Enemy the Dark in the Depth below. By chance, they were hurled one against the other and in the fray the Dark ventured to come up from the Depth to mingle together with them, 'thus introducing evil into the world'.[3] A convenient summary of Manichaean doctrine is given by Mr. Runciman, on the basis of the more elaborate treatment by Professor Burkitt:

[1] Irenaeus, *Against Heresies*, tr. Alexander Roberts and James Donaldson (Edinburgh, 1858), I, p. 31. Cf. F. C. Burkitt, *Church and Gnosis* (Cambridge, 1932), pp. 42–53.

[2] A. V. W. Jackson, *Zoroastrian Studies* (New York, 1928), p. 220. Cf. E. C. Blackman, *Marcion and His Influence* (London, 1948).

[3] Francis C. Burkitt, *The Religion of the Manichees* (Cambridge, 1925), pp. 76–7.

'From all eternity the two realms of Light and Darkness existed side by side. In the former dwelt the Eternal God, the Lord of Greatness with His light, His power and His wisdom, in His five dwellings of Sense, Reason, Thought, Imagination and Intention. In the latter dwelt the Lord of the Dark with his disorderly anarchical restless brood. Evil began when the denizens of the Dark, impelled by curiosity or some vague unregulated desire, began to invade the realm of Light. The realm of Light had no natural defences, so the Lord of Greatness evoked the Mother of All who evoked the Primal Man to ward off the attack.'

Primal Man, clothed in Light, Wind, Fire and Water, and the Air was defeated by the Archons of Darkness who swallowed the Five Bright Elements; Primal Man called on God to help and He created the Friend of Luminaries, the Great Ban, and the Living Spirit who in turn defeated the Archons of Darkness.

'But they had already digested the Five Pure Elements, and the Realm of Light was thereby the poorer. A wall had to be built to prevent the darkness spreading farther; then these mixed elements had to be localized. To do so, the Universe was created, held in place by five spirits evoked by the Living Spirit, of which Atlas is the most familiar. Here the Archons were placed.'

The Archons were forced to disgorge Light, particularly by God's Messenger who caused them to release the Light they held, thus allowing sin to go into the world. But the King of Darkness counterbalanced this threat by making a new creation in the image of the Messenger in which he concealed what Light there was remaining; this being was Adam, compounded of Darkness and Light.[1] Other heretical sects were influenced by the Manichees and developed dualist doctrines of their own: the Montanists, the Adoptionists, the Messalians, the Novatians, the Encratites, the Archontics, the Thonraki, the Paulicians, the Athingani, the Bogomils, the Patarenes, and, in its most impressive development, and from the point of view of the Church perhaps its most dangerous enemy, the Cathars in their various manifestations. Thus, from at least the third century to the fourteenth, the Church had to contend with dualist doctrine in an area ranging from Syria to northern Egypt to the Black Sea to the Atlantic.

Much as there is to condemn in the methods employed by the Church to stamp out the dualist heresies, it remains true that it was

[1] Steven Runciman, op. cit., pp. 12–16; cf. F. C. Burkitt, op. cit., pp. 16–32; and Dmitri Obolensky, *The Bogomils* (Cambridge, 1948), pp. 5–27.

the Church itself which was the more faithful adherent to the tradition of the myth and ritual pattern, for it saw deeper into its essential meaning. The dualism which lay at the basis of the heretical beliefs led the heretics into the position where they were forced to suspend the outcome of the combat between light and dark, good and evil, death and life. The effect of the failure to arrive at a resolution of the conflict was to minimize faith in the ultimate victory of light, good, and life, and even to deny them altogether. But a religion which makes this most important of all victories so uncertain must of necessity induce in its followers excesses in one of two opposite directions, so that it is not surprising when we learn that the heretics were accused on the one hand of practising the most strict and severe asceticism and on the other of indulging in the grossest of pagan cultic rites. If the Church did give greater prominence in its charges to the more sensational aspects of heretical worship, thus obscuring the undeniable moral fervour of many of the sects, nevertheless it was right in insisting that the outcome of the combat could not be too long delayed, that the world could not be so sharply divided, and that the motion of the pattern could not be stopped at its most awful moment, but had to be pushed on resolutely, no matter what the cost, to the settling of destinies, to the victory of the good. Without the small moment of doubt, scepticism cannot be converted into faith, but that small moment cannot last a second too long, lest men lose faith altogether. The heretics enlarged the small moment beyond the breaking point; the Church, in seeking to redress the balance, tipped the scales too far in the direction of faith at the expense of scepticism, thus destroying that tension between the two on which tragedy is poised. Unfortunately, action and reaction destroyed the very thing both sought to uphold, so that, while the tradition of the myth and ritual pattern was maintained, it was carried on in circumstances which prevented it from flowering into tragedy.

Finally, to complete our survey of the Christian exemplifications of the myth and ritual pattern,[1] we turn to the presence of the pattern

[1] Orthodox Christianity had at its disposal two versions of the paradox of the fortunate fall: the death and resurrection of Christ and the theme of Adam's fall and its subsequent benefits for mankind. The first version I have touched on; the second has been treated by Professor Lovejoy in his article on the paradox of the fortunate fall; see also, Norman P. Williams, *The Ideas of the Fall and of Original Sin* (London, 1927). Speculation about Adam's state in the Garden was frequent and detailed: see Arnold Williams, *The Common Expositor* (Chapel Hill, North Carolina, 1948), for the opinions of the medieval and Renaissance commentators on Genesis. This theme is likewise linked up with the idea of primitivism; see George Boas, op. cit., pp. 15–86.

in Christian ritual. Professor E. O. James has demonstrated the similarities in structure of the coronation ceremonies of the king, the ordination rites of the bishop, the installation of the individual into the Christian community, the ritual of the altar, the marriage rites, the last rites, and the processions of the Church.[1] Of the rituals of the Church, perhaps none is more important nor more moving than that associated with Easter; the attitude taken towards Easter by devout Christians has been feelingly expressed in a sonnet by Spenser in which the imagery, drawn from the Fathers of the Church, at the same time recalls the language of the myth and ritual pattern, only far more spiritualized:

*Most glorious Lord of Life, that on this day,*
*Didst make thy triumph over death and sin:*
*And having harrowed hell didst bring away*
*Captivitie thence captive, us to win:*
*This joyous day, deare Lord, with joy begin,*
*And grant that we for whom thou diddest die,*
*Beeing with thy deare blood cleane washt from sin,*
*May live for ever in felicitie:*
*And that thy love we weighing worthily,*
*May likewise love thee for that same again:*
*And for thy sake, that all like deare dost buy,*
*With love may one another entertaine.*
*So let us love, deare Love, like as we ought,*
*Love is the lesson which the Lord us taught.*

The ceremonies of Christian initiation were at an early date linked with Easter. At the beginning of Lent, the names of those who were to be baptized on Easter Eve were inscribed and the baptism was administered at the vigil of Easter Sunday, the last day possible being Pentecost. The convert entered into the catechumenate by presenting himself before the priest, who blew in his face, marked on his forehead the sign of the cross, prayed over him with his hand extended over his head, and administered salt which had been exorcized: the candidate was now a catechumen. He then went through seven scrutinies during the season of Lent, accompanied by exorcisms and instructions in the Gospel, the Creed, and the Lord's Prayer. The

[1] In *Christian Myth and Ritual*. Cf. also his essay, 'The Sources of Christian Ritual and Its Relation to the Culture Pattern of the Ancient East', in *The Labyrinth*, ed. S. H. Hooke (London, 1935), pp. 237–60.

last scrutiny took place on the vigil of Easter and was followed by the rite of the *Effeta* in which the priest touched the candidate on the upper part of the lip and ears with a saliva-moistened finger. The candidates now put aside their garments and were anointed with oil and then they formally abjured Satan. At the solemn vigil of Easter, the candidates were present and the lections read included passages from the Old Testament: the Creation, the Deluge, and the passage of the Red Sea. The 'elect' were then divested of their garments and were presented to the Pope, who put three questions to them to which the candidates replied in the affirmative three times and were then three times immersed. During the immersion ceremonies, the Pope withdrew to the *consignatorium*, to which the candidates, having put on new white garments, repaired, and had the sign of the cross placed on their foreheads by the Pope. All then returned to the basilica, where the Pope commenced the first Easter Mass and for the first time, just as day broke, the initiates were permitted to participate in the services. In the course of time the rites underwent some changes: on Holy Saturday the new fire was blessed and the paschal candle was lit: 'The death of Christ,' writes Duchesne, 'followed quickly by His resurrection, found an expressive image in the fire, candle, or lamp, which being extinguished, can be lit again.' Though the custom was not in use at Rome, three great lamps being used to light the candles borne before the Pope on Friday and Saturday, outside of Rome, in Northern Italy, Gaul, and Spain, the blessing of the candle was an ancient custom, and in the sixth century was permitted in the churches, except that of the Pope itself. The Easter candle was blessed by the archdeacon, who ascended the ambo and began to speak:

'O mira circa nos tuae pietatis dignatio! O inestimabilis dilectio caritatis! Ut servum redimeres filium tradidisti! O certe necessarium Adae peccatum, quod Christi morte delectum est. O felix culpa, quae talem ac tantum meruit habere redemptorem! O beata nox, quae sola meruit scire tempus et horam in qua Christus ab inferis resurrexit.'[1]

We have thus returned to the starting point of our inquiry.

[1] Mgr. L. Duchesne, *Christian Worship, Its Origin and Evolution*, tr. M. L. McLure (London, 1923), p. 254. For the account of the Easter ceremonies, I have followed Duchesne, ibid., pp. 247–57, 292–327, and E. O. James, *Christian Myth and Ritual* (London, 1933), pp. 99–122.

## CHAPTER VI

# *The Theory of Tragedy*

'What is the reason', asks St. Augustine in the third book of his *Confessions*, '. . . that a spectator desires to be made sad when he beholds doleful and tragical passages, which he himself could not endure to suffer? . . . and if the calamities of the person represented (either fallen out long since or utterly feigned) be so lamely set out, that no passion be moved in the spectator, he goes away surfeited and reporting scurvily of it. But if he be moved to passion, he sits it out very attentively, and even weeps for joy again. Are tears therefore loved, and passions?'[1] The happy combination of pagan learning and Christian compassion enabled Augustine to put his finger directly on the crucial spot of tragedy: why do we, the spectators, take pleasure in seeing a representation of suffering? Why are we both attracted to and repelled by the spectacle of the suffering of a fellow creature? This is indeed the paradox of tragedy, that we enjoy where we should suffer, that we suffer as we enjoy, that we should get so perverse a pleasure out of the depiction of human misery. Hitherto, we have considered this problem in its historical development; we have seen that our response to tragedy is a response deeply rooted in the past of man, which tragedy has the power to evoke afresh. I should like now to examine the problem from another angle of approach: this time from the point of view of the theory of tragedy, my intent being to show that both modes of procedure, the historical and the critical, though they start from opposite sides of the problem, so to speak, arrive in the end at the same destination.

[1] *St. Augustine's Confessions with an English Translation by William Watts*, 1631, ed. W. H. D. Rouse (London, 1912), I, pp. 101–3.

To begin with, there have been some theories of tragedy which quite candidly state that the pleasure taken in tragedy is indeed perverse, that it does unashamedly appeal to the brute and the mean in man. Such a view is very close to the Lucretian notion that we take pleasure in another's adversity, a notion to which Rousseau and Shelley inclined in some degree; but, while this theory of tragedy does recognize that man is not all angel, it does not come anywhere near an adequate explanation of the contradictory character of our response to tragedy. The pleasure in tragedy is not in the suffering *per se*, as though tragedy were merely an animated *grand guignol*, but in the use to which the spectacle of suffering is put. In tragedy, suffering is a means to an end, not the end in itself, and the tragic protagonist must be made to achieve victory at the moment of his deepest despair.

Nor does the Schopenhauerean theory that the end of tragedy is a fitting representation of the essential hopelessness of the human lot:

> '. . . the end of this highest poetical achievement is the representation of the terrible side of life. The unspeakable pain, the wail of humanity, the triumph of evil, the scornful mastery of chance, and the irretrievable fall of the just and innocent is here presented to us . . .'[1]

square with the actual effect of tragedy, which is ultimately optimistic in its character. But Schopenhauer sees in tragedy the complete extinction of the individual, the total loss of the ego in:

> '. . . resignation, the surrender, not merely of life, but the very will to live. Thus we see in tragedies the noblest men, after long conflict and suffering, at last renounce the ends they have so keenly followed, and all the pleasures of life forever, or else freely and joyfully surrender life itself.'[2]

Schopenhauer is indeed right in rejecting the siren claims of poetic justice, but in his reaction against it, he goes to the opposite extreme of denying justice altogether: 'The true sense of tragedy is . . . that . . . the hero atones for . . . the crime of existence itself.' Therefore for him that tragedy is best in which the mere necessity of living in itself

[1] Arthur Schopenhauer, *The World as Will and Idea* (London and New York, 1883), I, p. 326.
[2] Ibid., I, p. 327.

forces one man to injure another, not because he has provocation, but solely and precisely because of the very patternlessness of life itself:

'Lastly, the misfortune may be brought about by the mere position of the *dramatis personae* with regard to each other through their relations; so that there is no need either for a tremendous error or an unheard-of accident, nor yet for a character whose wickedness reaches the limits of human possibility; but characters of ordinary morality, under circumstances such as often occur, are so situated, with regard to each other that their position compels them, knowingly and with their eyes open, to do each other the greatest injury, without any one of them being entirely in the wrong.'[1]

But Schopenhauer is hard put to find examples of tragedy to prove his contention, and of the five plays he does instance he admits that one lacks the tragic conclusion, another he is forced to misread, two he quite completely misinterprets, and the fifth is scarcely of the stature as literature to be included with the others. Nevertheless, in justice to him, it can be said that he has described not tragedy but life before it is reformed by tragedy, though, even here, his larger view is open to serious question. The chaos of life is surely more obvious than its pattern, so that it comes as no surprise that the Schopenhaurean description, like that of Hobbes, should in our times seem to fit so well the appearance of things; it is as though Schopenhauer had laid down the programme for Kafka to follow: to create a world whose meaning is in its meaninglessness. But tragedy is at bottom man's most vehement protest against meaninglessness; it refuses to accept the dehumanization of man which the Schopenhaurean view of necessity entails; tragedy creates a pattern of human destiny in which man through suffering learns to live, not die. By striking at the freedom of man's will, by denying him freedom of choice, not even between good and evil, but the very possibility of choice at all, Schopenhauer denies the viability not only of tragedy but of life itself, at least as western man had always understood them.[2]

For Hegel, on the other hand, the ordering of experience is exactly

[1] Ibid., I, p. 329.

[2] Brunetière, certainly not as philosophical a critic as Schopenhauer, but with the willingness to consider more examples of tragedy than Schopenhauer did, in effect answered him when he insisted in *The Law of the Drama* on the primacy of free will in drama.

the pleasure to be derived from tragedy. For him, tragedy is the process and reconciliation; describing the nature of ancient tragedy, Hegel writes:

'. . . the twofold vindication of the mutually conflicting aspects are no doubt retained, but the *one-sided* mode under which they were maintained is cancelled, and the undisturbed ideal harmony brings back again that condition of the chorus, which attributes without reserve equal honour to all the gods. The true course of dramatic development consists in the annulment of *contradictions* viewed as such, in the reconciliation of the forces of human action, which alternately strive to negate each other in their conflict. Only so far is misfortune and suffering not the final issue, but rather the satisfaction of spirit, as for the first time, in virtue of such a conclusion, the necessity of all that particular individuals experience, is able to appear in complete accord with reason, and our emotional attitude is tranquillized on a true ethical basis, rudely shaken by the calamitous results to the heroes, but reconciled in the substantial facts.'[1]

For all the pontificality of his writing, Hegel has come very close to the understanding of the nature of the pleasure to be had from tragedy. His failure is not so much a failure of theory as it is his refusal to extend that theory from ancient tragedy to modern tragedy as well. His description of the essence of tragedy is intended to apply to ancient tragedy primarily:

'In ancient tragedy [he writes] it is the eternal justice which, as the absolute might of destiny, delivers and restores the harmony of the substantive being in its ethical character by its opposition to the particular forces which, in their strain to assert an independent subsistence, come into collision and which, in virtue of the rational ideality implied in its operations, satisfies us even where we see the downfall of particular men.'[2]

But instead of applying this principle to modern tragedy, Hegel chose instead to assert the differences rather than the similarities between ancient and modern tragedy, and thereby seriously qualified the value of his theory in its universal application. In their attempts

[1] G. W. F. Hegel, *The Philosophy of Fine Art*, tr. F. P. B. Osmaston (London, 1920), IV, p. 321.
[2] Ibid., IV, p. 340.

to distinguish themselves from their predecessors, the romantics were forced to rewrite the history of literature in terms of their special needs, and, as the men of the Renaissance, under the impetus of similar pressures, had devised a tripartite division of world history into ancient-medieval-modern and thereby established their unique place in history by means of this new scheme, so now the romantics recast history into a two-part arrangement based on these equations: ancient equals pagan equals classicism, and contrariwise, modern equals Christianity equals romantic; their position was thus secured and likewise made unique. It was therefore to their interests that the difference between the ancient and modern, that is, between the classical and the romantic, should be emphasized as much as possible and the similarities minimized. This thesis was a German romantic invention, though for its clearest expression we can turn to the English romantic critics, particularly those who were most impressed by the Germans.[1]

Modern tragedy, Hegel holds, emphasizes the unique individuality of its characters who are thereby rendered incapable of embodying ethical forces so that conflict has now become the result of the external accident of circumstances. Moreover, the objects of attention in modern tragedy are different from the ancient: they are not so much ethical powers as the history of Christ or of the saints; not so much the ethical implications of power, as the position of the king and his relation to his vassals; and the principal subject matters of the tragic drama have become questions of civic or private right, new aspects of family life, personal love or honour, with the chief emphasis on the uniqueness of the individual, his inner experience of heart and emotion; in short, the individuality of his distinct and separate personality. Conflict is, therefore, now lodged within the character itself and, as this character is marked by spiritual vacillation and distraction, it leads to weakness of indecision, fluctuations of reflection, and the endless weighing of reasons. Consequently, tragic reconciliation in the classic sense is made impossible; what justice there remains is more abstract and more cold than in ancient tragedy, and the protagonists '. . . are crushed by an actual force which they have defied in order to carry out their personal aims', and which they themselves must acknowledge to be just in its aims and results. To be sure, Shakespeare's characters represent the finest flowering of

[1] For the evidence for this statement see my article, 'English Treatment of the Classical-Romantic Problem', *MLQ*, VII (1946), pp. 477–88.

modern tragedy, but only within the limitations of this kind of tragedy:

'Unsupported by the sanction of the moral law, but rather carried onward by the formal necessity of their personality, they suffer themselves to be involved in their acts by the coil of external circumstances, or they plunge blindly therein and maintain themselves there by sheer force of will, even where all that they do is merely done because they are impelled to assert themselves against others, or because they have simply come to the particular point they have reached. The rise of insurgent passion, one essentially consonant with a certain type of character, one which has not as yet fully merged, but now secures its utmost expansion, this onward movement and process of a great soul, with all the intimate traits of its evolution, this picture of its self-destructive conflict with circumstances, human and objective conditions and results, is the main content of some of Shakespeare's most interesting tragedies.'[1]

Diversity, then, is the chief feature which distinguishes the modern from the ancient tragedy, but the price paid for variety is, in Hegel's opinion, too great; modern tragedy fails because, for all its fascinations, it is employed to exhibit the vagaries of the diverse characters of many individuals, and it does not have, nor can it have, the unifying ethical basis of ancient tragedy.

Hegel's theory of the pleasure taken in tragedy, profound as it is, seems to me to fail on three counts. In the first place, he does not see how his theory, designed to cover ancient tragedy, is also applicable to modern tragedy; more particularly, his error consists in identifying romantic tragedy, that is, the kind of tragedy written by Schiller, Goethe, Byron, and Shelley, with Shakespearean tragedy. His strictures apply well enough to the deficiencies of romantic tragedy; they do not apply to Shakespearean tragedy. For, as Bradley has shown in his essay, 'Hegel's Theory of Tragedy', Hegel glides too smoothly from the depiction of suffering to a reconciliation at once too easy and too complete; as a consequence, he does not realize that in the conclusions to Shakespearean tragedy, '. . . pain', as Bradley puts it, 'is mingled not merely with acquiescence, but with something like exultation'. Furthermore, Bradley continues, '. . . the tragic conflict is one not merely of good with evil, but also, and more essentially, of good with good', and he goes on to illustrate this

[1] G. W. F. Hegel, op. cit., IV, p. 340.

telling point with an analysis of *Macbeth* as a division of spirit involving conflict and waste. But the tragic catastrophe is more than a mere negation, as in Hegel; it has:

'. . . a second and affirmative aspect, which is the source of our feelings of reconciliation, whatever form they may assume. And this will be taken into account if we describe the catastrophe as the violent self-restitution of the divided spiritual unity. The necessity which acts and negates in it, that is to say, is yet of one substance with both the agents. *It* is divided against itself in them; they are *its* conflicting forces; and in restoring its unity through negation it affirms them, as far as they are compatible with their unity. The qualification is essential, since the hero, for all his affinity with that power, is, as the living man we see before us, not so compatible. He must die, and his union with "eternal justice" (which is more than "justice") must itself be "eternal" or ideal. But the qualification does not abolish what it qualifies. . . . He dies, and our hearts die with him; and yet his death matters nothing to us, or we even exult.'[1]

Hegel's second error, then, is his failure to utilize his own dialectic rightly; the reconciliation is not the mere addition of two opposites, but the creation on a higher level of a new and correspondingly more meaningful synthesis; the transformation is one of quality, not of quantity alone. Finally, Hegel lodges the effect of catharsis exclusively in the protagonist in the play so that it is with the protagonist's change alone that he is concerned. But the function of tragedy can be complete only with its effect on the spectator, with *his* change. Tragedy is essentially a social process, not a personal and individualistic act. Unfortunately, our romantic heritage of individualism has blinded us to the communal character of tragedy so that we have come to see it only as the pitiful protest of the overwhelmed, individual discreet unavailingly beating himself against a universe which is either relentless or indifferent, but which in any case cannot ever be amenable to man's noblest desires. The contemporary audience has been conditioned to accept as an accurate picture of the world the romantic rather than the classical view. No matter how harrowing were the scenes which they saw, no matter how severely their faith in God and man was questioned, the Greek and the Elizabethan audiences knew that as the outcome of the bitter passage they went through in the drama, as the price they had to pay, in the end, the way of the good

[1] Andrew C. Bradley, *Oxford Lectures on Poetry* (London and New York, p. 91).

would triumph over the way of the evil and they could continue to live in a world which they could understand as somehow participating in and even actively promoting their highest ends. But the members of the contemporary audience, like the protagonists of the tragedies they see, have been made the fools of time and terror; they are the strangers who come to the Castle, they are the accused in the Trial; they have been led to believe that they live in a universe which is indifferent to them and has no purpose beyond that of carrying out its inscrutable operations mechanically and efficiently; and they are alone, afraid, insecure, and unloved. Hence contemporary tragedy is rooted in a tremendous need for self-identification; the audience goes to the theatre not to judge and be judged, but to explain and be explained; it seeks endlessly to justify itself, to assert itself as made up of individuals who do count for something. It is Willy Loman, pathetically trying to explain away his failures, trying to amount to something, trying to be the unique Willy Loman and ending by being no man; it is Blanche Du Bois striving to satisfy desires she neither wants nor understands, finding her refuge in the womb of the warm bath. Like Willy and Blanche, the contemporary audience is the victim of a double doom: it is forced to live in an external universe which is hostile to it and it is tainted with an inner weakness not of its own making. To make choices, and to face the responsibilities of those choices, requires a strength which it has been led to believe it cannot have; it can only be the witness of its own weakness.

Instead of following the lead of Hegel and Bradley, contemporary criticism of tragedy has preferred to continue in the direction pointed out first by Hume and later by Coleridge. In his essay, 'Of Tragedy', Hume had suggested that the pleasure in tragedy is actually the pleasure of a composition so well executed as to seem more exciting and real than the representation itself; the pleasure to be had from the play, then, is in the appreciation of its eloquence. This idea, elaborated on by Coleridge and later by Croce, is the starting point for those critics of tragedy who wish to deny the ethical content of tragedy altogether.[1] In conformity with the definition of poetry he gave in the first lecture of the 1818 series on Shakespeare as:

[1] For an account of how the shift from the didactic interpretation of Aristotle in the Renaissance to the aesthetic rendering of Croce occurred, see A. H. Gilbert and H. L. Suggs, 'On the Relation of Horace to Aristotle in Literary Criticism', *JEGP*, XLVI 1947), pp. 233–47.

'. . . a species of composition, opposed to science, as having intellectual pleasure for its object, and as attaining its end by the use of language natural to us in a state of excitement,—but distinguished from other species of composition, not excluded by the former criterion, by permitting a pleasure from the whole consistent with a consciousness of pleasure from the component parts;—and the perfection of which is, to communicate from each part the greatest immediate pleasure compatible with the largest sum of pleasure on the whole, . . .'[1]

Coleridge thus laid the foundations of the organic theory of poetry and indicated the line which those who wished to avoid the traditional form-content problem were later to follow. So, for example, by defining a poem as '. . . a pattern of resolutions and balances and harmonizations, developed through a temporal scheme', Professor Cleanth Brooks is able to propose:

'. . . a kind of scale for determining the value of poetry. Low in the scale one would find a rather simple poetry in which the associations of the various elements that go to make up the poem are similar in tone and therefore can be unified under one rather simple attitude—poems of simple affection, positive, "external" satires, etc. Higher in the scale, one would find poems in which the variety and clash among the elements to be comprehended under a total attitude are sharper. In tragedy, where the clash is at its sharpest—where the tension between attraction and repulsion is most powerful—one would probably find the highest point in the scale.'[2]

The value of such a scale, he asserts, is that it utilizes criteria '. . . in terms of the organizations of the poems themselves—not by having to appeal to some outside scale of values'. But in practice the exponents of the organic theory must of necessity go outside the confines of the individual poem, and this is true not only when they apply their method to the exposition of a large poem, where it is almost inevitable that they must bring to bear on its elucidation a very large apparatus of information, but even to such a simple lyric as, for example, Herrick's 'Corinna's Going A-Maying', which Professor Brooks reads, rather astonishingly both in the light of his own

[1] Samuel Taylor Coleridge, *Essays and Lectures on Shakespeare and Some Other Old Poets and Dramatists* (London, 1909), pp. 10–11.
[2] Cleanth Brooks, *The Well-Wrought Urn* (New York, 1947), pp. 186, 229–30.

warning and of the simplicity of the poem itself, as '. . . a clash between the Christian and pagan world views'. I think that one can agree with him when he says that his analysis of the clothed daggers and naked babe images in *Macbeth* by no means expounds the whole of the meaning of the play, nor do the deliberate limitations of the method quite prepare us for such a statement concerning *Macbeth* as:

'. . . Macbeth is thus caught between the irrational and the rational. There is a sense, of course, in which every man is caught between them. Man must try to predict and plan and control his destiny. That is man's fate; and the struggle, if he is to realize himself as a man, cannot be avoided. The question, of course, which has always interested the tragic dramatist involves the terms on which the struggle is accepted and the protagonist's attitude toward fate and toward himself. Macbeth in his general concern for the future is typical—is Every Man. He becomes the typical tragic protagonist when he yields to pride and *hybris*.'[1]

This is well put, but the point is that in terms of Professor Brooks's own frame of reference it should not have been put at all.[2] But it is Professor John Crowe Ransom who goes the whole way in carrying out the formulae of Coleridge's organic theory of poetry as applied to tragedy. Professor Ransom does indeed recognize the ethical

[1] Ibid., p. 41.

[2] This tactic of severely bounding the frame of reference and then blithely going ahead to make whatever generalizations one wishes while at the same time insisting that everyone else remain within the circumscribed circle seems to be a favourite with those who pursue the method of imagery studies, which is a constituent part of the organic theory of poetry. For example, I find that for all the strictures he has heaped on Bradley's discussion of *Macbeth*, Mr. L. C. Knights finally manages to say pretty much the same things about the play as Bradley does, in words not so very different from Bradley's, and with nowhere near the same effect and penetration; see too how Mr. Edward A. Armstrong, after a most carefully guarded statement on the technique of investigation of Shakespeare's word-associations, *Shakespeare's Imagination, A Study of the Psychology of Association and Inspiration* (London, 1946), p. 41, comes to the conclusion, which is at once too narrow and too broad, that in Shakespeare's . . . 'imagination the ideas Life and Death were supreme. His thought constantly played between them, and other images ordered themselves in accordance with their relationship to these two supreme categories and the imagery most intimately associated with them. . . . There are certain other important contrasting images of almost equal relevance to Life and Death intimately connected with them and constantly like them such as Love and Hate, Light and Darkness.' Ibid., p. 44; cf. pp. 93–9. It is not easy to see how a writer of tragedy could very well avoid using such antitheses, and how this statement differentiates Shakespeare from other writers of tragedy I do not know. Cf. Lillian Hornstein, 'Analysis of Imagery: A Critique of Literary Method', *PMLA*, LVII (1942), pp. 638–53.

implications inherent in the Aristotelian catharsis, but manages to wrench the cause the other way:

'We must think of Aristotle as a true humanist, a Greek very close to his racial culture, and beyond Plato in his responsiveness, for having the noble and improbable insight that the tragic art purges men of their fears and makes them better men. But to grasp the technique of this purging, we have to make a configuration of our own, and go beyond Aristotle. I think the trick to try will be something like this: to see if the lavish, the all-but-incessant poetry with which the Greek dramatists invest their tragedy does not throw a decent obscurity over the terrible events and though of course if does not promise to avert these, at least it does immunize us against our terror.'[1]

But does the trick come off? Assuming for the moment the correctness of the description of the poetry of Greek drama as 'lavish and all-but-incessant', how does this analysis distinguish tragedy from, say, the epic? The skill in communication which is admired in tragedy is equally to be found in other genres and types as well, otherwise there is neither poetry nor poem to start with. Moreover, the language is here seen as something apart from and different from the text, as though it has an identity and independent motion of its own whose function it is to impress on the reader a sense other than that which is actually conveyed by the text and the pattern of the action. Finally, the concept of language as a curtain, or even a barrier, between the action and the spectator, if it has some degree of applicability to the work of those contemporary poets who are consciously using it for deliberate and recognized ends, is unknown to classical and Renaissance poetics and it implies a theory of the function of literature which goes counter to the main traditions of criticism from Plato onwards until it was redirected by the romantics.[2]

[1] John Crowe Ransom, 'The Literary Criticism of Aristotle', *The Kenyon Review*, X 1948), p. 393. By the way, is this a misreading of a passage in Mr. Kenneth Burke: 'The poet, in his pious or tragic rôle, would immunize us by stylistically infecting us with the disease. As we move towards the impious response, on the other hand, we get an 'allopathic" strategy of cure. We get the recourse to "antidote".' *The Philosophy of Literary Form* (Baton Rouge (La.), 1941), p. 65. But Mr. Burke's notion of stylistic immunization is here thought of as the mode of operation of tragedy and not as its end.

[2] There are some students of tragedy who, though unable to accept the non-judgment bias of the organic theory of poetry, yet cannot bring themselves to a whole-hearted commitment to the principle of ethicial judgment. Thus, Mr. F. L. Lucas defines tragedy as '. . . a representation of human unhappiness which pleases us notwithstanding by the

In view of the inadequacies of the theories of tragedy we have just considered here, we are left after all with Aristotle. I have deliberately gone this roundabout way to get to the *Poetics*, since it is necessary to see clearly what modifications and departures have been made in and from Aristotle's ideas on tragedy before they can be perceived in their own proper light. For the purpose of this discussion, the passage in the *Poetics*, 1452b30–1453a1, is, to my way of thinking, of crucial importance, and I use the translation of Professor Seymour Pitcher, which runs as follows:

'Since, then, the structure of the finest tragedy should not be simple, but complicated, and the tragedy should be imitative of fearful and pitiful events (for that is characteristic of this kind of imitation), first it is clear that the good and just men are not to be shown

truth with which it is seen and the skill with which it is communicated'. *Tragedy in Relation to Aristotle's Poetics* (New York, 1928), p. 60. Of course, the use of the word 'notwithstanding' completely begs the question since the problem of why a representation of human unhappiness should please us is still left unsettled. Professor Frye holds that Shakespeare's ultimate value lies in his having merely reproduced so faithfully and vividly the '. . . mutable many, the absolute illusion of throng, without attempting to inform it further than is essential to herding it into the five acts of a play'. *Romance and Tragedy* (Boston, 1922), p. 290, which rather gives the impression that Shakespeare, far from mastering the materials of his drama, was in fact mastered by them and just barely got them into the plays. Professor E. E. Stoll writes: 'And all that I can discover to alleviate our dismay when for the last time the curtain falls, is, apart from the life-giving spirit of poetry moving and hovering over the stage, the breadth and fairness, the exaltation and pity, in the presentation.' From *Art and Artifice in Shakespeare* in *Shakepeare Criticism*, 1919–35, ed. Anne Bradby (Oxford, 1936), pp. 75–6. Professor Theodore Spencer suggests that for the Elizabethans tragedy was merely a story that ended in death, *Death and Elizabethan Tragedy* (Cambridge (Mass.), 1936), pp. 232–3; on the other hand, Professor L. B. Campbell states that for the Elizabethans '. . . tragedies came to be regarded as indeed mirrors for magistrates and mirrors for all men whereby they might be either called to repentance or warned by the images of their own vices and passions to turn to virtue'. *Shakespeare's Tragic Heroes Slaves of Passion* (Cambridge, 1930), p. 37; the same conclusion is reached by Professor Bowers in his *Elizabethan Revenge Tragedy*, 1587–1642 (Prineton, 1940), p. 261. The most that Professor Willard Farnham grudgingly admits is that: 'All that Shakespeare alone will permit us to say is that the yoke of life is hard but supremely worth the bearing in the interest of the general good.' *The Medieval Heritage of Elizabethan Tragedy* (Berkeley (Cal.), 1936), p. 446; a view which is shared by Professor Howard Baker, *Induction to Tragedy* (Baton Rouge, La., 1939), p. 220. In his account of 'the penetration of Senecan sensibility', Mr. Eliot insists that the '. . . attitude of self-dramatization assumed by some of Shakespeare's heroes at moments of tragic intensity', an attitude characteristic of the Elizabethan dramatists as a whole, with the exception of Marlowe, is a terrible exposure of human weakness, the result of a philosophy which is '. . . the refuge for the individual in an indifferent or hostile world too big for him', 'Shakespeare and the Stoicism of Seneca' in Brady, op. cit., pp. 213, 215. But see on this Professor Charlton's Introduction to his edition of *William Alexander*.

changing from good fortune to bad (for that is neither fearful nor pitiful, but repulsive); nor the wicked man from obscurity to good fortune (for that is most unsuited to tragedy of all since it has none of the qualities it should have—that is to say, it is not friendly to mankind, it is not pitiful, and it is not fearful); nor, again, is the thorough scoundrel necessarily to fall from good fortune to bad (for although such a situation would show friendliness to mankind, it would have neither pity nor fear, since the one is that we feel concerning the man who does not deserve his misfortune, the other concerning the man who is like us—so that what happens will be neither pitiful nor fearful). The man who is in the midst, then, of these is left. Such a man is one who does not differ from us in virtue and sense of justice nor change from bad fortune through evil and wickedness, but through some error; he is of those who are in great repute and good fortune, like Oedipus and Thysetes and the notable men from such families.'[1]

The central problem raised in this statement of the nature of tragedy rests, it seems to me, in the paradox that 'the man in the midst' who does not differ from us in virtue and sense of justice should fall, and that this fall should be a source of aesthetic and ethical satisfaction to us as the spectators of that fall. It is, of course, perfectly clear that Aristotle at the very outset dismisses the idea of poetic justice, though it had respectable backing and offered an easy way out of the dilemma. A fragment from the *Aletes* of Sophocles is an excellent formulation of the idea of poetic justice which was available to Aristotle:

'Strange, that impious men, sprung from wicked parents, should prosper, while good men of generous breed should be unfortunate! It is not right that heaven should deal so with men. The gods should manifestly reward the pious, and the unrighteous should suffer some manifest punishment for their wickedness. Then the wicked man would not flourish.'[2]

But this notion, which received its classic expression in the medieval fall of princes and wheel of fortune themes, is quite explicitly rejected by Aristotle, for, though it shows friendliness to mankind, that is, though we cannot help but approve the punishment of mani-

[1] Seymour Pitcher, 'Aristotle's Good and Just Heroes', *PQ*, XXIV (1945), p. 6.
[2] Fragment 107, tr. F. M. Cornford.

fest wickedness, it is neither pitiful nor fearful; on the contrary, there is perhaps too much exultation in us. More important, this is too easy a solution to the problem of evil; experience all too bitterly teaches us that the way of the world is much too often quite otherwise. In other words, poetic justice is essentially a shabby device intended to intrude the moral element into tragedy at the expense of the medium; it is propaganda. When John Dennis in his outspoken way stated his credo:

'I conceive that every Tragedy ought to be a very solemn Lecture, inculcating a particular Providence, and showing it plainly protecting the good, and chastizing the bad, or at least the violent: and that if it is otherwise, it is either an empty amusement, or a scandalous and pernicious libel upon the government of the world.'[1]

he was merely making explicit a bias for the moral function of art which has exercised a continuous influence on art from the complaints of Theognis to the Motion Picture Production Code under which all Hollywood films are made to-day. Both poetic justice and tragedy look to the establishment of justice as the end which they seek to accomplish, but they differ completely in the means of achieving that end, and therein lies the measure of their difference. In bourgeois tragedy, for example, both hero and villain get their just deserts by virtue of a formula which is the aesthetic and ethical manifestation of a society which bases its values on accumulation, and which defines goodness and badness in terms of the mere quantity of that accumulation. In such a system of calculation, virtue is made to pay off as a result of a carefully made appraisal of the ostensible superiority of reward for the good done (or, more exactly, for the evil not done) over punishment precisely in the same manner as the business man calculates the risk in a deal of making or losing money. Theoretically, the maxim of 'nothing ventured, nothing gained' is supposed to govern the business ethic, but the venture is so hedged round with qualifications and assurances and manipulations that the element of risk has been reduced to its barest minimum. At the same time, the appeal to morality, the exhortation to be good, as an insurance proposition, a calculated risk that one ought not to take unnecessary chances (as Pascal so vulgarly argued), results in a kind of art which rivets man to a pattern of behaviour at once mean and small,

[1] John Dennis, *The Advancement and Reformation of Modern Poetry* (London, 1701), p. A6v.

the very antithesis of the true tragic pattern.[1] I have mentioned the Motion Picture Production Code; no consideration of the problem of poetic justice ought to omit taking into account the provisions of the Code for the simple and terrifying reason that, while plays affect at the most only thousands of spectators, and these constituting a fairly homogeneous and educated audience, the motion pictures produced under the Code are shown to something like 200,000,000 people weekly all over the world, an audience almost as diverse as is its numbers, and extremely susceptible to what they see. The general principles upon which the Code is based are as follow:

1. No picture shall be produced which will lower the moral standards of those who see it. Hence, the sympathy of the audience shall never be thrown to the side of crime, wrongdoing, evil or sin.
2. Correct standards of life, subject only to the requirements of drama and entertainment shall be presented.
3. Law, natural or human, shall not be ridiculed, nor shall sympathy be created for its violation.

Among the specific applications of these basic principles, I cull these:

Revenge in modern times shall not be justified.

The use of liquor in American life, when not required by the plot or for proper characterization, will not be shown.

Obscenity in word, gesture, reference, song, joke, or by suggestion (even when likely to be understood by only part of the audience) is forbidden.

Dances which emphasize indecent movements are to be regarded as obscene.

The treatment of bedrooms must be governed by good taste and delicacy.

[1] For Elizabethan bourgeois tragedy, see Louis B. Wright, *Middle-Class Culture in Elizabethan England* (Chapel Hill (North Carolina), 1935); and Henry H. Adams, *English Domestic or Homiletic Tragedy*, 1575–1672 (New York and Oxford, 1943). For eighteenth-century bourgeois tragedy, see Ernest Bernbaum, *The Drama of Sensibility* (Cambridge (Mass.), 1925); Clarence C. Green, *The Neo-Classic Theory of Tragedy in England During the Eighteenth Century* (Cambridge (Mass.) and Oxford, 1934); and Fred D. Nolte, *The Early Middle Class Drama* (1696–1774) (Lancaster, Pa., 1935). For the development of romantic sentimentalism which underlies the aesthetics of bourgeois tragedy, see Hoxie N. Fairchild, *Religious Trends in English Poetry* (New York and Oxford, 1939): '. . . the romanticism of the 1780–1830 period is simply Protestant Christianity in a more or less delightfully phosphorescent state of decay', p. 538.

And here are the complete sections on sex and religion:

II. Sex.

The sanctity of the institution of marriage and the home shall be upheld. Pictures shall not infer that low forms of sex relationship are the accepted or common thing.

1. Adultery, sometimes necessary to the plot, must not be explicitly treated, or justified, or presented attractively.
2. Scenes of passion.
   (*a*) They should not be introduced when not essential to the plot.
   (*b*) Excessive and lustful kissing, lustful embraces, suggestive postures and gestures, are not to be shown.
   (*c*) In general, passion should be so treated that these scenes do not stimulate the lower and baser element.
3. Seduction and rape.
   (*a*) They should never be more than suggested, and only when essential for the plot, and even then never shown by explicit method.
   (*b*) They are never the proper subject for comedy.
4. Sex perversion or any inference of it is forbidden.
5. White slavery shall not be treated.
6. Miscegnation (sex relationship between the black and white races) is forbidden.
7. Sex hygiene and venereal diseases are not subjects for motion pictures.
8. Scenes of actual childbirth, in fact or in silhouette, are never to be presented.
9. Children's sex organs are never to be exposed.

VIII. Religion.

1. No film or episode may throw ridicule on any religious faith.
2. Ministers of religion in their characters as ministers of religion should not be used as comic characters or as villains.
3. Ceremonies of a definite religion should be carefully and respectfully handled.

Now follows the arguments advanced for supporting the general principles of the Code; I have reduced them to simple propositions, though the language of the original is often retained:

1. Motion pictures are entertainment.
2. Entertainment can be helpful or harmful to the human race.
3. The moral importance of entertainment has been universally recognized.
4. Correct entertainment raises the whole standard of a nation; wrong entertainment lowers it.
5. Motion pictures, like all the arts, have the same object, that of presenting human thought, emotion, and experience, in terms of an appeal to the soul through the senses.
6. Art can be morally good or morally evil in its effects.

   *Note:* It has often been argued that art in itself is unmoral, neither good nor bad. This is perhaps true of the *Thing* which is music, painting, poetry, etc. But the thing is the *Product* of some person's mind, and the intention of that mind was either good or bad morally when it produced the thing. Besides, the thing has its *Effect* upon those who come in contact with it. In both these ways, that is, as a product of a mind and as the cause of definite effects, it has a deep moral significance and an unmistakable moral quality.
7. Motion pictures reproduce the morality of the men who make them and affect the moral standards of those who see them.
8. In view of the mass appeal of the movies, its moral effects are particularly striking.
9. The movies appeal to every class and reach all places; in this it differs from the other arts, which are limited in their appeal to the mature few.
10. In general, the mobility, popularity, accessibility, emotional appeal, vividness, straightforward presentation of fact in the film make for more intimate contact with a larger audience and for greater emotional appeal, and hence its greater responsibility.

From this it follows that, and here I quote fully:

1. No picture shall be produced which will lower the moral standards of those who see it. Hence the sympathy of the audience should never be thrown to the side of crime, wrongdoing, evil, or sin.

This is done:

1. When evil is made to appear attractive or alluring, and good is made to appear unattractive.
2. When the sympathy of the audience is thrown on the side of crime, wrongdoing, evil, sin. The same thing is true of a film that would throw sympathy against goodness, honour, innocence, purity or honesty.

*Note:* Sympathy with a person who sins is not the same as sympathy with the sin or crime of which he is guilty. We may feel sorry for the plight of the murderer or even understand the circumstances which led him to his crime. We may not feel sympathy with the wrong which he has done.

The presentation of evil is often essential for art or fiction or drama. This in itself is not wrong, provided:

(*a*) That evil is not presented alluringly. Even if later in the film the evil is condemned or punished, it must not be allowed to appear so attractive that the audiences' emotions are drawn to desire or approve so strongly that later the condemnation is forgotten and only the apparent joy of the sin is remembered.

(*b*) That throughout, the audience feels sure that evil is wrong and good is right.

The Code then goes on to detail various prohibitions and gives reasons for these prohibitions, the two fundamental arguments for them being, first, that motion pictures appeal to a vast, immature audience which must not be 'hardened', and second, that the effect of motion pictures on this audience is so stimulating that it must be kept in check:

'The effect of nudity or semi-nudity upon the normal man or woman, and much more upon the young and immature persons, has been honestly recognized by all lawmakers and moralists. Hence the fact that the nude or semi-nude body may be beautiful does not make its use in the films moral. For, in addition to its beauty, the effect of the nude or semi-nude body on the normal individual must be taken into consideration.'[1]

[1] These citations are taken from the mimeographed copy of the Motion Picture Production Code and from the Appendix to Ruth A. Inglis, *Freedom of the Movies* (Chicago 1947), pp. 205–19.

I have quoted these passages at some length since they are not easily accessible nor are they ordinarily found in critical discussions, yet they express the point of view of poetic justice so baldly and in such humorless detail and are, moreover, of such great influence on the most popular and influential of the arts, that they bring the problem of poetic justice in particular and of the relation of art to society in general into the sharpest focus. I leave out of consideration the fact that the Code was written in large part by a Jesuit priest (the language of the Code is obviously revealing) and is administered by a Catholic, for the reason that both Protestants and Jews co-operated with the Catholics in the Legion of Decency campaign to secure the adoption of the Code and have themselves organized to secure the ends which the Catholics have sought and have mainly gained. The sad truth is that the men who make motion pictures, and I do not mean by this the men who write and act out the scenarios, who direct the actors, or who turn the cameras, but the men who own the studios (for the most part, the New York and California bankers who gained control of the studios during the depression and have kept it ever since) and therefore control their output, these men do not need the guidance of the Code, for, like the men who own the newspapers and the radio stations and the mass circulation magazines, they are as anxious as the proponents of the Code that the image of life which the Code dictates be imposed as real on the minds of the mass of people and be accepted by them. It seems to follow that, when, as in the case of the motion pictures, a mass audience can be brought into regular and profitable contact with an art form on a mass scale, it becomes imperative that the outcome of the drama can never be left to chance and that the conventional code of behaviour must be upheld; the more attractive the appeal and the more responsive the audience, the more stringent the censorship which is justified by the conviction that the people cannot be trusted.

Poetic justice, then, stems from the distrust of the audience and is intended to bring about mass deception on a mass scale. But tragedy can exist only when the issue is left in doubt, when the conflict of forces is left free to play itself out, when the audience can be trusted to understand what is at stake; contrariwise, in an art form which is dominated by the concept of poetic justice, truth cannot be allowed freely to emerge from the clash of opposing forces, but is imposed on the process from the outside, so that what does finally appear is necessarily emasculated, narrowly defined, and partisan. Concealed behind the Motion Picture Production Code are alarming attitudes toward the people and the kind of life they are supposed to lead. In the first place, the Code is based on a rather open contempt for people, a lack of trust in their ability to recognize and resist corruption, and with this contempt is allied the desire to impose on the people by covert means what they would not accept if presented to them in its open state. Second, the Code deliberately wrenches the experience of life into a predetermined and sterile pattern; all the noble issues which confront man are dulled down, falsified, and made to fit into a predetermined and stifling parochialism. Third, virtue and vice are defined in a way at once narrow and vague; narrow in the sense that it is confined to the pettiness of custom; vague in the sense that it is based on amorphous moral stereotypes. Fourth, the provisions of the Code create in effect an artificial system of values which by prohibiting virtually every action which dares or questions results in holding up and making safe from criticism the *status quo*. Finally, the Code succeeds in accomplishing what it expressly seeks to avoid: it is so restrictive that unless means to circumvent had been found, no motion pictures could be made at all, yet to get around the provisions of the Code, recourse to hypocrisy, artificiality, and falsity had inevitably to be made, with the end that instead of exemplifying the moral values of the Code, the motion pictures made under its provisions are perfect demonstrations of what slyness, suggestiveness, and double-dealing can accomplish. This, then, is the final triumph of poetic justice.

Aristotle rejects poetic justice, if not for the social reasons I have advanced, then certainly for aesthetic reasons, and in rejecting poetic justice, he rejects propaganda as well, poetic justice being the expression in an art form of orthodoxy in any shape. For Aristotle, tragedy must fulfil three requirements: the protagonist must be capable of arousing our pity because he does not deserve his misfortune; he must be capable of arousing our fear, since he is a man like us, that is, he is not innately evil, and, but for an error committed not deliberately but rather through ignorance, would not suffer his fall; and, finally, the action must exhibit friendliness to mankind, that is, we must approve the ultimate wisdom of the design. All three must be present together, and Aristotle condemns those plays which have one or two of the elements in combination, but not all three together. Now, it is true that in the *Nicomachean Ethics* he says that: 'Works of art have their merit in themselves, so that it is enough if they are produced having a certain quality of their own,'[1] but the question remains, what is this intrinsic merit of works of art which produces their proper quality? At the outset of the *Ethics*, Aristotle had already made this observation:

'It is true that a certain variety is to be observed among the ends at which the arts and sciences aim: in some cases the activity of practising the art is itself the end, whereas in others the end is some product over and above the mere exercise of the art; and in the arts whose ends are certain things beside the practice of the arts themselves, these products are essentially superior in value to the activities.'[2]

Later on, he points out that the pursuit of good appears to be one thing in one pursuit of art and another in another, and he therefore asks, what definition of the Good will then hold true in all the arts? His answer succinctly stated is: '. . . that for the sake of which everything else is done'. He elaborates on this principle as follows:

'Now there appear to be several ends at which our actions aim; but as we choose some of them—for instance, wealth, or flutes, and instruments generally—as a means to something else, it is clear that not all of them are final ends; whereas the Supreme Good seems to be something final or perfect. Consequently, if there be some one thing which alone is a final end, this thing—or if there be several final ends, the one among them which is the most final—will be the Good which we are seeking. In speaking of degrees of finality, we mean that a thing pursued as an end in itself is more final than one pursued as a means to something else, and that a thing never chosen as a means to anything else is more final than things chosen both as ends in themselves and as means to that thing and accordingly a thing chosen always as an end and never as a means we call absolutely final. Now happiness above all else appears to be absolutely final in this sense, since we always choose it for its own sake and never as a means to something else; whereas honour, pleasure, intelligence, and excellence in its various forms, we choose indeed for their own sakes (since we should be glad to have each of them although no extraneous advantage resulted from it), but we also choose them for the sake of happiness, in the belief that they will be a means to our

[1] Aristotle, *The Nicomachean Ethics*, tr. H. Rackham (London, 1926), II, iv, 3.
[2] Ibid., I, i, 2.

securing it. But no one chooses happiness for the sake of honour, pleasure, etc., nor as a means to anything whatever other than itself.'[1]

In *The Rhetoric*, Aristotle carefully distinguishes between the right use, leading to the greatest benefit, and the wrong use, leading to an equal amount of harm, of all good things,[2] and he points out that what distinguishes the sophist in dialectics is not the faculty but the moral purpose. There are, therefore, two ends to be sought for all things: one, the immediate end of the form *per se* reaching its fullest expression and flowering, becoming perfect in itself; and the other, the ultimate end, which it shares with all things, tending toward and contributing to the ascent to the highest good, the two together being parts of the same process leading to the same goal. If we apply these criteria to tragedy, we find that it is ethical in its ends, both within the terms of the nature of its medium, that is to say, the pattern of action of characters who choose and avoid on the basis of their moral bent, for '. . . it is always in actions that goodness is present',[3] for of the six constituent parts on which the quality of tragedy depends:

'The most important of these is the arrangement of the incidents, for tragedy is not a representation of men but a piece of action, of life, of happiness and unhappiness, which comes under the head of action, and the end aimed at is the representation not of qualities of character but of some action; and while character makes men what they are, it is the scenes they act in that make them happy or the opposite.'[4]

and within the terms of the larger scheme of things, since all things that men do are done for the sake of happiness which is '. . . a certain activity of soul in conformity with perfect virtue'.[5] So, without once mentioning Plato, Aristotle has restored art to its proper place.

Repugnant as Plato's ideas on the relations of art to society may be to us, there is no doubt that the problems he raised are of tremendous concern to us still and cannot be easily settled; certainly, neither the notion of the poet as the unacknowledged legislator of the world, as Sidney and Shelley would so enthusiastically have us believe,

[1] Ibid., I, vii, 2–5.
[2] Aristotle, *The 'Art' of Rhetoric*, tr. John H. Frere (London, 1926), I, i, 13.
[3] Aristotle, *The Metaphysics*, XIII, iii, 10, 1078a.
[4] Aristotle, *The Poetics*, tr. W. Hamilton Fyfe (London, 1927), VI, 12.
[5] *Ethics*, I, xiii, 1.

nor the recourse to poetic justice, is adequate to the solution of the dilemma posed by Plato, nor will it do to take refuge in a quasi-Coleridgean poetics which excludes the content of literature altogether. From the *Ion* to the *Laws*, the problem of the poet's function in society is never far from Plato's thought. In the *Ion*, he shows that the method of inspiration by which the poet works, noble as it is, does not, however, lead to accurate and useful knowledge: 'And why in Heaven's name, Ion, if you are the best man among the Greeks as an elocutionist and as a general, do you travel around reciting to the Greeks, but never lead an army?'[1] though Ion quite misses the irony of the question. In the *Meno*, Plato goes on to assert an absolute standard of truth attainable only by one kind of approach which is certainly not the method of poetry, and in the *Symposium* he begins to cut out from under the feet of the artist his preoccupation with the things of this world by proclaiming '. . . that life above all others which man should live, in the contemplation of beauty absolute'.[2] This distinction between the body and the soul is carried to an even greater length in the *Phaedo*, which, though it contains no specific references to poetry, leads to certain conclusions about it which are unmistakable; in the words of Professor Greene, these are:

> 'Knowledge of the truth must mean knowledge of universals; to concern oneself only with the world of sense is to shut oneself off from the only region where truth can be found. Therefore the poet who attempts to convey truth simply by the use of sensible images is lending himself to deception. In order to make sure that his poems give some sort of knowledge or truth, he must choose his images in such a way that the reader or hearer shall be reminded by the particulars of the universals. Further, Plato would deprecate any attempt by the poet to appeal so strongly to the emotions that the mind would think only of the sensible images, and forget to pass beyond them to the realities that can be apprehended only by the mind.'[3]

With the *Republic*, all the implications with regard to poetry are brought clearly to the surface and there subjected to a barrage of criticisms, ethical, metaphysical, and epistemological, but not strictly aesthetic, in their nature. However, a distinction of this sort is actually irrelevant both on historical and methodological grounds, since

[1] *Ion*, 54O*d*, tr. A. H. Gilbert.
[2] *Symposium*, 211, tr. Jowett.
[3] William Chase Greene, 'Plato's View of Poetry', *HSCP*, XXIX (1918), p. 28.

it played no important rôle in the history and practice of criticism from Plato on; indeed, the refusal to make this distinction may well be Plato's legacy to criticism, as Mr. Eliot has rather wryly observed in *A Dialogue on Dramatic Poetry*: 'You can never draw the line between aesthetic criticism and moral and social criticism; you cannot draw a line between criticism and metaphysics; you start with literary criticism, and however rigorous an aesthete you may be, you are over the frontier into something else sooner or later.'[1] To return to the *Republic*: first, the poets are accused of telling lies about the gods as well as depicting them in their worst moments, but, Plato argues, since God is both good and invariable, he should not be presented as being the cause of evil, nor as subject to other powers, nor as a deceiver. Particularly should neither gods nor heroes be shown in fearful moods nor lamenting, not because such passages are '. . . unpoetic and displeasing for the rabble to hear, but because the more poetic they are the less fit they are for the ears of boys and men trained to be free and to fear servitude more than death'.[2] In short, harmful stories must be forbidden '. . . that they may not produce in the young a strong inclination to evil'. But the guardians are to imitate '. . . the characters of the courageous, wise, holy, free, and the like' and the law must be laid down:

'. . . that the immoral and unrestrained and false and ungraceful cannot be presented in the images of animals or in architecture or in any other art, and that a person of that sort of character shall not be allowed to work among us, in order that our guardians may not be brought up among ugly forms as though in a bad pasture, where every day they pluck and feed on all manner of things, a little at a time, until at last they have unwittingly gathered into their souls a great mass of ills.'

But another kind of art is eminently desirable, for, Socrates continues:

'Are we not rather to seek for artists of a higher genius who are able to discover the nature of the beautiful and the graceful, in order that the young men, as though living in a healthful spot, may suck virtue in everywhere, and the influence of beautiful works may always be exercised on their sight and hearing, like breezes bringing

[1] T. S. Eliot, *Selected Essays*, 1917–32 (London and New York, 1932), p. 92.
[2] *The Republic*, III, 386A, tr. A. H. Gilbert.

health from happy climes, and may lead them unconsciously to resemble and love the beauty of reason with which they are in accord?'[1]

Thus, not all artists are to be expelled from the state but only those whose art is not conducive to the best interests of the state; Gulley Jimson, however, must go. But in Book X there is a shift in the reasons for the condemnation of poetry; now the ground of criticism is that it is imitative, for it is thrice removed from reality and is therefore incapable of leading us to the truth. Plato here repeats and amplifies the arguments already given in the *Ion* in order to draw the opposition between poetry and dialectic and, in point of fact, between every other means of attaining knowledge and dialectic, as sharply as he can. We must realize to the full how completely committed to the supremacy of dialectic Plato is to appreciate why his opposition to the poets is so bitter. For him, there exists a sure body of knowledge which can lead to the attainment of virtue; this body of knowledge is fixed, permanent, and accessible to man by the exercise of the right mode of apprehending it, but by that mode alone, that is, by dialectic. In the *Phaedo*, Socrates gets Simmias to admit that there exist absolute beauty, absolute justice, and absolute truth, but none of these has ever been or ever can be reached through the senses; they can be reached only by the mind alone, undistracted by the senses: '. . . if we would have pure knowledge of anything we must be quit of the body—the soul in herself must behold things in themselves; and then we shall attain the wisdom which we desire, and of which we say that we are lovers', nor does he shrink from the logical consequence of this position, '. . . not while we live, but after death'.[2] Therefore, the real world is not the world of sense, but the world of pure essences which we can but imperfectly grasp while in our bodily state. Here, of course, we reach the twin doctrines of ideas and of recollection which at first glance would seem to place insuperable obstacles in the path of obtaining knowledge, but Plato draws quite the opposite conclusions from his epistemology, for, says Socrates, since this knowledge does exist, and since the soul must always have possessed it, therefore '. . . we shall be better and braver and less helpless if we think that we ought to inquire, than we should have been if we indulged in the idle fancy that there was no knowing and no use in seeking to know what we do not know;—that is a theme upon which I am ready to fight, in word and deed, to the ut-

[1] Ibid., III, 400D. [2] *The Phaedo*, II, pp. 205–6, tr. Jowett.

most of my power.'[1] But we can inquire only by the method of dialectic which in the *Republic* is described now as the means of attaining to the truth and now as the truth itself, that is, dialectic is both the means to the good life and the way of the good life itself. Hence, Plato's repudiation of the poets is not the result of a perverse whim but the logical deduction from the very intent of his philosophy. Indeed, one can almost say that for Plato the rejection of the poets is associated in his mind with the rejection of the doctrine of flux, against which, as Aristotle later pointed out, he so violently revolted:

> 'Nor can we reasonably say, Cratylus, that there is knowledge at all if everything is in a state of transition and there is nothing abiding; for knowledge too cannot continue to be knowledge unless continuing always to abide and exist. But if the very nature of knowledge changes, at the same time when the change occurs there will be no knowledge; and if the transition is always going on, there will always be no knowledge, and, according to this view, there will be no one to know and nothing to be known: but if that which knows and that which is known exists ever, and the beautiful and the good and every other thing also exists, then I do not think that they can resemble a process of flux, as we were just now supposing.'[2]

Stability and order, then, underlie Plato's whole thought, so much so that, in the *Timaeus*, they are imposed on the universe at the very moment of its creation, and in the *Symposium* are made to constitute the very essence of being, that is, of God. Thus, Plato's attitude toward the poets is no light thing, and in the *Laws*, where he gets down to rock-bottom cases and is not so much concerned with a theoretical defence of dialectic as with instituting a workable state, he has the Athenian Stranger say: 'The argument affirms that any change whatever except from evil is the most dangerous of all things; this is true in the case of the seasons and the winds, in the management of our bodies and the habits of our minds—true of all things except, as I said before, of the bad.'[3] Therefore even the plays of children are to be used to implant 'a reverence for antiquity', and their rhythms and their music, their dances and their songs, are to be imitative only of the good. Words which inspire despondency, evil omens, and fore-

[1] *The Meno*, II, p. 47, tr. Jowett. [2] *The Cratylus*, I, p. 388, tr. Jowett.
[3] *The Laws*, V. p. 178, tr. Jowett.

bodings are to be avoided and the poet '. . . shall compose nothing contrary to the ideas of the lawful, or just, or beautiful, or good, which are allowed to the state'.[1]

It is easy enough to dismiss Plato's state as 'outrageously totalitarian', 'a mechanical monster', and 'a totalitarian nightmare',[2] but if there is a fault to be found in Plato's treatment of the poets, it is the fault of a too logical consistency, for, if the ultimate end of society is indeed order and stability—and it is difficult to find many who will question that proposition—then Plato is certainly right in being so wary of any social force whose effects cannot be predicted or controlled, and the artist is just such a social force. In any case, the objection to Plato has very seldom been on the grounds that his state is so totalitarian, this being a rather recent argument; on the contrary, the criticism has almost always been that Plato erred in singling out the poets for his special disapproval, and almost every reply to him has been put in these terms, that he failed to understand the true nature of the poet, which was that the poet could and would do exactly what Plato wanted of him, if indeed not more so. Roughly speaking, until the time of the romantics, the artist was not conceived of, nor did he conceive of himself, as a critic of society; on the contrary, his duty lay in enhancing by the power and pleasure of his art those values upon which society traditionally rested. There is a striking passage in the *Statesman* which illustrates this attitude quite neatly. The Eleatic Stranger is talking with the younger Socrates about the problem of obeying the law. Suppose, he says, that everyone recalls the countless indignities he has suffered at the hands of physicians and pilots; suppose that we were to determine that they should no longer be allowed to exercise their crafts without regulation; and so let us suppose that we call an assembly of all those people who are interested in these crafts, whether they know anything about these crafts or not, and that this assemblage then lays down the rules of the practice of these crafts, obedience to which the pilots and doctors are to be tested annually in open court; in addition, says the Stranger:

'. . . we shall have to enact that if anyone is detected enquiring into piloting and navigation, or into health and the true nature of medi-

[1] Ibid., V, p. 182.

[2] These phrases are from Herschel Baker, *The Dignity of Man* (Cambridge (Mass.), 1947).

cine, or about the winds, or other conditions of the atmosphere, contrary to the written rules, and has any ingenious notions about such matters, he is not to be called a pilot or physician, but a cloudy prating sophist;—further, on the ground that he is a corrupter of the young, who would persuade them to follow the art of medicine or piloting in an unlawful manner, and to exercise an arbitrary rule over their patients or ships, anyone who is qualified by law may inform against him, and indict him in some court, then if he is found to be persuading any, whether young or old, to act contrary to the written law, he is to be punished with the utmost rigour; for no one should be presumed to be wiser than the laws; and as touching healing and health and piloting and navigation, the nature of them is known to all, for anybody may learn the written laws and the national customs. If such were the method of procedure, Socrates, about these sciences and about generalship, and any branch of hunting, or about painting or imitation in general, or carpentry, or any sort of handicraft, or husbandry, or planting, or if we were to see an art of rearing horses, or tending herds, or divination, or any ministerial service, or draught-playing, or any science conversant with number, whether simple or square or cube, or comprising motion,—I say, if all these things were done in this way according to art, what would be the result?'

And the younger Socrates bravely and democratically answers:

'All the arts would utterly perish, and could never be recovered, because enquiry would be unlawful. And human life, which is bad enough already, would then become utterly unendurable.'[1]

At first hearing, one would think that Plato has himself utterly demolished his own state, and with it come tumbling down all the totalitarianisms of our own day. But it transpires that the Stranger is not at all interested in defending freedom of inquiry. Quite the opposite; in fact, it turns out that he is arguing for the right of the scientific ruler to transcend the law in the light of his superior knowledge; the real enemies of the state are precisely freedom and the unrestrained voice of the people. The Stranger asks:

'May not any man, rich or poor, with or without laws, with the will of the citizens or against the will of the citizens, do what is for

[1] *The Statesman*, IV, pp. 502–3, tr. Jowett.

their interest? Is not this the true principle of government, according to which the wise and good man will order the affairs of his subjects? . . . Nor can wise rulers ever err while they, observing the one great rule of distributing justice to the citizens with intelligence and skill, are able to preserve them, and, as far as may be, to make them better from being worse.'[1]

Wisdom and rulership confirm themselves; truth resides not with the artist, not with the people, but with the ruler, so that, in effect, power and truth have become interchangeable entities.

The problem of the ethical content of art turns out to be not the wholesale rejection of the artist, which would be a problem easily disposed of, but the much more subtle and difficult one of determining the direction of the content of art. Even the most severe and stringent polemics against art, from those of the Church Fathers to the Puritan tracts to our own totalitarian dogmas, have not failed to make this fundamental and significant distinction. The fulminations against art made by the Christians were directed not against art itself so much as against the kind of art which did not meet their needs, and there is no real evidence for a thorough-going demand for the complete cessation of art; rather, the demand was for a Christian redirection of art. In criticizing the decorations of the school library in which he worked, St. Bernard of Clairvaux does not object to them as art objects but rather to their distracting effects: '*In fine*,' he writes in the *Apologia ad Willelmum*, 'on all sides there appears so rich and so amazing a variety of forms that it is more delightful to read the marbles than the manuscripts, and to spend the whole day in admiring these things, piece by piece, rather than in meditating on the Law Divine.'[2] Indeed, the Platonic conception of the fecundity of God, introduced into Christianity via Neo-Platonism, could not but counterweigh the ascetic repudiation of art, for, if out of God's plenitude had come all the diverse forms around us, how can we fail to see in them the evidences of God's goodness? The doctrine of lights, given its form by Dionysius the Areopagite and its Christian cachet by John the Scot, perpetuated the love of art in the face of persistent iconoclastic revulsions. In his poem describing the doors of the central west portal of St.-Denis, the Abbot Suger writes:

[1] Ibid., V, p. 500.

[2] Translated by Professor Erwin Panofsky in the Introduction to his *Abbot Suger on the Abbey Church of St.-Denis and its Art Treasures* (Princeton, New Jersey, 1946), p. 5.

*Whoever thou art, if thou seekest to extol the glory of these doors,*
*Marvel not at the gold and expense but at the craftmanship of the work.*
*Bright is the noble work; but, being nobly bright, the work*
*Should brighten the minds so that they may travel, through the true lights,*
*To the True Light where Christ is the true door.*
*In what manner it be inherent in this world the golden door defines;*
*The dull mind rises to truth through that which is material*
*And, in seeing this light, is resurrected from its former submersion.*[1]

Art serves the useful and necessary function of leading the dull mind, incapable of rising to the highest truths, to the True Light. Indeed, while a respectable anthology of citations from the Fathers can be made of their opposition to art, which is just about what Jeremy Collier did, it is apparent that this opposition is to pagan art in particular and not to art in general. Yet, though the arguments advanced by Plato in the tenth book of the *Republic* would seem to provide all the weapons which the Christians needed to direct against art, it was rather the flights of the *Symposium* and of the *Timaeus*, especially developed by Dionysius and Erigena, which laid the basis for a more tolerant Christian view of the arts.[2]

The problem of the ethical content of art, then, needs restatement, not in terms of the traditional opposition between total acceptance and total rejection, nor between the absolute antagonism of the artist to society and the absolute indifference of society to the artist, but rather in terms of the exact delimitation of its employment. No society has been willing to give up the use of so powerful and persuasive a means of moulding men's minds as art is. To those who rule, and to those who study rule, art has too important a social function ever to be dismissed lightly, and neither Plato nor the Church nor the Communist Party has ever made that mistake. If anything, they have taken art perhaps more seriously than even its most partisan adherents might wish, and one cannot conceive any of

[1] Ibid., p. 23. Professor Panofsky's introduction should be read in connection with the third chapter of Professor Lovejoy's *The Great Chain of Being* (Cambridge (Mass.), 1948), pp. 67–98.

[2] See Frederick A. Norwood, 'Attitudes of the Ante-Nicene Fathers toward Greek Artistic Achievement', *JHI*, VIII (1947), pp. 431–3, for the evidence that these Fathers were far from rejecting art out of hand, and Gretchen Finney, 'Ecstasy and Music in Seventeenth Century England', *JHI*, VIII (1947), pp. 153–86, where the attitude of the Fathers toward music is shown to be even more liberal than toward the other arts. Cf. Frances A. Yates, *The French Academies of the Sixteenth Century* (London, 1947), pp. 36–40.

them narrowing down the consideration of poetry to its mode of expression or of asserting its arcane uniqueness or of converting it into the darling of a coterie. Nevertheless, Plato, and those of his way of thinking, have had to be answered, and they have been answered in one of three ways, as I have already suggested. The first is the Renaissance assertion that the poet is a teacher even superior to the philosopher; that is, he can do what the philosopher does, but better. Unfortunately, this argument goes against the grain of certain of the new critics, who seek to avoid the dilemma implied in the form-content problem by removing art altogether from the realm of social responsibility by the denial that art can properly produce social and ideological effects. The result has been that these opposite approaches tend to cancel each other out, and they leave the field to be held pretty much by what can be called the liberal defence of art.

As with Plato, the liberal defence of art begins with a theory of the state, but this state, instead of accepting the concepts of order and stability as its sole end, accepts them as only one half of a balance, the other being precisely that principle to which Plato was so strongly opposed, the principle of flux. The liberal point of view believes that change is a good in itself; it encourages development, variety, and multiplicity, both in the individual in his own thought and action and in the programmes and actions of the state itself. The liberal state is, then, a kind of tension between the need for order and stability on the one hand and the equal and opposite need for change and variety on the other; it meets and solves its problems in motion. Instead of accepting a position as true eternally and, therefore, fixed forever, it seeks its answers through the competition of conflicting forces, for, when there are a number of conflicting claims, in the long run the best of these will ultimately emerge victorious because it is the best; it has proved itself in action and carries its authority, not because it is the decision of the wisest or oldest or most powerful, but because it has survived the competition; if it had not been the best, it would not have survived, and it is the best because it has survived. If the principle of competition is extended to the realm of ideas, it becomes apparent that the liberal defence of art is an adaptation of the concept of the free exchange of commodities to the free exchange of ideas. That is, the true and the best will win out over the false and the worst by virtue of their intrinsic merits; the best ideas, as well as the best works of art, will survive the competition and they will survive the competition because they are the best. Let Truth and Falsehood grapple, said Milton in the *Areopagitica*, and who ever knew Truth put to the worse in a free and open encounter? When truth and error have fair play, said Benjamin Franklin in *An Apology for Printers*, the former is always an overmatch for the latter. But the market must be free; its natural and self-regulating mechanism cannot be tampered with; the artist must be free to do what he wishes in the way he wishes, his audience must be free to choose what it wants and, in the long run, the best art will be produced, recognized, and rewarded. The analogy between the free market-place of commodities and the free exchange of ideas has been pithily put by Mr. Justice Holmes:

'But when men have realized that time has upset many fighting faiths, they may come to believe even more than they believe the very foundations of their own conduct that the ultimate good desired is better reached by the free trade in ideas—that the best test of truth is the power of thought to get itself accepted in the competition of the market, and that truth is the only ground upon which their wishes safely can be carried out.'[1]

Appealing as this defence of the freedom of ideas and of the arts is, its ultimate justification rests on an analogy, and that analogy is simply not true. The free market-place of commodities never existed, and has become less free with the passing of time. The buyer and seller have not and do not meet on equal terms, and competition has always tended to be replaced by combinations in restraint of competition. It is only the economic romantics of the Austrian school, the N.A.M., and the editors of *Time* who wistfully live in an economic past which never was; they have created a picture of the nineteenth century which has all the nostalgia of the Golden Age as well as all its unreality. When we look at the market-place of ideas, we find that, far from being free, it has become increasingly dominated by fewer and larger combinations whose control over the channels of communication has in effect given them control over the production of art. I cite the sad statistics recently compiled by Mr. Morris L. Ernst: ten states have not a single city with competing daily papers, fourteen companies control about one quarter of the daily total circulation of the press, one company dominates more than 3,000 weeklies, there are only 117 cities where competing dailies exist, four networks have 95 per cent of night-time broadcasting power, eleven adver-

[1] Abrams *v.* U.S., 250 U.S. 616 (1919).

tisers account for 50 per cent of network income, five companies control 2,800 theatres, two companies produce 90 per cent of the raw film stock, and so on.[1] It is such statistics as these which set the backdrop against which the drama of the competition of ideas must be played; unfortunately, instead of a drama, we have a puppet play and the wires show all too clearly.

The impasse which the liberal defence of ideas has reached is nowhere better illustrated than in the discussion concerning the defence of civil liberties. I begin first with the more restricted problem of the legal censorship of books. Professor Iredell Jenkins has pointed out that artistic freedom has been defended in the courts on three grounds: the first, which he terms the doctrine of dual appreciation, holds that the work of art may be seen in two different ways, as obscene by some, but when properly understood by others, as salutary in its effects. This position leads to the second defence, which is based on the principle of mature or sophisticated normality, that is, the proper reader of a book is mature and sophisticated enough not to be affected by passages which when read by less mature readers might be inflammatory. Finally, there is the third argument, the one now most often advanced, which is the appeal to the artist's motive; this has been stated by Judge Woolsey in his decision on *Ulysses*:

'. . . in any case where a book is claimed to be obscene it must first be determined whether the interest with which it was written was what is called, according to the usual phrase, pornographic,—that is, written for the purpose of exploiting obscenity. If the conclusion is that the book is pornographic, that is the end of the inquiry and forfeiture must follow. But in *Ulysses*, in spite of its unusual frankness, I do not detect anywhere the leer of the sensualist. I hold, therefore, that it is not pornographic.'[2]

The critic will immediately see the fallacy of the argument of the artist's intent and even the courts have been uneasy over this matter since the argument has more recently been made that '. . . truth should always be accepted as a justification of literature'.[3] But again this criterion is as unsatisfactory legally as it is aesthetically, for, as Professor Jenkins points out, all these arguments give the show

[1] Morris L. Ernst, *The First Freedom* (New York and London, 1946), pp. xii–xiii. These conclusions have been reinforced by the Reports of the Commission on the Freedom of the Press.

[2] U.S. *v.* One Book called *Ulysses* and Random House. 5 Fed. Supp. 182.

[3] People *v.* Viking Press. 264 N.Y.S. 534, the decision on *God's Little Acre.*

away since they admit that art is a force which can be applied in any direction: 'Art is a goddess', he writes, 'who lends herself easily to prostitution: viewed properly, she exerts an influence which is altogether beneficial; viewed improperly, her effects are violent and harmful.'[1] If this is so, which group should the court protect: those who can be influenced by the bad and must be shielded from it, an attitude given classic expression by Judge Thayer:

'There is to be found in every community a class of people who are so intelligent and so mature that their minds are not liable to be affected by reading matter, no matter how obscene, lewd, or indecent it may be. Then there is another large class to be found in every community—the young and the immature, the ignorant, and those who are sensually inclined—who are liable to be influenced to their harm by reading indecent and obscene publications. The statute under which this indictment was framed was designed to protect the latter class from harm, and it is a wholesome statute. Hence, in judging of the tendency of the publications to deprave or corrupt the mind, or to excite lustful and sensual desires (which are the test of obscenity and lawlessness), you should consider the effect that the publications would have on the minds of that class of persons, rather than the effect such publications would have on people of a high order of intelligence, and those who have reached mature years, who by reason of their intelligence or their years are steeled against such influences.'[2]

or, on the other hand, must the reading habits of those capable of true understanding and appreciation be protected from the safeguards imposed on the others? 'To put thought in leash', declared Judge Learned Hand, 'to the average conscience of the time is perhaps tolerable, but to fetter it by the necessities of the lowest and least capable seems a fatal policy.'[3] Admirable as this statement is, what are its consequences? The assumption upon which this position rests is that, while art does exercise its effects, art is the concern only of those capable of not being wrongly affected by it; the majority of people, since they do not have much to do with art in the first place, are not going to be hurt by it in any event. There is a kind of gentle-

[1] Iredell Jenkins, "The Laisser-Faire Theory of Artistic Censorship', *JHI*, V (1944), p. 79.

[2] U.S. *v.* Clarke, 38 Fed. 734.

[3] U.S. *v.* Kennerley, 209 Fed. 119.

men's agreement that, while art may under extreme circumstances become a dangerous social phenomenon should the masses get to accept and understand it, by and large they are not likely to do either and art can be safely left in the hands of those able to deal with it properly, that is, not to take it seriously. Yet this patrician paternalism does not even serve its own purposes, for, as soon as men do take seriously ideas and their consequences, the positions they hold *vis-à-vis* each other harden, and what had seemed merely amusing and speculative, the tolerated aberrations of somewhat queer and unconventional people, suddenly become fraught with the deepest significance. 'The degree of tolerance obtainable at any moment depends', Shaw observes in the preface to *Saint Joan*, 'on the strain under which society is maintaining its cohesion.' But once the strain begins to tell, once the breaking-point is reached, the toleration of toleration is no longer a matter of maintaining a polite social fiction; its defence requires more than a blind trust in the gyrating ball of competition coming up at the right time with the right belief.

This difficulty is revealed even more clearly in the area of the free communication of ideas where the theory of the free market-place crumbles under the tug of the strain of cohesion. Mr. Justice Jackson has declared: 'If there is one fixed star in our constitutional constellation, it is that no official, high or petty, can prescribe what shall be orthodox in politics, nationalism, religion, or other matters of opinion or force citizens to confess by word or act their faith therein.'[1] But the prescription of opinion is not the prerogative of the state alone; we have here no more than an echo of the eighteenth-century distrust of the state. The formation of opinion is as much in the hands of agencies outside the state, if indeed not more so, and in a society whose members have been instructed sufficiently to be propagandized but not educated enough to know it, the opinion manufactured by the press, radio, and motion pictures is not in the statute books and cannot be attacked legally; it is pervasive and cannot be exposed: it is omnipresent and cannot be held responsible. Mr. Justice Holmes's famous dictum, that while every man has freedom of expression, that freedom does not mean that he can falsely shout 'Fire' in a theatre and cause a panic, intended to preserve freedom of expression, contains in it the seeds from which the repression of expression may in fact grow. In an artificially-induced atmospheer of hysteria, everyone can too easily be convinced that shouts of

[1] West Virginia *v.* Barnette, 319 U.S. 624 (1943).

'Fire' are indeed being raised and can be heard, and the courts can in time do no more than agree that their hearing has not been affected. 'The question in every case', stated Mr. Justice Holmes, 'is whether the words used are in such circumstances and are of such a nature as to create a clear and present danger that they will bring about the substantive evils that Congress has a right to prevent.'[1] Under normal and ideal conditions, the rule of clear and present danger is, as Mr. Justice Brandeis has said:

'. . . a rule of reason. Correctly applied, it will preserve the right of free speech both from suppression by tyrannous, well-meaning majorities and from abuse by irresponsible, fanatical minorities. Like many other rules of human conduct, it can be applied correctly only by the exercise of good judgment; and to the exercise of good judgment, calmness is, in times of deep feeling and on subjects which excite passion, as essential as fearlessness and honesty.'[2]

But who is to define what the danger actually is, to whom is the danger dangerous, how do we know that the danger has become clear and present, who is to have the responsibility of uttering the cry of danger? A reform which may have constituted a clear and present danger to our ancestors is now taken for granted by us as a right, and may it not be equally true that a clear and present danger to us may be blithely accepted as a good to our descendants? But the siren call of the clear and present danger, shrieked aloud until we are deafened by its clamour to all else, may close our ears to the quiet voice of reason, urbanely if vainly, calling to us through the din of the market-place of ideas.[3]

What happens when authority is convinced that a clear and present danger exists can be illustrated by a case which took place in the simple times of World War I; the case rejoices in the ironic title of U.S. *v.* The Spirit of '76, and the story has been told by Professor Zechariah Chafee in this way:

'Robert Goldstein, who had been connected with D. W. Griffith in producing *The Birth of a Nation*, a well-known moving-picture

[1] Schenck *v.* U.S., 249 U.S. 47 (1919).

[2] Schaefer *v.* U.S., 251 U.S. 468 (1920).

[3] A symptom of national deafness is the recent decision of Judge Learned Hand, chief judge of the U.S. court of appeals in New York, upholding the constitutionality of the Smith Act.

film of the Civil War, planned a similar presentation of the Revolution in a film called *The Spirit of '76*, which contained such scenes as Patrick Henry's Speech, the Signing of the Declaration of Independence, and Valley Forge. After a year and a half of work the picture was finished, just before the outbreak of our war with Germany. The film was displayed in Los Angeles to the usual audience, which was not shown to contain either soldiers or sailors. The government thereupon indicted Goldstein for presenting a play designed and intended to arouse antagonism, hatred, and enmity between the American people (particularly the armed forces) and the people of Great Britain (particularly their armed forces) when Great Britain was "an ally" of the United States, because one scene, the Wyoming Massacre, portrayed British soldiers bayoneting women and children and carrying away girls.'

The reason for the indictment had been stated by Judge Bledsoe as follows:

'Great Britain is an ally of the United States . . . this is no time . . . for the exploitation of those things that may have the tendency . . . of creating animosity or want of confidence between us and our allies, because to do so weakens our efforts, weakens the chance of our success, impairs our solidarity. . . . No man should be permitted, by deliberate act, or even *unthinkingly* [italics mine] to do that which will in any way detract from the efforts which the United States is putting forth or serve to postpone for a single moment the early coming of the day when the success of our arms shall be a fact.'[1]

The end of the tale is swiftly told by Professor Chafee:

'The film was seized, the business was thrown from prosperity into bankruptcy with a loss of over $100,000, and Goldstein was convicted of attempting to cause insubordination, etc., in the armed forces and sentenced to ten years in the federal penitentiary at Steilacoom, Washington. His punishment for depicting the origin of this nation was commuted to three years.'[2]

Of course, anything can and does happen in California, but the case of the U.S. *v.* the Spirit of '76 illustrates what can and does happen when the policy of the clear and present danger is put to the

[1] U.S. *v.* Spirit of '76, 252 Fed. 946 (Cal., 1917).

[2] Zechariah Chafee, *Free Speech in the United States* (Cambridge (Mass.), 1941), p. 55.

test of experience; in the competition of the market place of ideas, it is not all certain that the truth will prevail, especially when those who run the market-place do not want it to prevail. The dilemma of the liberal defence has been succinctly stated by Mill in two different passages. 'An opinion the corn-dealers are starvers of the poor, or that private property is robbery, ought to be unmolested when simply circulated through the press,' he writes in *On Liberty*, 'but may justly incur punishment when delivered orally to an excited mob assembled before the house of a corn-dealer, or when handed about the same mob in the form of a placard.'[1] But in the later essay, *On Social Freedom*, he says: 'That man seems to me to act with freedom who yields to the impulse of the *highest motive* which demands his obedience, or which presents itself to his consciousness, at the moment of determination.'[2] Is the man whose highest motive impels him to hand about a placard denouncing corn-dealers to an excited mob a clear and present danger to the state as well as to the corn-dealer? Freedom of discussion, says Bagehot in his essay on 'The Metaphysical Basis of Toleration', must not be used to destroy society,[3] but this very limitation puts an effective end to all freedom of discussion, for experience shows that in troubled times the expression of even the most innocent opinions may be construed as tending toward the destruction of society; the free market-place of ideas chokes up.

The liberal defence of art fails, then, because in seeking to assure that all points of view shall be expressed, none can prevail, and judgment goes by the board. With the abdication of responsibility, action is paralyzed, and when man loses the exercise of responsible action, he loses his status as man. For men must act, and they must act on the basis of what they believe, and they must believe while they act that what they believe is true, that is, can and must be acted on. To be sure, we know only too well that while we believe and act on that belief, the belief and the act may at that very moment be in the process of being proved false, still we must act; this is the risk of accepting the responsibility of being man. That is why the heart and centre of the myth and ritual pattern is the small moment of doubt and indecision, when, for that moment, victory and defeat are poised in the balance, and only the moral force of man wills him on in

[1] J. S. Mill, *On Liberty*, ed. R. B. McCallum (Oxford, 1946), p. 49.
[2] J. S. Mill, *On Social Freedom* (New York, 1941), p. 56.
[3] Walter Bagehot, *Works*, ed. Forrest Morgan II (Hartford, 1891), pp. 339–59.

action to success. The tragic protagonist acts in the conviction that his action is right and he accepts the responsibility for that action; for him to do less than that means the loss of his stature as a moral, responsible agent. For this reason does Aristotle insist over and over again on the primacy of action and, by doing so, has infused ethos into medium, thereby giving the lie to Plato's denunciation of the poets. In the pattern of tragedy, the protagonist falls because of some excess, but the presumption which marks this excess must be understood as reflecting more than a mere personal disability. The fall of a great man through pride of will or the desire for power, while affecting enough, is at the most pathetic; certainly it is not tragic. We are swept away by the violence of personal passion, we are saddened by the uselessness of the destruction of one whom we pity, but we do not go beyond; we do not reach out, question, wonder. The tragic occurs when by the fall of a man of strong character we are made aware of something greater than that man or even mankind; we seem to have a new and truer vision of the universe. It is to be admitted that the tragic hero suffers for his *hybris* and we, the spectators, suffer too, but we are willing to suffer; indeed, we take pleasure in that suffering, if only that suffering be made intelligible to us. But suffering can be made bearable only when it is made a part of a rational world order into which it fits and which has an understandable place for it. Something of the calm which comes when suffering has been shown not to have been in vain is apparent in Adam's speech at the end of *Paradise Lost*:

> *Henceforth I learn that to obey is best,*
> *And love with fear the only God, to walk*
> *As in his presence, and in him sole depend,*
> *Merciful over all his works, with good*
> *Still overwhelming evil, and by small*
> *Accomplishing great things.*

Here is to be found, I think, the core of greatness in tragedy, the mark by which it may be recognized: the sense of assurance, achieved through suffering, of rational order. Tragedy occurs when the accepted order of things is fundamentally questioned only to be the more triumphantly reaffirmed. Pity, terror, awe: these are the emotional responses, the aesthetic bridge, as it were, which makes possible the passage from the action on the stage to the heightened ethical consciousness in the mind of the spectator: pity for the tragic hero who, a man like us, must suffer that we may learn to live rightly; terror that he has dared to question the justness of the order of nature; and awe because that order has been re-established more convincingly than ever before. But the tragic dramatist does not work by the methods of logical proof; he does not try, in the words of Mr. Eliot: '. . . to persuade the readers to an intellectual assent, but to convey an emotional equivalent for the ideas',[1] to make the spectator who intellectually accepts '. . . *feel* . . . as a matter of personal experience'.

Fifth-century Greece and Elizabethan England were both ages of faith: faith in the justice of the gods in the one, faith in the justice of God in the other. Both were profoundly religious periods; the establishment of the nature of man's relation to God was for each a real and moving need. Yet, at the same time, both ages were equally sceptical. The winds of new doctrine swept through the streets of Athens and London and left the old and conventional modes of religious thought bare to the probing of doubt. It became the function of the Greek dramatists to reconcile the old religion with its unpredictable and arbitrary gods to the new philosophy with its beliefs in a reasonable world order. They did this by effecting a new synthesis, which combined the concept of inevitable retribution for evil done with a rational mode of justice; that is, they provided a simultaneously religious and humanistic solution to the union of faith and reason, a union which Aristotle expressed in aesthetic terms. Somewhat in the same way, Shakespeare took the concept of an ordered and static society with its corresponding hierarchy of stratified values and infused it with the vitality of Renaissance humanism, the insistence on man's goodness and freedom. He combined the need for order with the need for life. He thrust aside ritual, but retained faith; at the same time, he avoided the extremes of Renaissance politics and science, which enabled him to see through the shams of convention to the reality beneath; finally, he created a vision of free men responsible to a just order of things. In both the Athenian and Elizabethan climates of ideas, tragedy emerges when what is dead in the old is eliminated and what is good retained, when what is viable in the new is kept and what is extreme rejected, and when the fusion of the best in each is effected in a new synthesis on a plane more ethically satisfying than either taken singly. Tragedy, therefore, cannot exist

[1] T. S. Eliot, 'The Social Function of Poetry', in *Critiques and Essays in Criticism, 1920–48*, ed. Robert W. Stallman (New York, 1949), p. 107.

where there is no faith; conversely, it cannot exist where there is no doubt; it can exist only in an atmosphere of sceptical faith. The protagonist must be free to choose: Oedipus must be free to choose between the demands of his own reason and those of the gods; Hamlet must be free to choose between taking justice into his own hands, thereby partaking of the very evil which he wishes to expunge, and God's own way of establishing justice; Adam must be free to choose between his own will and that of God. In each case, the protagonist is left free and, in each case, he chooses wrongly, yet in each case still, the result of the wrong choice is our own escape and our enlightenment, and this is the paradox and irony of tragedy. Yet nothing less than this sacrifice will do, and only the symbolic sacrifice of one who is like us can make possible our atonement for the evil which is within us and for the sins which we are capable of committing. Nevertheless, in western thought, if man is free to choose, in the end he must choose rightly. He is free to choose his salvation, but he is punished for his wrong choice. Man is free, but he is free within the limits set for him by his condition as man: 'Man's are the heart's plans; from Yahweh the tongue's answer.' And: 'Whosoever would save his life shall lose it; and whosoever shall lose his life for My sake and the Gospel's shall save it.' The paradox is resolved in action: the good which Paul so despaired of doing is done in the act of walking in the right way.

# *Conclusion*

HAVING arrived at the stage where historical evidence and aesthetic theory begin to confirm each other, I must stop. I began with the postulate that our response to tragedy is not a single one, but rather a series of responses. This chain of responses may be looked on as the gradual unfolding of successive layers of experience, at least six in number: first, the impact of experience which produces the archetypes of belief; second, the formation of the archetype of rebirth; third, the crystallization of the archetype of rebirth in the myth and ritual of the ancient Near East; fourth, the infusion and transformation of myth and ritual into and in the religions of the ancient world, including Christianity; fifth, the concretization and formalization of the archetype of rebirth into the concept of *felix culpa*, the paradox of the fortunate fall; and finally, the secular utilization of the paradox of the fortunate fall as the substance out of which tragedy, and particularly Shakespearean tragedy, is made. Of these, our concern here has been with the third, fourth, and fifth links, the first two lying outside the present state of our knowledge of man's deepest past, both historical and psychological, and the sixth being reserved for separate treatment.

The paradox of the fortunate fall recapitulates in terse form a long and complicated line of development in the history of ideas. It is the shorthand symbol for the meaning of the myth and ritual pattern as a whole; compressed into it is the entire range of significance of a complex of belief and action which for many centuries and in many forms has been able to provide a satisfactory answer to a deeply rooted need of man, his longing for order, for rationality, and, above all, for life. What spiritual and aesthetic power the paradox of the fortunate fall possesses, it owes to its origins in the myth and ritual of the ancient world, so that, in responding to the concept of *felix culpa*, we are at the same time responding to all the layers of association embedded in the myth and ritual pattern in the long course of its development. Though at first glance there appears to be little, if anything, in common between the sophisticated expression of the idea in its form as the paradox of the fortunate fall on the one hand and the crudities of the myth and ritual of the ancient Near East, especially in their earliest manifestations, on the other, nevertheless, when we try to account for the spiritual force of the concept of *felix culpa*, we are impelled to retrace, step by step, the laboriously slow evolution of one of the most tenaciously held faiths which man has ever grasped. The basis of that faith is a twofold conviction, as much the result of intuition as of observation: first, that the most fundamental and significant rhythm of nature is the cycle of birth, death, and birth again; and second, that by mimetically reproducing this rhythm, man can, to some degree, control nature, and by so controlling it, if only for the moment, achieve a victory, fleeting and transitory as it may be, but a victory none the less, over the forces of chaos and disorder which ever threaten to engulf him from all sides. The sun rises after the night; the grain sprouts after the winter; the waters run after the drought; the dead god lives again; and man falls, but not in vain.

As we have seen, the myth and ritual pattern takes the form of a drama in which the divine king in his own person engages in combat with an opposing force, suffers, is defeated, dies, is reborn triumphantly, celebrates his victory by the act of creation in the divine marriage and by the sacred procession, and grants the fruits of that victory in the settling of destinies in which the people, for whom and with whom he undergoes his suffering, death, and rebirth, are raised to a new and higher stage of understanding and justice. To be sure, the order of acts in the drama is not everywhere the same, nor are all the scenes necessarily enacted; with the passage of time, some scenes are subordinated to others, some given increased prominence, while others are eliminated altogether, but whatever changes have been made, the shape and intent of the pattern remain the same: the depiction of the triumph of light, life, and good through suffering over dark, death, and evil. But it must be obvious by now that the central figure in the drama is not the god, nor the divine king, nor the hero, but man himself, projected as god, divine king, or hero, but in the end and always man, man struggling desperately and endlessly to carve out of a chaotic and cruel cosmos a world of order and justice. In a sense, man has never succeeded in that effort, nor, in the very nature of the situation, can he possibly succeed. Yet, precisely because he is man, he struggles; he plunges into the terrors of the small moment, he suffers, he dies, but he lives again. For the very struggle to succeed is a success in itself; as long as he struggles against the dark, death, and evil, he holds them off, and for every moment that they are held off, he has succeeded. It is not the engagement itself which alone makes man; it is rather the kind of engagement which he chooses to encounter which distinguishes him as man. For he chooses what battle he shall fight and he takes on thereby the responsibility of responsibility; he selects not any engagement, nor looks forward to any victory, but this one alone, and precisely this: the victory of light, life, and good over dark, death, and evil. He dies that he may live, he falls that he may rise, he suffers that he may learn.

He suffers that he may learn and he learns through suffering to mitigate suffering. At first, a man is slain that another may live; man is still too close to the cruelty he wishes to overcome to be free from it. But in time he learns that a substitute for the slain man can be made and a great step forward is taken, for, once this idea has taken root, he proceeds from the living substitute to the inanimate to the symbol; he has bridged the gap between magic and religion. But one more step can be taken. In both the physical and symbolic forms of learning through suffering, the effective force lies in the act; except in the most sophisticated religions, the catharsis takes place outside the spectator; it takes place not so much in him as for him. But in tragedy, catharsis is produced in the mind of the spectator; the purgation is internal; and whatever suffering is presented on the stage is the representation of suffering and not suffering itself. Tragedy, therefore, represents the highest stage in the development of the myth and ritual pattern as regards the method by which its ends are secured.

Similarly, tragedy represents the highest stage of development of the form of the myth and ritual pattern. The paradox of the fortunate fall places the totality of experience behind the myth and ritual pattern at the disposal of tragedy; it is the filter through which the form and meaning of the pattern are passed so that they can reach tragedy in their most concentrated and purified state. By the time the myth and ritual pattern has been compressed into its expression as the paradox of the fortunate form, its basic structure has been clearly revealed, its essential meaning has been sharply formulated, and it remains for the artist to reshape the pattern in terms of his own particular medium and of his individual genius. This, then, is the double heritage of the myth and ritual pattern, through the agency of the paradox of the fortunate fall, to the making of tragedy: on the one hand, the structure of tragedy, from the succession of acts in the movement of the myth and ritual drama; on the other hand, the content of tragedy, from the purpose of the myth and ritual pattern, the triumph of life through suffering over death; the two being fused into a single shape.

It must not be thought that the impulse behind the myth and ritual pattern has been exhausted. It is true that the examples with which we have been concerned here have been drawn mainly from religion and are intended to explain why we take pleasure in the pleasure peculiar to tragedy. But we must remember that one of the chief characteristics of the pattern is its ability to take on new shapes in response to the demands created by new needs in new circumstances. If in the past, the pattern showed itself in the forms of religion, and later in the form of tragedy, it does not mean that these alone are the only media of its expression. Accordingly, we ought to expect it to appear in new guises, and in view of the direction of our interests today, it would not be surprising if we found the myth and ritual pattern being expressed both in fiction and in politics. I would suggest, therefore, that, as examples, Mann's Joseph series and Joyce's *Finnegan Wake* might be considered as deliberate restatements of the pattern in the form of the novel and that Marxism would well repay study as another version of the pattern now expressed in sociopolitical terms. These are only a few examples of many which might be suggested, and the method could with profit be applied to other examples drawn from other fields.

A final word about the methodological intent of this study. I have long felt that there is need of a bridge between the scholar and the critic in which the methods of the one lead into the methods of the other to the point where the two merge into one continuous and single mode of analysis and judgment. I do not pretend that I have been able to construct such a bridge here, but I hope I have been able to throw a little light on the way such a bridge might be constructed. I have taken an idea first described by Professor Lovejoy, an idea which made the critics unhappy because it would seem to have no aesthetic consequences whatsoever, and have traced what I think are its origins in the myth and ritual pattern of the ancient Near East. From this analysis of its origins, I tried to indicate the source of the power of the idea, a power not merely ideological in nature but emotional as well, a power which accounts for its persistent use by many people in many ways, diverse in its manifold shapes, yet one in its fructifying force. The method used has been historical, yet from this method, I trust to have extracted those emotional overtones of the idea which give it its aesthetic potency, thus enabling us to respond not only to its ideological content, but also to its aesthetic stimulation, so that as we understand, so simultaneously are we able to participate in the aesthetic experience of it. Thus I hope I have been able to forge both the historical and critical approaches into a single method which partakes of the strength of each, the one anchoring the idea to the deepest roots of human aspiration and need, the other apprehending on the basis of that knowledge its full aesthetic significance.

# *Bibliography of Works Cited in the Text*

ABBREVIATIONS

*AJA—American Journal of Archaeology.*
*AJSL—American Journal of Semitic Languages and Literatures.*
*AO—Acta Orientalia.*
*BASOR—Bulletin of the American Schools of Oriental Research.*
*CP—Classical Philology.*
*ELH—English Literary History.*
*HSCP—Harvard Studies in Classical Philology.*
*HTR—Harvard Theological Review.*
*HUCA—Hebrew Union College Annual.*
*JAOS—Journal of the American Oriental Society.*
*JBL—Journal of Biblical Literature and Exegesis.*
*JEGP—Journal of English and Germanic Philology.*
*JHI—Journal of the History of Ideas.*
*JNES—Journal of Near Eastern Studies.*
*JPOS—Journal of the Palestine Oriental Society.*
*JRAS—Journal of the Royal Asiatic Society of Great Britain and Ireland.*
*JWI—Journal of the Warburg and Courtauld Institutes.*
*KR—Kenyon Review.*
*MLQ—Modern Language Quarterly.*
*PAPS—Proceedings of the American Philosophical Society.*
*PMLA—Publications of the Modern Language Association.*
*PQ—Philological Quarterly.*
*RR—Review of Religion.*
*SMSR—Studi e materiali di storia delle religioni.*
*ZAW—Zeitschrift fur die alttestamentliche Wissenschaft.*

Adams, Henry H., *English Domestic or, Homiletic Tragedy*, 1575–1642, New York and Oxford, 1943.

## *Bibliography*

Adams, Joseph Q., *Chief Pre-Shakespearean Dramas*, London, 1924.

Albright, William F., 'Historical and Mythical Elements in the Story of Joseph', *JBL*, XXXVII (1918), pp. 111–43.

'New Light on Early Canaanite Language and Literature', *BASOR*, XLVI (1932), pp. 15–20.

'More Light on the Canaanite Epic of Aleyan Baal and Mot', *BASOR*, L (1933), pp. 13–20.

'New Canaanite Historical and Mythological Data', *BASOR*, LXIII (1936), pp. 23–32.

'Recent Progress in North-Canaanite Research', *BASOR*, LXX (1938), pp. 18–24.

*From the Stone Age to Christianity*, Baltimore, 1940.

*Archaeology and the Religion of Israel*, Baltimore, 1942.

Allen, Grant, *The Evolution of the Idea of God*, London, 1901.

Angus, S., *The Mystery-Religions and Christianity*, London and New York, 1925.

*The Religious Quests of the Graeco-Roman World*, London and New York, 1929.

*Ante-Nicene Fathers, The*, ed. A. Robertson and J. Donaldson, 10 vols., Buffalo, 1885–97.

*Apostolic Fathers, The*, ed. K. Lake, 2 vols., London, 1913.

Apuleius, *The Golden Ass*, ed. W. Adlington, rev. S. Gasalee, London, 1915.

Aristophanes, *The Frogs*, ed. B. Rogers, London, 1902.

Aristotle, *The 'Art' of Rhetoric*, ed. J. H. Frere, London, 1926.

*The Metaphysics*, ed. H. Tredemick, 2 vols., London, 1933–5.

*The Nicomachean Ethics*, ed. H. Rackham, London, 1926.

*The Poetics*, ed. W. H. Fyfe, London, 1927.

Armstrong, Edward A., *Shakespeare's Imagination*, London, 1946.

*St. Augustine's Confessions with an English Translation by William Watts*, 1631, ed. W. H. D. Rouse, 2 vols., London, 1912.

Aulen, Gustaf, *Christus Victor*, tr. A. G. Herbert, London, 1940.

Bagehot, Walter, 'The Metaphysical Basis of Toleration', *The Works*, ed. F. Morgan (Hartford, 1891), II, pp. 339–59.

Baker, Herschel, *The Dignity of Man*, Cambridge, Mass., 1947.

Baker, Howard, *Induction to Tragedy*, Baton Rouge, La., 1939.

Baynes, H. G., 'On the Psychological Origins of the Divine Kingship,' *Folk-Lore*, XCVIII (1936), pp. 74–104.

Bernbaum, Ernest, *The Drama of Sensibility*, 1696–1750, Cambridge, Mass., 1925.

Blackman, E. C., *Marcion and His Influence*, London, 1948.

Boas, George, *Essays on Primitivism and Related Ideas in Antiquity*, Baltimore, 1948.

Bodkin, Maud, *Archetypal Patterns in Poetry*, London, 1934.

# Bibliography


Bowers, Fredson T., *Elizabethan Revenge Tragedy*, Princeton, 1940.

Bowra, C. M., *Sophoclean Tragedy*, Oxford, 1944.

Bradby, Anne, ed., *Shakespeare Criticism*, 1919–35, Oxford, 1936.

Bradley, Andrew C., 'Hegel's Theory of Tragedy', *Oxford Lectures on Poetry*, London, 1917.

Brandon, S. G. F., 'The Problem of Change in the Ancient World', *Folk-Lore*, LXI (1950), pp. 88–97.

Breasted, James H., *Development of Religion and Thought in Ancient Egypt*, London and New York, 1912.

*The Dawn of Conscience*, New York, 1934.

Briffault, Robert, *The Mothers*, 3 vols., London, 1927.

Brooks, Cleanth, *The Well-Wrought Urn*, New York, 1947.

Buchler, A., *Studies in Sin and Atonement in the Rabbinic Literature of the First Century*, Oxford, 1928.

Burke, Kenneth, *The Philosophy of Literary Form*, Baton Rouge, La., 1941.

Burkitt, Francis C., *The Religion of the Manichees*, Cambridge, 1925.

*Church and Gnosis*, Cambridge, 1932.

Butler, Eva M., *The Myth of the Magus*, Cambridge, 1948.

Campbell, Joseph, *The Hero with a Thousand Faces*, New York, 1949.

Campbell, Lily B., *Shakespeare's Tragic Heroes*, Cambridge, 1930.

Cantor, Helene J., 'The Aegean and the Orient in the Second Millenium B.C.', *AJA*, LI (1947), pp. 1–103.

Chafee, Zechariah, *Free Speech in the United States*, Cambridge, Mass., 1941.

Chambers, Edmund K., *The Medieval Stage*, 2 vols., Oxford, 1903.

*The English Folk Play*, Oxford, 1933.

Charles, R. H., *A Critical History of the Doctrine of a Future Life*, London, 1899.

Charlton, H. B., 'Introductory Essay on the Growth of the Senecan Tradition in Renaissance Tragedy', in *The Poetical Works of Sir William Alexander* (Edinburgh, 1921), I, pp. xvii–cc.

Chase, Richard, 'Myth as Literature', *English Institute Essays*, 1947 (New York, 1948), pp. 3–22.

Chew, Samuel, 'Time and Fortune', *ELH*, VI (1939), pp. 83–113.

Childe, V. Gordon, *New Light on the Most Ancient East*, London and New York, 1934.

*Man Makes Himself*, London, 1948.

Cioffari, V., *Fortune and Fate from Democritus to St. Thomas Aquinas*, New York, 1935.

Coleridge, Samuel T., *Essays and Lectures on Shakespeare*, London, 1909.

Cornford, Francis M., *The Origins of Attic Comedy*, Cambridge, 1934.

'The Unconscious Element in Literature and Philosophy', in *The Unwritten Philosophy and Other Essays*, ed. W. K. C. Guthrie (Cambridge, 1950), pp. 1–13.

# *Bibliography*

Cumont, Franz, *The Oriental Religions in Roman Paganism*, London and Chicago, 1911.
*Lux Perpetua*, Paris, 1949.

Dante, *The Comedy of Dante Alighieri*, tr. Dorothy Sayers, Penguin Books, 1949.
Danthine, Hélène, *Le palmier-dattier et les arbres sacrés dans l'iconographie de l'Asie Occidentale ancienne*, 2 vols., Paris, 1937.
Dawson, Christopher, *Religion and Culture*, London, 1948.
Dennis, John, *The Advancement and Reformation of Poetry*, London, 1701.
*Diodorus of Sicily*, ed. C. H. Oldfather, 3 vols., London, 1939.
Duchesne, L., *Christian Worship*, tr. M. L. McLure, London, 1923.
Dussaud, René, *Les découvertes de Ras Shamra (Ugarit) et l'Ancien Testament*, Paris, 1941.

Edelstein, Emma J. and Ludwig, *Asclepius*, 2 vols., Baltimore, 1948.
Eliot, Thomas S., *Selected Essays*, 1917–32, London and New York, 1932.
Engnell, Ivan, *Studies in Divine Kingship in the Ancient Near East*, Uppsala, 1943.
Erman, Adolf, *The Literature of the Ancient Egyptians*, tr. A. M. Blackman, London, 1927.
Ernst, Morris L., *The First Freedom*, London and New York, 1946.
Euripides, *The Bacchae*, tr. G. Murray, London, n.d.
Eusebius, *Ecclesiastical History*, ed. K. Lake, 2 vols., London, 1926.
Evans, Arthur, *The Palace of Minos at Knossos*, 3 vols., London, 1921–30.

Fairchild, Hoxie N., *Religious Trends in English Poetry*, 2 vols., Oxford and New York, 1939–42.
Farnell, Lewis R., *The Cults of the Greek States*, 5 vols., Oxford, 1896–1909.
'Cretan Influences in Greek Religion', in *Essays in Aegean Archaeology Presented to Sir Arthur Evans*, ed. S. Casson, Oxford, 1927.
Farnham, Willard, *The Medieval Heritage of Elizabethan Tragedy*, Berkeley, Cal., 1936.
Finney, Gretchen L., 'Ecstasy and Music in Seventeenth-Century England', *JHI*, VIII (1947), pp. 153–86.
Frankfort, Henri, 'Gods and Myths on Sargonid Seals', *Iraq*, I (1934), pp. 2–29.
*Cylinder Seals*, London, 1939.
*Kingship and the Gods*, Chicago, 1948.
review of G. R. Levy, *The Gate of Horn*, *JNES*, IX (1950), pp. 48–50.
and H. A. Frankfort, John A. Wilson, Thorkild Jacobsen, and William A. Irwin, *The Intellectual Adventure of Ancient Man*, Chicago, 1946.
Frazer, James G., *The Golden Bough*, 12 vols., New York, 1935.

Freud, Sigmund, *Moses and Monotheism*, tr. K. Jones, London and New York, 1939.

*Totem and Taboo*, tr. J. Strachey, London, 1950.

Frye, Prosser H., *Romance and Tragedy*, Boston, 1922.

Furlani, C. G., 'L'umilizanione del re durante la festa di capoduno a Babele', *SMSR*, IV (1928), pp. 51–6, 105–7.

Gadd, C. J., *Ideas of Divine Rule in the Ancient East*, The Schweick Lectures of the British Academy 1945, London, 1948.

Gaster, Theodor H., 'The Battle of the Rain and the Sea: An Ancient Semitic Nature-Myth', *Iraq*, IV (1937), pp. 22–31.

'New Light on Early Palestinian Religions', *Religions*, XVIII (1937), pp. 7–36.

' "Baal Is Risen . . ." An Ancient Hebrew Passion-Play from Ras Shamra-Ugarit', *Iraq*, VI (1939), pp. 109–43.

'Divine Kingship in the Ancient Near East', *RR*, IX (1945), pp. 267–81.

'A Canaanite Ritual Drama: The Spring Festival at Ugarit', *JAOS*, LXVI (1946), pp. 49–76.

'Ugaritic Mythology', *JNES*, VII (1948), pp. 184–93.

*Thespis Ritual, Myth and Drama in the Ancient Near East*, New York, 1950.

Gilbert, Allan H., ed., *Literary Criticism from Plato to Dryden*, New York, 1940.

and H. L. Suggs, 'On the Relation of Horace to Aristotle in Literary Criticism', *JEGP*, XLVI (1947), pp. 233–47.

Glotz, Gustave, *The Aegean Civilization*, tr. M. R. Dobie and E. M. Riley, London and New York, 1925.

Goetze, Albrecht and E. H. Sturtevant, *The Hittite Ritual of Tunnawi*, New Haven, Conn., 1938.

Goodenough, Erwin R., 'Kingship in Early Israel', *JBL*, XLVIII (1929), pp. 169–205.

*By Light, Light The Mystic Gospel of Hellenistic Judaism*, New Haven, Conn., 1935.

Gordon, Cyrus H., 'A Marriage of the Gods in Canaanite Mythology', *BASOR*, LXV (1937), pp. 29–33.

Graham, William C. and Herbert G. May, *Culture and Conscience*, Chicago, 1936.

Graves, Robert, *The White Goddess*, New York, 1948.

Gray, G. B., *Sacrifice in the Old Testament*, Oxford, 1925.

*The Greek Bucolic Poets*, ed. J. M. Edmonds, London, 1912.

Green, Clarence C., *The Neo-Classic Theory of Tragedy in England during the Eighteenth Century*, Cambridge, Mass. and Oxford, 1934.

Greene, William C., 'Plato's View of Poetry', *HSCP*, XXIX (1918), pp. 1–76.
*Moira Fate, Good, and Evil in Greek Thought*, Cambridge, Mass., 1948.
Guterbock, Hans, 'The Hittite Version of the Hurrian Kumarbi Myths', *AJA*, LII (1948), pp. 123–34.
Guthrie, W. K. C., *Orpheus and Greek Religion*, London, 1935.
*The Greeks and Their Gods*, London, 1950.

*Hammurabi Code, The*, ed. C. Edwards, London, 1904.
Harrison, Jane E., *Prolegomena to the Study of Greek Religion*, Cambridge, 1908.
*Themis A Study of the Social Origins of Greek Religion*, Cambridge, 1912.
*Ancient Art and Ritual*, Oxford, 1948.
Hawkes, C. F. C., *The Prehistoric Foundations of Europe*, London, 1940.
Hegel, G. W. F., *The Philosophy of Fine Art*, tr. F. P. B. Osmaston, 4 vols., London, 1920.
Heidel, Alexander, *The Babylonian Genesis*, Chicago, 1942.
*The Gilgamesh Epic and Old Testament Parallels*, Chicago, 1946.
Heidel, William A., *The Day of Yahwah*, New York, 1929.
Hocart, A. M., *Kingship*, Oxford, 1927.
Hooke, Samuel H., ed., *Myth and Ritual*, Oxford, 1933.
ed., *The Labyrinth*, London, 1935.
*The Origins of Early Semitic Ritual*, The Schweich Lectures of the British Academy, 1935, London, 1938.
Hornstein, Lillian, 'Analysis of Imagery: A Critique of Literary Method', *PMLA*, LVII (1942), pp. 638–53.
Hyatt, J. Philip, 'The Ras Shamra Discoveries and the Interpretation of the Old Testament', *JBR*, X (1942), pp. 67–75.
'The Sources of the Suffering Servant Idea', *JNES*, III (1944), pp. 79–86.
Hyman, Stanley E., *The Armed Vision*, New York, 1948.
'Myth, Ritual, and Nonsesnse', *KR*, XI (1949), pp. 455–75.

Inglis, Ruth A., *Freedom of the Movies*, Chicago, 1947.
Irenaeus, *Against Heresies*, ed. A. Robertson and J. Donaldson, Edinburgh, 1858.

Jackson, Abraham V., *Zorastrian Studies*, New York, 1928.
Jacobsen, Thorkild, *The Sumerian King List*, Chicago, 1939.
'Sumerian Mythology', *JNES*, V (1946), pp. 128–52.
James, Edwin O., *Christian Myth and Ritual*, London, 1933.
*The Origins of Sacrifice*, London, 1933.
*The Old Testament in the Light of Anthropology*, London, 1935.
*The Origins of Religion*, London, 1937.
*Comparative Religion*, London, 1938.

James, William, *The Varieties of Religious Experience*, New York, 1902.
Jayne, Walter A., *The Healing Gods of Ancient Civilizations*, New Haven, Conn., 1925.
Jenkins, Iredell, 'Laisser-Faire Theory of Artistic Censorship', *JHI*, V (1944), pp. 71–90.
Josephus, *Jewish Antiquities*, ed. R. Marcus, 6 vols., London, 1943.
Jung, Carl G., *Contributions to Analytical Psychology*, tr. H. G. and C. F. Baynes, London, 1928.
*Introduction to a Science of Mythology*, tr. R. F. C. Hull, London, 1951.

Kantor, Helen J., 'The Aegean and the Orient in the Second Millenium B.C.', *AJA*, LI (1947), pp. 1–103.
Kelsen, Hans, *Society and Nature*, London and Chicago, 1943.
Kluckholm, Clyde, 'Myth and Ritual: A General Survey', *HTR*, XXXV (1942), pp. 45–79.
Knights, L. C., *Explorations*, London and New York, 1947.
Kraeling, C. H., 'The Wall Decorations', in *The Excavations at Dura-Europas*, ed. M. I Rostovtzeff et al, New Haven, Conn., 1936.
Kraeling, E. G., 'The Real Religion of Ancient Israel', *JBL*, LXVII (1928), pp. 133–59.
Kramer, Samuel N., *Lamentation over the Destruction of Ur*, Chicago, 1940.
'Sumerian Literature', *PAPS*, LXXXV (1942), pp. 293–323.
'The Babylonian Genesis. By Alexander Heidel', *JAOS*, LXIII (1943), pp. 69–73.
'The Epic of Gilgames and Its Sumerian Sources', *JAOS*, LXIV (1941), pp. 7–23.
*Sumerian Mythology*, Philadelphia, 1944.

Lactantius, *The Divine Institutes*, ed. W. Fletcher, Edinburgh, 1871.
Langdon, Stephen, *Tammuz and Ishtar*, Oxford, 1914.
*Babylonian Menologies and the Semitic Calendars*, The Schweich Lectures of the British Academy 1933, London, 1935.
Langhe, R. de, *Les textes de Ras Shamra-Ugarit et leurs rapports avec le milieu biblique de l'Ancien Testament*, 2 vols., Paris, 1945.
Lawrence, D. H., *Etruscan Places*, Penguin Books, 1950.
Levy, Gertrude R., *The Gate of Horn*, London, 1948.
Linforth, Ivan M., *The Arts of Orpheus*, Berkeley, Cal., 1941.
Lovejoy, Arthur O., *The Great Chain of Being*, Cambridge, Mass., 1948.
*Essays in the History of Ideas*, Baltimore, 1948.
and George Boas, *Primitivism and Related Ideas in Antiquity*, Baltimore, 1935.
*Loves and Wars of Baal and Anat, The*, ed. C. H. Gordon, Princeton, 1943.
Lucas, F. L., *Tragedy in Relation to Aristotle's 'Poetics'*, New York, 1928.
*Lucian*, ed. A. M. Harman, 5 vols., Cambridge, Mass., 1936.

Malinowski, Bronislaw, *Magic, Science and Religion and other Essays*, ed. R. Redfield, London and Glencoe, Ill, 1948.

Mallowan, M. E. L., 'Kingship and the Gods', *Antiquity*, XC (1949), pp. 93–99.

Matthews, J. G., 'Tammuz Worship in the Book of Malachi', *JPOS*, XI (1931), pp. 42–50.

May, Herbert G., 'The Fertility Cult in Josea', *AJSL*, XLVIII (1932), pp. 73–98.

'The Departure of the Glory of Yahweh', *JBL*, LVI (1937), pp. 309–21.

'Some Aspects of Solar Worship at Jerusalem', *ZAW*, LV (1937), pp. 269–81.

McEwan, Calvin W., *The Oriental Origin of Hellenistic Kingship*, Chicago, 1934.

Meek, Theophile, J., 'Canticles and the Tammuz Cult', *AJSL*, XXXIX (1922), pp. 1–14.

'The Song of Songs and the Fertility Cult', in *The Song of Songs, A Synposium*, ed. W. A. Schoff (Philadelphia, 1924), pp. 48–79.

Mellinck, Machteld J., *Hyakinthos*, Utrecht, 1943.

Mill, John S., *On Social Freedom*, New York, 1941.

*On Liberty and Considerations on Representative Government*, ed. R. B. McCallum, Oxford, 1946.

Minucius Felix, *Octavius*, ed. G. H. Rendall, London, 1931.

*Mishnah, The*, ed. H. Danby, Oxford, 1933.

Montefiore, C. G. and H. Loewe, ed., *A Rabbinic Anthology*, London, 1938.

Moore, George F., *Judaism in the First Centuries of the Christian Era, The Age of the Tannaim*, 3 vols., Oxford and Cambridge, Mass., 1927–30.

Morgenstern, Julian, 'The Source of the Creation-Story Genesis 1:1–2:4', *AJSL*, XXXVI (1920), pp. 169–212.

'The Gates of Righteousness', *HUCA*, VI (1929), pp. 1–37.

'The New Year for Kings', *Gaster Anniversary Volume*, ed. B. Schindler and A. Marmorstein (London, 1936), pp. 439–56.

'Amos Studies', *HUCA*, XII–XIII (1937–8), pp. 1–34.

'A Chapter in the History of the High-Priesthood', *AJSL*, LV (1938), pp. 1–24, 183–97, 360–77.

'Psalm 48', *HUCA*, XVI (1941), pp. 1–95.

'Psalm 8 and 19A', *HUCA*, XIX (1945–6), pp. 491–523.

'The Chanukkah Festival and the Calendar of Ancient Israel', *HUCA*, XX (1947), pp. 1–136; XXI (1948), pp. 365–496.

Muller, W. Max, *Egyptian Mythology*, London and Boston, 1923.

Murray, Gilbert, *Five Stages of Greek Religion*, London and New York, 1925.

*The Classical Tradition in Poetry*, Oxford, 1927.

*Stoic, Christian and Humanist*, London, 1940.

Murray, Margaret A., *The Witch-Cult in Western Europe*, Oxford, 1921.

Niebuhr, Reinhold, *Faith and History*, New York, 1949.
Nilsson, Martin P., *A History of Greek Religion*, tr. F. J. Fielden, Oxford, 1925.
*The Minoan-Mycenaean Religion and its Survival in Greek Religion*, London, 1927.
*The Mycenaean Origin of Greek Mythology*, Berkeley, Cal., 1932.
Nock, A. D., *Conversion The Old and the New in Religion from Alexander the Great to Augustine of Hippo*, Oxford, 1933.
'Orphism or Roman Philosophy', *HTR*, XXXIII (1940), pp. 301–15.
Nolte, Fred D., *The Early Middle Class Drama* (1696–1774), Lancaster, Pa., 1935.
North, Christopher R., 'The Religious Aspects of Hebrew Kingship', *ZAW*, L (1930), pp. 8–38.
*The Suffering Servant in Deutero-Isaiah*, Oxford, 1948.
Norwood, Frederick A., 'Attitudes of the Ante-Nicene Fathers toward Greek Artistic Achievement', *JHI*, VIII (1947), pp. 431–8.

Obermann, Julian, 'How Daniel was Blessed with a Son', *Supplement to JAOS*, LXVI (1946), pp. 1–30.
Obolensky, Dmitri, *The Bogomils, A Study in Balkan Neo-Manichaeism*, Cambridge, 1948.
Oesterley, W. O. E., *The Sacred Dance*, Cambridge, 1923.
*An Introduction to the Books of Apocrypha*, London, 1935.
*A Fresh Approach to the Psalms*, London and New York, 1937.
*Sacrifice in Ancient Israel*, London, 1937.
and G. H. Box, *The Religion and Worship of the Synagogue*, London and New York, 1907.
and T. H. Robinson, *Hebrew Religion Its Origin and Development*, London and New York, 1937.

Patai, Raphael, 'The "Control of Rain" in Ancient Palestine', *HUCA*, XIV (1939), pp. 251–86.
'Hebrew Installation Rites', *HUCA*, XX (1947), pp. 143–225.
*Man and Temple in Ancient Jewish and Ritual*, London, 1947.
Patch, Howard R., *The Goddess Fortuna in Medieval Literature*, Cambridge, Mass., 1927.
Patton, J., *The Canaanite Parallels to the Book of Psalms*, Baltimore, 1944.
Pedersen, J., 'Canaanite and Israelite Cultus', *AO*, XVIII (1940), pp. 1–14.
*Israel, Its Life and Culture*, 2 vols., Oxford, 1946–7.
Perrot, Nell, *Les représentations de l'arbre sacre sur les monuments de Mesopatamie et d'Elam*, Paris, 1937.

Persson, Axel W., *The Religion of Greece in Prehistoric Times*, Berkeley, Cal., 1942.

Pettazzoni, Raffaele, *La Confessione dei Peccati*, 3 vols., Bologna, 1929–35; Rome, 1936.

'Confession of Sins in Hittite Religion', in *Gaster Anniversary Volume*, ed. B. Schindler and A. Marmorstein (London, 1936), pp. 467–71.

Pickard-Cambridge, A. A. W., *Dithyramb Tragedy Comedy*, Oxford, 1927.

Pindar, *The Odes*, ed. J. Sandys, London, 1915.

Pitcher, Seymour M., 'Aristotle's Good and Just Heroes', *PQ*, XXIV (1945), pp. 1–11, 190–1.

Plato, *The Dialogues*, ed. B. Jowett, 4 vols., Oxford, 1892.

Pollard, Alfred W., *English Miracle Plays, Moralities and Interludes*, Oxford, 1927.

Radin, Paul, *Primitive Man as Philosopher*, London and New York, 1927.

Raglan, Lord, *The Hero*, Oxford, 1937.

*Death and Rebirth*, London, 1945.

Rankin, Oliver S., *The Origins of the Festival of Hanukkah*, Edinburgh, 1930.

Ransom, John C., 'The Literary Criticism of Aristotle', *KR*, X (1948), pp. 382–402.

Rashdall, Hastings, *The Idea of Atonement in Christian Theology*, London, 1918.

Robertson, John M., *Pagan Christs*, London, 1928.

Robinson, David, 'The Wheel of Fortune', *CP*, XLI (1946), pp. 207–16.

Roheim, Geza, *Animism, Magic, and the Divine King*, New York, 1930.

Rostovtzeff, Michael I., *Mystic Italy*, London and New York, 1927.

*Dura-Europos and its Art*, Oxford, 1938.

Rowley, H. H., 'The Song of Songs; An Examination of Recent Theory', *JRAS*, 1938, pp. 251–76.

Rugg-Gunn, Andrew, *Osiris and Odin, The Origin of Kingship*, London, 1940.

Runciman, Steven, *The Medieval Manichee*, Cambridge, 1947.

Russell, Bertrand, 'A Free Man's Worship', in *Mysticism and Logic and other Essays*, London, 1921.

Schaeffer, Claude F. A., *The Cuneiform Texts of Ras Shamra-Ugarit*, The Schweich Lectures of the British Academy 1936, London, 1939.

Schauss, Hayyim, *The Jewish Festivals*, tr. S. Jaffe, Cincinnati, 1938.

Schmitt, Nathaniel, 'Is Canticles an Adonis Litany?' *JAOS*, XLVI (1926), pp. 154–64.

Schopenhauer, Arthur, *The World as Will and Idea*, London and New York, 1883.

*A Select Library of Nicene and Post-Nicene Fathers*, ed. P. Schaff, 14 vols., New York, 1886–90.

*Service of the Synagogue New Year Day of Atonement*, ed. H. M. Adler, 3 vols., London, n.d.

Shaw, George B., *Saint Joan*, New York, 1924.

Smith, J. M., 'Traces of Emperor-Worship in the Old Testament', *AJSL*, XXXIX (1929), pp. 32–9.

Smith, W. Robertson, *Lectures on the Religion of the Semites*, London, 1901.

Snaith, Norman H., *The Jewish New Year Festival*, London, 1947.

Sonne, Isiah, 'The Paintings of the Dura Synagogue', *HUCA*, XX (1947), pp. 324–9.

Speiser, E. A., 'An Intrusive Hurro-Hittite Myth', *JAOS*, LXII (1942), pp. 98–102.

Spence, Lewis, *Myth and Ritual in Dance, Game and Rhyme*, London, 1947.

Spencer, Theodore, *Death and Elizabethan Tragedy*, Cambridge, Mass., 1936.

Review of Arthur O. Lovejoy, *Essays in the History of Ideas*, in *JHI*, IX (1948), pp. 439–46.

Stallman, Robert W., ed., *Critiques and Essays in Criticism* 1920–48, New York, 1949.

Staples, W. E., 'The Book of Ruth', *AJSL*, LIV (1937), pp. 145–57.

*Abbot Suger on the Abbey Church of St. Denis and its Art Treasures*, ed. Erwin Panofsky, Princeton, 1946.

Sukenik, E. L., *Ancient Synagogues in Palestine and Greece*, The Schweich Lectures of the British Academy 1930, London, 1934.

*The Babylonian Talmud Rosh Hashanah*, ed. I. Epstein, tr. M. Simon, London, 1938.

Tertullian, *Apology*, ed. T. R. Glover, London, 1931.

Thomson, George, *Aeschylus and Athens*, London, 1941.

*Studies in Ancient Greek Society, the Prehistoric Aegean*, London, 1949.

Toynbee, Arnold J., *A Study of History*, 6 vols., Oxford, 1939.

Underhill, Evelyn, *Mysticism*, London, 1923.

Van Buren, E. Douglas, *The Flowering Vase and the God with the Streams*, Berling, 1933.

'The Sacred Marriage in Early Times in Mesopotamia', *Orientalia*, n.s., XIII (1944), pp. 1–72.

'The Dragon in Ancient Mesopotamia', *Orientalia*, n.s., XV (1945), pp. 1–45.

Virolleaud, Charles, 'Un poème phénicien de Ras-Shamra. La lutte de Môt, fils des dieux et d'Alein, fils de Baal', *Syria*, XII (1931), pp. 193–224, 350–57.

'Un nouveau chant du poème d'Alein-Baal', *Syria*, XIII (1932), pp. 113–63.

'La naissance des dieux gracieux et beaux. Poème phénicien de Ras Shamra', *Syria*, XIV (1933), 128–51.

'Nouveau fragment du poème de Môt et d'Aleyn-Baal', *Syria*, XV (1934), pp. 226–43.

'La mort de Baal, poème de Ras-Shamra (IXAB)', *Syria*, XV (1934), pp. 305–36.

'La révolte de Koser contre Baal. Poème de Ras Shamra (III AB, A)', *Syria*, XVI (1935), pp. 29–45.

'Les chasses de Baal. Poème de Ras Shamra', *Syria*, XVI (1935), pp. 247–66.

'Hyme phénicien au dieu Nikal et aux déesses Kosarot, provenant de Ras Shamra', *Syria*, XVII (1936), pp. 209–28.

'Anat et la génisse. Poème de Ras Shamra (IV AB)', *Syria*, XVII (1936), pp. 150–73.

'La déesse Anat. Poème de Ras Shamra (V AB)', *Syria*, XVII (1936), pp. 335–45; XVIII (1937), pp. 85–102 (V AB, B); pp. 256–70 (V AB, C).

'Les Rephaïm. Fragments de poèmes de Ras Shamra', *Syria*, XXII (1941), pp. 1–30.

'Le roi Kéret et son fils (II K). Poème de Ras Shamra', *Syria*, XXII (1941), pp. 105–36, 197–217; XXIII (1942), pp. 1–20.

'Le mariage du roi Kéret (III K). Poème de Ras Shamra', *Syria*, XXIII (1942–3), pp. 137–72.

Waterman, Leroy, ed., *Royal Correspondence of the Assyrian Empire*, 2 vols., Ann Arbor, Mich., 1930.

Weisinger, Herbert, 'English Treatment of the Classical-Romantic Problem', *MLQ*, VII (1946), pp. 477–88.

Welsford, Enid, *The Fool His Social and Literary History*, London, 1935.

Wensinck, A. J., 'The Semitic New Year and the Origins of Eschatalogy', *AO*, I (1923), pp. 158–99.

Weston, Jessie L., *From Ritual to Romance*, Cambridge, 1920.

Widengren, George, *The Accadian and Hebrew Psalms of Lamentation as Religious Documents*, Stockholm, 1937.

Williams, Arnold L., *The Common Expositer*, Chapel Hill, N.C., 1948.

Williams, Norman P., *The Ideas of the Fall and of Original Sin*, London, 1927

Williamson, Hugh R., *The Arrow and the Sword*, London, 1947.

Willoughby, Harold R., *Pagan Regeneration*, Chicago, 1929.

Wischnitzer, Rachel, *The Messianic Theme in the Paintings of the Dura-Synagogue*, Cambridge, 1949.

Wittkower, Rudolf, 'Eagle and Serpent: A Study in the Migration of Symbols', *JWI*, II (1938–9), pp. 293–325.

Wolfson, Harry A., *Philo Foundations of Religious Philosophy in Judaism, Christianity, and Islam*, 2 vols., Cambridge, Mass., 1947.

Wright, Louis B., *Middle-Class Culture in Elizabethan England*, Chapel Hill, N.C., 1935.

Yates, Frances A., *The French Academies of the Sixteenth Century*, London, 1947.

Young, Karl, *The Drama of the Medieval Church*, 2 vols., Oxford, 1933.

# Index



T

# *Index*

# Index

# Index

# Index

# Index

# Index

# Index

# Index

# Index

# *Index*